# CAPTURE THE FLAG

# CAPTURE
## THE
# FLAG

*A Political History of
American Patriotism*

**WODEN TEACHOUT**

BASIC

BOOKS
A Member of the Perseus Books Group
New York

*For Mark,*

*my favorite patriot*

Published by Basic Books,
A Member of the Perseus Books Group

Books published by Basic Books are available at special discounts for
bulk purchases in the United States by corporations, institutions, and
other organizations. For more information, please contact the Special
Markets Department at the Perseus Books Group, 2300 Chestnut Street,
Suite 200, Philadelphia, PA 19103, or call (800) 810-4145, ext. 5000,
or e-mail special.markets@perseusbooks.com.

Designed by Brent Wilcox

Library of Congress Cataloging-in-Publication Data
Teachout, Woden.
    Capture the flag : a political history of American patriotism /
Woden Teachout.
        p.   cm.
    Includes bibliographical references and index.
    ISBN 978-0-465-00209-2 (alk. paper)
    1. Flags—United States—History.   2. Patriotism—United States—
History.   3. Patriotism—Political aspects—United States.
I. Title.
    CR113.T43 2009
    929.9'20973—dc22
                                                                    2009005811

10 9 8 7 6 5 4 3 2 1

# CONTENTS

# INTRODUCTION

A winter wind swept across New York Harbor in late afternoon the day after Christmas in 1971. Tourists riding the
last two ferries from Manhattan to the Statue of Liberty huddled
against the bulkheads, sheltering themselves from the gusts.
Among the passengers were clusters of long-haired adults in well-
used army-surplus clothing, looking for all the world like hippies
taking in the world-famous landmark. The mission of these fifteen men, however, was not tourism.[1]

Immediately upon docking at the island, the men performed a
quick reconnaissance. They wedged open a few doors and then
took refuge from sight; some crouched behind the massive supporting columns in the base of the statue. Some found storage
closets and tucked themselves away. A few climbed the stairs toward the crown with the tourists, hurriedly pulled back a metal
grate, and crawled into the arm. They waited as darkness fell.[2]

The men were members of Vietnam Veterans Against the War,
a rapidly growing organization with over twenty thousand members. VVAW—composed of military personnel who had served in
Vietnam—had gained great traction over the past two years, carrying out a series of public actions in opposition to continued

American military presence in Vietnam. Members had called on symbols of American patriotism to draw attention to the Vietnam War and make a political plea for its immediate end: They had marched in George Washington's footsteps from Morristown to Valley Forge; they had held a public ceremony of mourning at Arlington National Ceremony. Eloquent members of the group, including a young John Kerry, had testified before congressional committees. Now a small group had decided to occupy the classic, signal symbol of American liberty.

As evening came on, the veterans in the statue listened to the sounds of the island closing down. They heard the voices of tourists receding as the day's last ferry departed from the dock. They heard park rangers shutting down the monument, and relaxed a little when the lights went out. After a watchful interval, they emerged from hiding and carefully made their way to their agreed-on meeting place, the main desk downstairs. One vet startled the lone night watchman, who stared for a moment in disbelief at the unexpected visitor and then dropped his flashlight and fled. Unmooring his private boat in haste, the watchman motored off into the darkness.[3]

The group was now alone at the Statue of Liberty. Down on the public plaza, they approached the extensive row of flags. One by one, they turned each flag upside down, the standard signal of distress or a country under siege. They set wooden beams in front of the entrances, forming a kind of barricade. Then, from the long bank of pay phones, they called newspapers, televisions, and radio stations. Soon the vets heard the chug, chug, chug of a vessel, and a *New York Times* reporter appeared out of the dark. Other reporters followed in tugboats.[4]

The veterans stood at the base of the statue, speaking to reporters through the barricaded doors. They described their intention to hold the statue without violence, both to protest the war and to call attention to the mistreatment of veterans. The reporters were sympathetic. A French journalist, inspired by the upended flags on the plaza, suggested that the men also fly a distress flag from the statue's head. If they draped an upside-down flag from that iconic copper brow, he promised, the photograph would appear on the front page of every major newspaper. The veterans liked the idea. Taking one of the flags from the base of the statue, they climbed the long spiral stairs to the crown, and high over the harbor, they hung the flag upside down.[5]

The Frenchman hired a helicopter and captured the image. And the following day, there it was on the front page of newspapers worldwide: "Liberty in Distress," read the headlines. The veterans issued a statement:

> The reason we chose the Statue of Liberty is that since we were children, the statue has been analogous in our minds with freedom and an America we love.
>
> Then we went to fight a war in the name of freedom. We saw that freedom is a selective expression allowed only to those who are white and who maintain the status quo.
>
> Until this symbol again takes on the meaning it was intended to have, we must continue our demonstrations all over the nation of our love of freedom and of America.[6]

"The meaning it was intended to have." One of the hallmarks of the Vietnam era was faith: faith that the democratic system would work, faith that action and organizing and revealing the horrors would shift government policy. To activists, who saw the huge swell of public opinion rising against the war, it seemed not only that the government might end American involvement, but also that the government must. If wrongheaded policies like segregation could be dismantled, then surely so could wrongheaded policies like Vietnam. Many war protesters worked for years organizing, speaking, teaching, and marching against the war, confident that if they could only get the truth out, the government would withdraw. But the war continued. The country kept bombing, body bags kept coming home—and the activists' faith in their democracy began to fail. When it became obvious that the people were unable to change those government policies—ones that clearly subverted American ideals of liberty, equality, and republicanism—the antiwar organizers felt betrayed. The flag, which had been a symbol of so much hope, became a terrible symbol of hypocrisy. The legacy of that period still shapes the way many Americans approach both patriotism and the flag.

. ∾∘∾

This book is a history of the flag, but it is not the story of Betsy Ross or Francis Scott Key. It is the story of the flag's political history: the ways in which it has been pulled back and forth, from one political party to another, from one social movement to another. For more than two centuries, our fellow citizens—patriots all—have harnessed the flag's power in service to disparate visions, and in doing so, they have made those visions part of the American dream. The flag is not powerful in spite of its ambiguity; it is powerful because of its ambiguity. It has stood, at different times, for radical democracy, opposition to immigration, the abolition of slavery, unregulated capitalism, segregation, integration, and a hawkish war policy, among many other things.

The story of the flag is also the story of American patriotism, and the book traces two threads of patriotism—humanitarian and nationalist—that run through the past two and a half centuries.[7] Both strands claim their origins in the principles of the Declaration of Independence and the Bill of Rights, and both are incontestably, inarguably American. They are also very different. Humanitarian patriotism represents an ideological commitment to democracy as a political and social system. It emphasizes government as the source of civil liberties and the result of participatory democracy. The state exists as a means, not an end in itself; it is a vehicle for realizing the potential of each of its citizens. Patriots of this type frequently invoke the Declaration of Independence when speaking of individual equality and individual rights. They watch their governments with a mixture of tolerance and suspicion, tolerant because the state exists to serve them, suspicious because the overwhelming power of the state poses a potential risk to individual citizens. They love their country because of what it offers. Some privilege the political possibility inherent in democratic government, others the ability to improve economic fortunes or the freedom to worship. But in each case, humanitarian patriots honor their country not unequivocally but as an expression—however incompletely realized—of ideals. For this reason, they value dissent as a key patriotic activity, a necessary check against the power of the state.

The humanitarian form of patriotism dominated American civic life until the turn of the twentieth century. When Jefferson sat in Philadelphia in 1776 and hammered out draft after draft of the Declaration of Independence, his ringing phrases—"All men are created equal"; "endowed by their Creator with inherent and inalienable rights"; "life, liberty, and the pursuit of happiness"—

articulated the foundations of humanitarian patriotism. Lincoln called on this tradition when he stood before Congress in 1861 and described the Union as a government "whose leading object is to elevate the condition of men—to lift artificial weights from all shoulders—to clear the paths of laudable pursuit for all—to afford all, an unfettered start, and a fair chance, in the race of life." In the same vein, Martin Luther King Jr., in his iconic speech at the March on Washington in 1963, described the Declaration and U.S. Constitution as "a promissory note to which every American was to fall heir . . . a promise that all men—yes, black men as well as white men—would be guaranteed the unalienable rights of life, liberty, and the pursuit of happiness." This was a classic articulation of patriotism in the humanitarian strain.

Nationalist patriotism came to prominence around the turn of the twentieth century with the rise of the nation-states across Europe and the world. It presupposed a citizenry defined not only by a political covenant but also by a shared cultural, social, economic, ethnic, and geographic heritage. Nationalist patriots sought to eliminate the gap between the state—the political entity—and the nation, the cultural collectivity. They imagined the nation-state as a transcendent thing, far more than the sum of its individual citizens. When faced with the inevitable conflicts between national ideals and real government policy, these patriots chose to protect the security of the state, seeing it as the best long-term guarantor of those ideals. They were more likely to think in terms of duty and to subsume their own needs to a perceived higher good; they were more willing to sacrifice the rights of individuals for what they perceived to be the good of the country, privileging loyalty above skepticism. Their patriotism reflected this deference, using songs, rituals, and symbols to create a culture of reverence.

Elements of nationalist patriotism existed in the United States as early as the Declaration of Independence—indeed, the nationalist impulse was necessary to forging an independent country—and grew throughout the nineteenth century. The tradition took ascendance with the writing of the Pledge of Allegiance and its first mass performance on Columbus Day in 1892. All across the country, schoolchildren stood at attention before the flag, raised their right hands in the straight-armed salute, and moved their lips in unison, their small voices pledging allegiance first to the flag and then to the republic. When Teddy Roosevelt gave his inaugural address in 1905, he described his "new nationalism" by saying, "We have become a great nation.... Much has been given us, and much will rightfully be expected of us." Forty-six years later, John F. Kennedy proclaimed, "Ask not what your country can do for you, but what you can do for your country." And Ronald Reagan accepted the Republican nomination in 1980 by invoking "the American compact" of "shared values" and the "American spirit . . . that flows like a deep and mighty river through the history of our nation." Each was calling on the nationalist form of patriotism.

Humanitarian and nationalist patriotism are ideal types. In practice, they often intertwine, existing side by side in each historical era; few people subscribe exclusively to one or the other. Yet the two threads are helpful in teasing out the convictions that underpin patriotic emotions as well as the implications that flow from those convictions. They give us a way to map historical changes in patriotism onto shifts in the flag's meaning and onto the dominant political and cultural concerns of each era.

It was once possible to imagine an American patriotism without reference to the flag: The Continental Congress did just that.

But throughout the nineteenth century, the flag crept ever more deeply into the national consciousness, moving from the margins of patriotism to its center. With the Civil War, the flag gained personal meaning for most ordinary Americans. With the crisis of capitalism at the end of the nineteenth century, citizens flew the flag from their houses, saluted it, and sang to it. And in the twentieth century, the flag came to possess the iconic, nearly spiritual power that it has today.

In the last forty years, the cynicism born in the Vietnam era also turned the flag into a bitter symbol of tremendous loss. Believing that the United States no longer stood for government by the people, for the people, and of the people, many Americans found it hard to claim the flag as their own. It seemed to fly solely over the so-called right, standing for nationalism, economic imperialism, laissez-faire capitalism, and unquestioning support for U.S. policy. Beneath a tenacious alliance between the flag and conservative Americans lay an understanding of patriotism—an understanding that the left did not share. There was an emphasis on loyalty, a wariness of political protest, and an almost religious faith in the idea of an American nation. The humanitarian impulses of Revolutionary America had given way to the nationalist patriotism of the twentieth century. And now, in the twenty-first century, politicians must pin a flag on their lapel and take care to position themselves for the cameras: Any absence of the Stars and Stripes calls their patriotism into doubt. This posturing may be absurd, but it points to a larger truth. The American flag is a symbol, yet it is also a catalyst, an object lesson in the transformative power of symbols.

The story of the American flag is the story of a country in search of itself, a country led sometimes by one sort of patriot and at other times by another, both kinds laying claim to the same American values and both claiming the flag as a powerful symbol. Telling this story reveals that ascendant groups invariably use the flag as a way to make their case. Those who claim it engage its tremendous political and cultural power in service to their version of the American dream. Those who relinquish the flag give up one of the most powerful ways to define a national vision.

But the story of the American flag also reveals the flag's potential for reinterpretation. It asks us to understand the varied impulses of American patriotism, to reexamine the categories of "right" and "left"—both of which have at one time or another laid claim to the flag—and to reacquaint ourselves with our shared American values. Seen within the context of our history, the flag has the ability to displace our constructed categories and established political parties and to focus on the common values beneath. It can point to a shared heritage, a common source of pride, a language of connection.

Ultimately, the flag is a challenge. As generations of Americans have pointed out from the late eighteenth century through the present, the Revolution remains unfinished: The democratic vision of liberty and justice for all remains the country's promise, not its reality. The flag reveals this gap. In the hands of many Americans before us, it has insisted that we reexamine our national path and has called on the power of patriotism to move our country closer, step by step, to what we hope it can be.

The opportunity beckons.

# ~1~

# FLAG OF RESISTANCE

## Rowdy Boys, Liberty, and the American Revolution

In 1769, Benjamin Franklin drafted a map for the British mail service, one that depicts the world as the colonists saw it. Landmasses form the map's margins. To the west, North America's coastline curves in a graceful swoop from Halifax down to Savannah and then out again along the Caribbean islands. To the east, Great Britain's islands straddle Europe and Africa. The curving coastlines, pocked with port cities, frame the map's centerpiece: the Atlantic Ocean. The ocean is densely inscribed. A grid marks latitude and longitude, and a star emits rays of magnetic direction that extend in precise gradations: west, southwest, south-southwest, and beyond. The Gulf Stream sweeps from Florida to the Azores in a great arc of clouded ink. It is in this ocean world that the origins of the American flag lie.[1]

Flags were a rare sight on land in the British North American colonies. The streets boasted a rich visual tapestry, but no flags. There were no flags on the expansive brick mansions on the hills or the ramshackle wooden homes along the coasts, no flags on the cobbler's shops or haberdasheries, and no flags on the few independent school buildings. Flagpoles had yet to be imagined. Only down on the wharf were there flags, waving from the ships bobbing up and down in the harbor.

The eighteenth-century ocean was filled with vessels flying their identifying flags. British cargo ships carried tea and window-panes, silk and stockings to North America, then took cod and tobacco back to London—all under the red, blue, and white geometry of the Union Jack. Dutch slave traders steered an ominous course from the west coast of Africa to the sugar plantations of Barbados and on to the docks of Charleston, flying their prince's flag: thick horizontal stripes of red, white, and blue. French ships flew gold fleurs-de-lis on a blue field; Spanish ships featured a white field boldly crossed with red.[2]

For these ships and the men who sailed them, flags played a critical role: not so much as symbols but as a means of communication and as a homing beacon. Sailors hoisted "the colors" as a sign of national allegiance visible across long stretches of water, turning encounters between two ships into international events. The colors answered that critical question: friend or foe? Was it the Union Jack? The familiar design of a fellow countryman meant safety and comradeship—a chance to trade provisions and resupply. Was it a dark pirate flag? The warning flash of enemy or pirate colors meant a chase and possibly a battle. When sailors landed in a port town, the flag became part of their cityscape. The masts in the harbor rose up, visible from the lower streets, so sailors emerging from taverns or bawdy houses in the light of dawn could find their way back through the cobbled streets.

The flag's Revolutionary usage originated in the sailing culture born in these towns and on these ships. There were hundreds of thousands of sailors, nearly all of them men, most in their twenties, the majority of them working-class. They were "rowdy boys"—farm boys, free blacks, escaped slaves, and convicts—from up and down the coast. They came from Massachusetts port towns, New York Harbor, the wharves of Philadelphia, Charleston's steamy waterfront, and farther afield from the Indies, Ireland, and Africa. They stood muscular and proud in big beaver hats, short blue peacoats, and striped pants tarred for waterproofing against the ocean waves. They had signed on for adventure, money, and in many instances, an incipient form of patriotism.[3]

Long before separation from Great Britain was considered, American colonists felt a kind of apolitical pride in their native land. For some, this was a spiritual pride, the sense that America was the promised land and that New Englanders were God's chosen people. For others, it was pride in the tremendous natural resources of the North American continent. Such pride allowed the colonists to think of themselves as a people apart. The term *American* was already in vogue, describing all those who lived in the geographic area and including both Native Americans and those of European ancestry. These ideas had no political ramifications as yet: None of them caused the colonists to seriously question their relationship with Great Britain.[4]

But in the eighteenth century, radical ideas about politics, liberty, and national allegiance began to emerge, appearing with particular strength on the colonial waterfront. Sailing culture held the seeds of political consciousness. Sailors stood on the bottom rung of the hierarchical social ladder of colonial society: They were caricatured as Jack Tar, a derogatory nickname that married the term for a common working man—Jack—with the dark, sticky substance that waterproofed sails and characterized the waterfront. When John Adams agreed to defend the British soldiers who had shot into the crowd at the Boston Massacre, he dismissed that crowd as "a Rabble of Saucy Boys, Negroes and Mulattoes, Irish Teagues, and Outlandish Jack Tars."[5] Their lowly status, paradoxically, gave sailors a freedom to shape their own culture. Except for the captains who employed them—and whom they could always leave when the voyage was finished—they did not have to answer to anyone. The transient nature of their work allowed them a great deal of autonomy, allowing them to move from port to port and country to country. Onshore, they could do as they pleased. And their numbers gave them the power they lacked in social terms: They were, apart from slaves, the first collective workers.[6]

Not surprisingly, freedom was a central conceit of sailing culture, threading through the men's songs, what they read, and their political convictions. Sailors' concepts of liberty and freedom were elastic, ranging from the very personal—the freedom to spend their gold coins at whichever "dance hall" they pleased—to the deeply political. Through their travels, they were exposed to Enlightenment concepts of liberty pulsing through British and European cities. Both Benjamin Franklin and Thomas Paine spent their young manhood as sailors, forming their passion for liberty during their time at sea. One of the most popular mid-century sailing songs, "Hearts of Oak," proclaimed this fundamental value:

Hearts of oak we are still;
For we're sons of those men
Who always are ready—
Steady, boys, steady—
To fight for freedom again and again.[7]

In the mid-eighteenth century, the sailors' attachment to liberty was sharpened by the constant clash between their ideology and their experience. The British constitution guaranteed, in the popular phrase, "the rights of free born Englishmen," but the British government was a constant threat to their personal liberty through the Royal Navy's policy of impressment, in which sailors were "pressed" into service on warships for undefined amounts of time. Captains could simply kidnap sailors in North American ports: The shipmasters sent armed press gangs into ships, taverns, boardinghouses, and even private homes, with directions to seize any men they found there and bring them back to the naval ship. This practice was widespread and widely deplored.[8]

Impressment created the first and one of the strongest sources of colonial resistance to British imperialism, as whole waterfront communities joined sailors in acting against the press gangs. In the mid-1700s, the port towns along the Atlantic coast were the most developed and most populous centers in the North American colonies. Thousands of colonists—often as many as 20 or 30 percent of a city's population—joined the sailors in resistance, rioting in the streets. Some feared being taken themselves; others went out to defend their sons, brothers, cousins, uncles, and friends. The period from the 1740s to the 1760s saw nearly twenty anti-impressment riots in the colonies. These riots conditioned men who had no political power into taking up arms against representatives of their own government and laid the foundation for a form of political resistance that would become central to the American experience of patriotism.[9]

Flags brought from the waterfront would become key symbols of colonial resistance to a number of acts passed by Parliament in the mid-1760s. The Currency Act of 1764 prohibited the colonies from issuing paper money, which tightened the economy: British sterling was nearly impossible to come by. The Sugar Act of the same year reinforced the early Navigation Acts, a series of laws passed by the British parliament to protect British shipping. These cracked down on the smuggling of molasses, which stifled the colonies' profitable rum business and shut down their trade with the Caribbean. The Stamp Act provoked the strongest reaction. The law, passed in March 1765, required colonists to purchase tax stamps for all legal documents, contracts, newspapers, and pamphlets: It threatened to further slow an economy that was already dangerously depressed. The protests against it were the first in which large numbers of North Americans across the social spectrum began defying British policies wholesale. Like the impressment riots before them, the Stamp Act protests drew on a culture of working-class protest among sailors and waterfront people.

It is no coincidence that popular colonial resistance to the Stamp Act began in Boston, nor that the city was the site of so many important protests in the coming decade. Boston was the quintessential sailing city, and its shipbuilding industry gave it the most highly concentrated waterfront culture in the colonies. In 1765, it boasted fifteen thousand people, the third-largest population in the colonies, after Philadelphia and New York. It was a hilly, crowded city built on an island and oriented to the sea. A long, wooden wharf, stuck like a welcoming arm out into the ocean, was lined with fishing boats and coastal traders at anchor. Boats rocked alongside the dock, their holds full of imported goods: necessities for the poor, including firewood from Maine, and luxuries for the rich, such as Madeira wines from Teneriffe. Even in good times, sailors outnumbered members of any other occupation in all port towns; in Boston, the proportion of sailors was even higher. All kinds of other waterfront workers, too, depended on the shipping trade: merchant marines and fishermen, stevedores and ropewalkers, ships' carpenters and caulkers.[10]

The city's North End and South End faced the harbor: working-class neighborhoods where small wooden houses pressed tightly together. Here, the boardinghouses and taverns were filled with sailors, nearly all of them unemployed. Since 1760, the town had suffered through a devastating fire and smallpox epidemic; most recently, British policies had abruptly strangled colonial trade. A 1764 crackdown on smuggling meant that the molasses trade, so crucial to the North American rum distilleries, had ground to a near halt. For every five ships that had sailed from Boston Harbor the year before, only one sailed now; the seamen who did manage to get work found their wages docked by half. The Stamp Act threatened to make the situation even more dire. With its duties on every piece of paper, the act would drive up the cost of exporting goods to the point that most ships would not be able to sail.[11]

Along the waterfront, men were angry. Their anger was heard by Ebenezer MacIntosh, the popular leader of the South End. A short, sandy-haired man in his late twenties, he was by trade a cordwainer, a man who pressed leather into shape for shoes and boots. But he was also an organizer of Boston's sailors and waterfront workers, and he established a cadre of two thousand loyal followers. Lawyer and Stamp Act critic James Otis labeled MacIntosh "a bold fellow" and granted him a grudging respect, calling him a man who "with his mobbish eloquence prevails in every motion." MacIntosh was accustomed to the public display of power. Every year, Boston's workers came out in force for Pope Day, a version of the Guy Fawkes Day celebrated in England. Stuffing old clothing and hammering together crude wooden shapes, the workers made effigies of Fawkes, a Catholic revolutionary who had plotted to blow up the king and Parliament in the early seventeenth century. MacIntosh led the South End gang as it paraded through the streets with these figures and clashed with a rival parade of North End workers, an event that usually culminated with brawls and bonfires. Large and theatrical processions were his finest hour.[12]

Observing MacIntosh's influence among the waterfront workers, a group of nine merchants approached him. For the moment, they called themselves the Loyal Nine; later, they would become the Sons of Liberty. Among their ranks were artisans, a ship's captain, several distillers, and the printer of the *Boston Gazette*. They were also close associates of Sam Adams, the tavern keeper and tax collector who led Boston town meetings and petitioned against the Stamp Act. The Loyal Nine saw a confluence between their interests and those of the working class, one that might bear political fruit. The sailors found themselves unemployed; the merchants feared that the rising costs of the Stamp Act would make shipping altogether unaffordable. Both groups wanted the act stopped. The merchants knew they had no legal recourse, but they saw possibility in the popular anger all around them. If they could channel waterfront grievances into political protest, they might be able to repeal the act.

The Loyal Nine, working in concert with Sam Adams, convinced MacIntosh to use his considerable political power in a joint protest against the Stamp Act. MacIntosh had fallen into debt and received a citation, which might have landed him in jail. But Adams, in his role as tax collector, suspended the sentence and enlisted MacIntosh's cooperation.[13]

In the days leading up to August 14, the men plotted their demonstration. They gathered the necessary materials: a boot, green fabric and other cloth, rope, thread, needle, and pins. They composed patriotic doggerel, transcribing it onto little slips of paper, and stitched up various figures out of the cloth. On the night of August 13, they stuffed their handiwork with rags and slipped out into the darkness to hang it up.

The next morning, the Stamp Act protests began on a theatrical and playful note. A large elm—soon to be known as the Liberty Tree—rose from the corner of Orange and Essex Streets along the city's spine, and passersby noticed unusual objects dangling from its branches. The first was an effigy, a life-sized cloth figure pinned all over with paper labels. One read "A. O.," the initials of the stamp distributor Andrew Oliver; another label, pinned to the effigy's left arm, read: "What greater pleasure can there be than to see a stamp-man hanging on a tree." Still another read: "He that takes this down is an enemy to his Country." Many other slips of paper referenced liberty. The second figure was a boot with a bright green sole, stuffed with the figure of a devil peeking out of the top, a reference to King George's former tutor and chief adviser Lord Bute. Bute was widely vilified in Britain and the colonies, and his presence in the tableau invoked secret influence and disastrous decision making. Together, the figure of "A. O." and the boot linked the Stamp Act to an incompetent king and a villainous adviser, suggesting that British liberty was best served by resisting the legislation.[14]

The scene was intended to draw a crowd, and it did. Wednesday was market day, when farmers drove their carts full of cheeses and vegetables in from the surrounding countryside. The elm stood directly along this route, well within walking distance of the market. All morning, people gathered in the space beneath its branches, talking and pointing. MacIntosh was there with an organized group of South End men. When the sheriff arrived under orders to take down the display, they turned him away. Sam Adams, standing under the tree, was asked who the effigy represented. Straight-faced, he responded that "he did not know—he could not tell—he wanted to enquire."[15]

The Loyal Nine hovered in the crowd, disguised in the trousers and jackets of workingmen, along with several dozen other gentlemen. They watched as the scene took on the elements of a popular protest. Several men set up a mock stamp office and began "stamping" the farmers' wares in a charade of what the Stamp Act would entail when it came into effect in November. Hundreds of boys from the neighboring schools held a parade, marching in orderly procession to the tree. They carried a flag, most likely a plain red banner, a traditional symbol of defiance. By afternoon, between 2,500 and 5,000 people—1 out of every 3 to 6 people in the city—had come to see the sight.[16]

Toward evening, the threat of violence sharpened. Led by MacIntosh, the crowd carried out a symbolic funeral of the Stamp Act. Men cut down the effigy of the stamp distributor and carried it as though it were a dead body through the streets. The cheering crowd shouted out, "Liberty and property for ever!" and "No stamps!" Outside the town house the crowd gave three cheers "for defiance"—an old sailors' custom—as the governor and council listened anxiously inside. Then their protest took a more concrete turn. They headed down Kilby Street to Andrew Oliver's dock, where a future stamp office was being constructed. The crowd mock-stamped the wood and bricks and destroyed the structure. The people then hauled the wooden beams to Fort Hill, next to Oliver's elaborate estate, for a bonfire. In front of Oliver's mansion, they sawed off the effigy's head. The stamp office beams were turned into a burning pyre, and the beheaded effigy was placed on top. The crowd cheered as the effigy was devoured by the flames.[17]

The waterfront crowd continued its pressure the next day. That evening, the crowd returned to Fort Hill carrying tar barrels, which they piled into a pyramid ready for burning. On top they raised a flagstaff and hoisted the Union Jack. They had lit the conflagration when word of Oliver's resignation arrived. He would not announce it himself, but he wrote a note requesting "the Liberty of being excused from his new office." It was startling: One of the colony's most powerful men, a wealthy British agent, had relinquished a coveted post because of pressure from a crowd of waterfront workers.[18]

∽०∾

It is premature to call the sentiments that emerged on August 14 an American patriotism. The colonists were Britons; none, even the most radical, had any ideas of separating from England. They sought merely to change the administration's policies. Nonetheless, the waterfront crowd's major concerns did hearken back to Greek and Enlightenment ideals of patriotism, in their emphasis on a common good and on improving the lives of the suffering. And they articulated a new, distinctly colonial tradition of humanitarian patriotism.[19]

The first of these concerns was an embrace of political liberty. Liberty, one of the best-loved terms in the English language, was the cornerstone of the political philosophy that would come to be known as republican ideology. Britons boasted of being free-born Englishmen, claiming that the superiority of their monarchical republic was the liberty it guaranteed its citizens. They saw their constitution as protection against the assaults of political corruption that wore away at liberty. Anglo-American political thinkers articulated a belief in natural rights, an emphasis on government and society as social contracts, and a deep concern about government corruption. To them, as to other colonists across the social classes, the British government appeared foolish and vindictive. Educated citizens published pamphlets and debated Enlightenment ideas; working people rallied under liberty poles. As Thomas Oliver, a Boston Tory, commented: "The People, even to the lowest Ranks, have become more attentive to their liberties."[20]

The second concern present on that day was a growing rejection of hierarchy. Colonial society was deeply stratified: Poor people were known as "the meaner sort," and a poor man was expected to take off his hat to gentlemen when he met them in the street. This social structuring did not change overnight, but the Stamp Act protest was a decisive moment in the relationship between social classes. For the first time, gentlemen and waterfront workers combined forces. The merchants hid behind the crowds, allowing the workers to raise the threat of direct action. When Oliver resigned his office, the crowds were faced with the startling realization that they—who earned less than Oliver spent on his horses—had forced the British agent's hand.

The workers also took the protest in a direction that the Loyal Nine hadn't anticipated. After the effigy of the stamp distributor went up in flames on Fort Hill, many of the crowd, including the gentlemen, departed. But others, led by MacIntosh, returned to the stamp distributor's house. Andrew Oliver was a wealthy and privileged man. He lived in a mansion on a hill, where his household staff served meats off silver plates. The rioters who returned to the house that night targeted the symbols of this opulence. They shattered the imported glass windows, broke mirrors, smashed china, and set fire to Oliver's elegant driving coach. Before leaving, they drank his fine wine. These actions manifested an anger at social hierarchies—an anger that surprised the merchant class. The Loyal Nine, who had not sanctioned or imagined this as part of the protest, were dismayed and alarmed: One of them described the crowd as an "amazingly inflamed people."[21]

The incident, and the Loyal Nine's response, revealed the complexity of colonial emotions about social privilege. On its face, the joint effort of workers and merchants seemed to soften class distinctions: Their invocation of liberty, their critique of the monarchy, and their unusual cooperation all worked against the social hierarchies. But the events that followed also deepened the class differences. The Massachusetts governor spoke of the Stamp Act protests as "a War of Plunder, general leveling, and taking away the Distinction of rich and poor." And as Stamp Act crowds took action in state after state, their members became more articulate about their newfound egalitarianism. In Newport, Rhode Island, a crowd told the governor, who was trying to disperse them, "that they lookt upon this as the cause of the people, and that they did not intend to take directions from any body." Such sentiments were implicit in the attack on Oliver's finery, and they were deeply worrying to merchants like the Loyal Nine. These men believed in dismantling certain hierarchies, but were not so much egalitarian as antimonarchical. They were ready to strip King George's power, but they found it inconceivable to give up any of their own. They found themselves in the midst of forces they had hoped to channel but which had escaped them.[22]

∽◦∾

The Stamp Act protest started a raft of popular resistance. Within months, maritime crowds gathered and called for resignations and repeal all up and down the coast, from New Hampshire to South Carolina. In Charleston, two thousand people held a funeral procession for "American Liberty."[23] In Newport, a Rhode Island crowd threatened the distributor's house and forced customs collectors onto a ship in the harbor for safety. In New York, sea captains led a procession of several thousand people, at least a quarter of them sailors, which intimidated the lieutenant governor and kept him from issuing stamps. In 1768, Bostonians armed themselves and stopped customs officials from enforcing the Navigation Acts. In 1772, a Rhode Island crowd boarded the British schooner *Gaspée* in Narragansett Bay, wounded its captain, and sank the ship to protest the Navigation Acts. The next year, hundreds of citizens protested the British government's Tea Act, which gave preferential treatment to the East India Tea Company and undercut colonial merchants. The angry Americans boarded ships in Boston Harbor and dumped tea into the waves.[24] The act of patriotic dissent began to foster a different kind of patriotic sentiment: a growing sense of "nation," a sense of a community that could stand politically separate from Great Britain.

These acts drew on the tradition of anti-impressment riots, but they added a theatrical element. As American resistance became more explicitly political, it also developed its own iconography of protest. The events that British loyalists described as riots were frequently highly choreographed events involving parades, effigies, bonfires, and ritual gatherings—all hallmarks of working-class ritual celebrations like Pope's Day. Nautical influences appeared as well. Tarring and feathering, for example, was a sailing tradition; it incorporated the old folk symbolism of feathering with the traditional black pitch that seamen used to waterproof sails and clothing.

Two of these theatrical elements expressed an emergent political flag culture. Most obvious were the flags themselves. Dozens of different flags were used by colonists in the years from 1765 to 1775. In Boston, the Sons of Liberty attached a "liberty pole" up through the branches of the Liberty Tree; from it, they flew a flag of nine vertical red and white stripes. Protestors also hoisted rattlesnake flags: solid-colored flags, frequently yellow, depicting a coiled serpent preparing to strike and the words "Don't Tread on Me." Other citizens flew white flags on which were appliquéd the image of a green pine tree, a symbol of New England, with the words "An Appeal to Heaven." Still other banners were solid red flags, traditional British symbols of protest, bearing slogans like "George Rex" and "Liberties of America." It hardly mattered which image appeared on the field. To both the British and Americans, the very flying of a flag, backed up by the threat of the waterfront crowds who raised them, communicated defiance.[25]

"Liberty poles," tall ships' masts erected in public spaces, were the second theatrical expression of this protest culture. The masts were tall enough to be seen across the city and were easily available to the sailors and ships' carpenters who formed the nucleus of these crowds. Waterfront crowds gutted the central masts from old vessels or selected new spars from the piles of white pine destined for the king's ships, and hauled the spires up from the docks. Inspired by the Liberty Tree in Boston, liberty poles were the earliest flagpoles. The Liberty Tree had become a kind of alternate public space: the ground underneath it was called Liberty Hall and became an important place for meetings. Unlike the town house a half mile away, this space clearly belonged to the working people of Boston. When the Stamp Act was repealed in 1766 because of the protests, New Yorkers celebrated by erecting a liberty pole, and crowds in many other towns soon followed suit. Places like Taunton, New Jersey, and Poughkeepsie, New York, erected their own.[26]

Liberty poles quickly became public gathering spots. They were dramatic monuments by mere virtue of their height, and they were used as a public signal system. A flag flying high signified developing news: an alert of a mass meeting, for example, or reports in from England. The liberty poles' significance as an affront to the British made them even more compelling. In New York, the liberty pole became a central point of contention between waterfront crowds and British soldiers: Crowds erected a mast, and soldiers deliberately cut it down on three separate occasions. Boston's Liberty Tree fell during the winter of 1775–1776, when British soldiers chopped it down for firewood. In Charleston, the Liberty Tree was so noxious to the British that they cut it when they occupied the town.[27]

These popular forms of protest catalyzed the colonies, laying the foundation for an increasingly political American sense of patriotism. "Our Brethren in Boston have indeared themselves more than ever to all the colonies in America," wrote the *New York Gazette*. Calling the protest a "Noble Example," the paper hoped it "will be unanimously follow'd by all the Colonies." Ten years later, the colonies had followed that noble example all the way to the Declaration of Independence.[28]

∽∘∾

The two most famous images of the Revolutionary flag, both of them painted in the nineteenth century, reveal its symbolic importance in the 1800s but little about what flags meant during the Revolution. Emanuel Leutze's painting of Washington crossing the stormy waters of the Delaware, flag billowing in a halo of light at the center, is wholly inaccurate: Not only did the party actually cross the river at night, and in a high-sided transport vessel, but the men would also have flown a regimental flag if they carried one at all. Likewise, C. G. Weisgerber's *Birth of Our Nation's Flag* depicts Betsy Ross sitting in her parlor across from George Washington and two other congressmen, proffering a flag for their approval as sunlight streams through the window. There is no evidence that a congressional committee ever visited Ross or that she sewed the flag with a circle of stars in the canton: Like the Leutze painting, the scene is imaginary.

The so-called prisoner's flag, however, is real. This is a small flag made by an American seaman or seamen held captive in a British jail during the Revolution. Its rectangular backing is red wool, onto which are stitched seven strips of white silk. The navy canton is pocked with thirteen white stars, embroidered idiosyncratically in a host of different orientations: They seem to spin on their field. These are not the delicate seams of an accomplished seamstress; they are the strong, straight stitches of a seaman mending a sail. One can imagine a sailor bending over his materials day after day, having scavenged the red wool from an officer's greatcoat and purchased the white silk ribbon at the prison gate. The flag must have meant a great deal to him.[29]

The Revolution had begun in earnest with the open rebellion of the Declaration of Independence in 1776, as thousands joined the Continental army. For the first part of the war, it had seemed inconceivable that the new government would win: It was up against the strongest military power in the world, and British troops seized New York and captured the colonial seat at Philadelphia. But the decisive American victory of the Battle of Saratoga in 1777 proved a turning point, as American troops forced British General John Burgoyne to surrender. After a long campaign in the South, ending with Washington's decisive 1781 defeat of Lord Cornwallis at Yorktown, the British troops left the continent.

Of all those who fought in the Revolutionary War, it was seamen who embraced the flag most fervently. Imprisoned sailors were among the flag's earliest and most earnest private champions, the first to develop their own ceremonies and rituals around the flag. These men drew on the long strands of history to infuse the new flag with their own powerful and personal version of patriotism. There are intermittent records of this new culture: the hand-sewn prisoner's flag, lyrics of the popular sailing songs, prisoners' accounts of flag recognition. The most complete version is in a sailor's diary that describes a defiant Fourth of July ceremony in a British prison courtyard featuring military drills and handmade flags. It is the first recorded instance of American flag use that was popular and spontaneous, rather than quasi-official and organized. And it reveals the overlapping meanings of the new flag: as a tool of popular, humanitarian resistance and as a nationalist symbol of a new and separate government.

The first American flag appeared in the rigging of the *Alfred* as the warship sailed from Philadelphia in early December 1775. This was the Continental Colors: a flag bearing the red and white Sons of Liberty stripes in the field, and a miniature Union Jack in its canton. The complexity of the design made it hard to distinguish: One observer deemed it "English Colours but more Striped." Future commodore and naval hero John Paul Jones claimed to have been the first to raise it: "I hoisted with my own Hands the Flag of Freedom the First time that it was displayed on board the Alfred on the Delaware." The *Alfred* was the flag-ship of the new navy that had just been commissioned by the Continental Congress. It was a tiny fleet—only four ships—and Congress feared that it would be attacked by friendly forces without a distinct flag announcing its American sympathies. The authorization of a new flag design was a highly practical affair, without fanfare. The measure took place within the bounds of the Marine Committee and did not even arrive on the floor of the full Congress. The design of this flag, with both British and colonial elements, reflected the ambivalent political status of the rebellious colonies.[30]

Eighteen months later, on June 14, 1777, Congress adopted the Flag Resolution. With that act, the Continental Colors of the defiant colonies became the Stars and Stripes of the United States. There was little ceremony, but it was an important moment and one that would become more significant with time. For the first time, the American nation—the human community linked by shared territory, culture, and ideals—had become congruent with the state, the political entity. And the flag stood for three entities now woven together: the state, the nation, and the nonnational patriotism of the waterfront crowds.

The Stars and Stripes was not yet properly *a* flag: There were constituent elements but no standardized design. The most recognizable element was the red and white stripes, which echoed the protest flags of the Sons of Liberty. Each stripe symbolized one of the thirteen colonies, and together they symbolized the power of united resistance. Accompanying the stripes were white stars, which appeared in a blue canton in the upper left corner; their exact origin is unclear, though they may have come from the Masonic tradition of using stars or from the family military standard of George Washington. Within this basic structure, there were endless variations. Sometimes the stars were arranged in a circle, sometimes in rows, sometimes forming a square frame around a blue center, sometimes in an arch over the number seventy-six. Sometimes they had six or seven points, as in the heraldic tradition; sometimes they had five, which would become the American standard. The stripes, too, were variable: More than one flag showed red and blue stripes, or red, white, *and* blue. And while most flags showed thirteen stripes, some showed nine. Nine was a volatile number in the colonies. As the sum of four and five, it referred to the forty-fifth edition of the North Briton newspaper in which publisher John Wilkes had lambasted King George; Wilkes's subsequent arrest by the king caused an uproar about British constitutional freedoms. Whatever the number and significance of stripes, all traces of the Union Jack had disappeared.[31]

These new flags flew over the official navy, as well as over a host of private and commercial vessels. The official Continental navy was a negligible force, sailing only fifty-seven boats over the course of the war, many of which were small and in poor condition. But naval culture, as opposed to the navy, was broad and pervasive. Large numbers of Americans took to the seas in private ships that acted in quasi-official roles and served as an adjunct to the official fleet. More than 200,000 men sailed on these ships, almost as many as the 230,000 enlistments on the active rolls of the Continental army. The impact of naval culture becomes clearer with the realization that the population numbered 2.5 million at the beginning of the war. Of every 13 people (men, women, and children included), 1 person was a sailor.[32]

Most of these men served on the several thousand commercial vessels known as privateers. Trimmed with fast sails and carrying little burden, they served an important offensive function: They raided British ships and kept the profits. Privateers tracked down slower-moving vessels laden with British supplies for His Majesty's forces in the colonies. The raiding vessels' speed and large crews enabled the sailors to quickly move alongside, swarm onto the British decks, and subdue their crews. Then the raiders hauled off prizes, sometimes military supplies like cannons, guns, and powder, and sometimes casks of rum or shipments of food. Sometimes, the privateers themselves got taken, but as a whole, they succeeded in harassing the powerful Royal Navy. Their nips and stings forced convoy vessels into a defensive posture and kept the British navy from having the full run of the high seas.

Any self-respecting young man of the eighteenth century looking for fortune and adventure found himself down at the waterfront. The waves knocking on the wooden wharves prom-ised a magical world of adventure and fortune. The ships he saw anchored would soon steer for London, Savannah, Santo Domingo—magical cities he could only imagine. He saw the sailors swaggering down the cobblestones in their big beaver hats, clinking the coins in their pockets. As he passed the waterfront dance halls, he could hear the violins and tambourines within; when doors swung open, he saw the flash of dancing girls. On street corners, he was hailed by ships' recruiters in shining uni-forms. "Ha shipmate," they called out, "don't you wish to take a short cruise in a fine schooner and make your fortune?"[33]

By the time the Declaration of Independence was signed, many men were motivated by patriotism as well. Record num-bers signed up for service, and recruiting posters testified to this patriotic allure, especially when combined with profit. On broadsides depicting woodcut images of ships, they called out:

> to all the JOLLY TARS who are fighting for the RIGHTS and
>     LIBERTIES of AMERICA:
> make your Fortunes now, my Lads, before its too late,
> Defend, defend, I say defend an Independent State.[34]

Many of these sailors were ultimately captured by the Royal Navy, and nearly twenty-five hundred were held in British pris-ons over the course of the war. Despite their lack of official affil-iation, the seamen remained staunchly loyal to the American cause, refusing to join the Royal Navy and risking death for their convictions. When one Revolutionary sailor was hauled before a panel of British judges and asked why he had gone to sea, his reply was clear and direct: "We were out to fight the enemies of the thirteen United States." And these imprisoned seamen found meaning in the American flag, investing it with symbolic qualities far beyond its previous usage. Their improvised ceremonies around it reveal that sailors had begun to adopt the new flag in ways that were both national and personal.[35]

Old Mill Prison, a stone fortification on the English coast, was one of two British prisons and many prison ships that held the captured Americans. It was a dismal place. From the windows, the prisoners could glimpse the grassy headlands of Plymouth and the windswept Devon coast. Between the captives and these free fields stood a series of four gray stone walls, each ten to twenty feet high, their tops studded with shards of glass. The central yard was littered with nettles, old shoes, bones, and stones. Stench rose from the open sewage pits, where the men dumped their daily waste.[36]

On the morning of July 4, 1778, approximately two hundred captured American sailors gathered in the central prison yard. Once straight-backed and jaunty, they had enlisted during the fever of American patriotism in the summer of 1776. Now they were a motley crew, shoeless and ragged. Their bodies were weakened from a prison diet of bread, cabbage soup, and maggoty beef. Disease had ravaged them. Elias Hart lay dying of consumption, and Joseph Barnum, weakened from smallpox, would have his white and swollen knee amputated within the week. The prisoners hardly seemed the stuff of which nations were made.[37]

And yet the sailors were stubbornly loyal to the United States. King George would shortly announce himself willing to pardon any rebel who would sign on with a British man-of-war. The sailors knew that, aside from turning to the British, they had little hope. American ships would never be able to free them on the

British coast, and Benjamin Franklin was working for a prisoner exchange but had had no success. Their trials, which would take place before a British panel of judges, were a foregone conclusion. The men would be charged with high treason, summarily tried, and found guilty. They would make the long, slow walk to the gallows and make their last brief statements, and then their bodies would swing in the wind. But most American sailors were willing to accept this fate to die as an American, rather than turn traitor on a British warship. Nine out of ten chose to stay in prison and face an almost certain hanging. They were, in the words of one of them, "true sons of America."[38]

That morning of July 4, each of the several hundred prisoners wore a hat, folded out of paper into a distinctive three-corner construction. At a signal, they raised paper discs, cut into half-moon shapes, and set them into the notches on these hats. The guard, watching carefully, might have been able to see the image of the American flag: thirteen stars and thirteen stripes on each of the discs. And under this distinctive pattern, he would have just been able to make out Revolutionary slogans—"Independence" and "Liberty or Death"—printed in large capital letters.[39]

Few of the prisoners had served in the official army or navy, and many had already been captured when Congress had passed the Flag Resolution. They had sailed under the Continental Colors and had only learned of the Stars and Stripes in prison. But these symbols evoked a strong and personal sense of patriotism. The flags communicated the sailors' American allegiance and their defiance of British rule. Their three-corner hats, also known as cocked hats, were a replica of those worn by American officers. The paper discs were a handmade version of military cockades: circular knots of ribbon worn on one's hat as a badge of loyalty. It was well known that Washington wore a black cockade, as did many of the American troops. The printed words invoked what had become a specifically American tradition of resistance. They conjured up the spectacle of the Continental Congress ratifying the Declaration of Independence, and resonated with the mythic speech on the floor of the Virginia House of Burgesses, in which Representative Patrick Henry was said to have urged military action against the British by crying, "Give me liberty or give me death!"

Just past midday, at one o'clock, the prisoners assembled in the prison yard. They had spent the morning in their usual activities; now they gathered to show their self-discipline and their united strength. The prison guard, watching, saw a strange choreography evolve. The two hundred prisoners suddenly moved apart. They arranged themselves, still wearing their paper hats and flag cockades, into a number of smaller clusters. If the guard had thought to count, the number of clusters—thirteen—would have enlightened him.[40]

The guard watched as, one after another, each of the thirteen groups gave three cheers: Huzzah! Huzzah! Huzzah! As simple as the ceremony was, it was threatening, too. After the first three groups had cheered, the guard knew that ten more would have their turn before the prisoners were done. When the ceremony ended with the whole company cheering together, the guard must have feared the collective power of those two hundred prisoners, even against the locks and walls that kept them in. The prison agent, too, was concerned. He sent the guard to bring him one of the hats and doubled the watch at the gate.[41]

Among the prisoners was Charles Herbert, a twenty-year-old man from coastal Massachusetts. He was a typical recruit: young, white, landless. Like so many of his contemporaries, he had enlisted at the news of the Declaration of Independence, served first in his local militia and then on a privateer, and bonded deeply with his fellow sailors in prison. Herbert's diary—which he kept hidden in his shoe, since inmates were not allowed pen and paper—chronicled his years in prison. In it, the young captive described how the men tracked American military progress through smuggled newspapers, how they dug underground tunnels from which they escaped and were frequently brought back, and how they cooperated with one another against the hated prison agent. "The Americans unanimously hang together," he wrote.[42]

Two passages in Herbert's diary illuminate his developing patriotism with particular clarity. The first is the simple record of a book purchase: He spent precious money on a copy of Thomas Paine's *The American Crisis*. Herbert was certainly familiar with Paine's thinking, as all Americans were. Paine's *Common Sense,* published in January 1776, was the single most powerful articulation of American nationhood and the most popular work in all the colonies. It was written in plain language and read aloud in homes, workshops, and taverns. Within a few months of publication, it had outstripped all other pamphlet sales by ten to one.[43]

Paine was himself a sailor. Like many other seamen, he came from a working-class family, and as a young man, he had shipped on board a privateer. He had been profoundly shaped by his time at sea, admiring the solidarity of seamen, their cooperation, and their culture of egalitarianism. Paine's American vision, as articulated first in *Common Sense* and then in *The American Crisis*, infused republican ideology with a strong sense of these values. He sought to dismantle social hierarchies. He criticized monarchy not simply because it was corrupt, but also because of the very fact that it was a monarchy. "In America," he wrote, "the law is king." He developed the concept of "the people" more fully than ever before, basing his vision on a broad, inclusive franchise. "The case of America is in a great measure the cause of all mankind," he wrote. "We have it in our power to begin the world over again. The birth-day of a new world is at hand." In recording his purchase, Herbert carefully noted that he had bought it "on purpose to lend it to a friend without." Paine was the only political thinker whom sailors honored in this way. His vision, with its strongly egalitarian ethos, was the closest to the one that the sailors themselves embraced.[44]

A second passage, from March 1778, was written as news of the British army's struggles brought hope. Herbert often wrote at night, after other prisoners were sleeping. He must have sat in a small pool of light in the darkened prison, a marrow-bone candle flickering at his elbow, and laid out his vision of what he wanted the war to achieve:

> I hope that our long wished for prize is just at hand—a prize that is preferable to any other earthly enjoyment. I hope our days of trouble are nearly at an end, and after we have borne them with a spirit of manly fortitude, we shall be returned to a free country, to enjoy our just rights and privileges for which we have been so long contending. This will make ample satisfaction for all our sufferings.[45]

This was the language of republican ideology. Nowhere in the diary did Herbert write that he wished the war were simply over so that he could go home. Rather, his vision was deeply egalitarian.

He assumed that the free country was *his* as well as others'. Sailors had no economic, cultural, or political power. They were subject to captain's orders on ship and to impressment in port. They were not allowed to vote. And yet, Herbert spoke of rights that belonged specifically to him and other sailors when he wrote of "our just rights and privileges." He saw himself as part of a political system in which he too could participate. And he saw the sailors' suffering not only as a form of loyalty to the colonies but also as a loyalty to themselves. Their love of country was inextricable from what it promised them.

Before the Old Mill Prison flag ceremony, the prisoners had governed themselves with the rough egalitarianism they had on board ship. When someone stole, they formed a gauntlet around the prison yard and forced the thief to run through while they beat at him with nettles from the yard. They hung together, too, using a boycott to punish a cook whose wife had betrayed an escaping prisoner. After the flag ceremony, the men's relationship with one another changed. Instead of the implicit comradeship of sailors' culture, they began to act as a government: formal, deliberate, representative. The change was swift and striking. Within two weeks, they began to act as a democratic body, making joint decisions and issuing proclamations. They provided for the needy, raising money to support a prisoner's wife and contributing to a fund for the sick. Most strikingly, they drew up formal "articles" banning gambling and cursing and posted them in the yard. This was prison democracy, enforced by tying violators to a post and pouring cold water down their necks for half an hour.[46]

The sailors' new sense of self-determination culminated in a different ceremony in the prison yard, held six months after the first. On the second anniversary of their capture, on a December day, the men gathered again. This time, there were no cocked hats, no cockades, no Stars and Stripes, no division into thirteen colonies. Instead, there were words. The men gathered around a paper that was read aloud.

> We, whose names are hereunto subscribed, do, of our own free and voluntary consent, agree firmly with each other, and hereby solemnly swear, that we are fully determined to stand, and so remain as long as we live, true and loyal to our Congress, our country, our wives, children and friends, and never petition to enter on board any of His Majesty's ships or vessels or into any of service whatsoever.[47]

More than one hundred men signed this statement. The prisoners had petitioned before, but it had always been a supplication for better food or treatment. This petition did not ask. It was a declaration of independence. It was also the fullest expression of the liberty claimed by the sailors when they had raised the flags on their hats. Their patriotism was defined by what they articulated: their loyalty to their Congress and their country, clearly distinguished, and to their own families. It was also defined through their expression. American patriotism meant the ability to represent one's own self in a political context. It allowed the sailors to imagine themselves not simply as the men who fought the war but also as the men who governed the community.

The colonists as a whole underwent a similar transformation. At the moment of the Stamp Act in 1765, most colonists simply wanted the offensive measure repealed. At the moment of the

Declaration in 1776, they wanted political independence from Great Britain. By the end of the war, they had effected a social revolution. The process of effective group opposition was transformative: It turned what might have been merely a republic into a democracy. Like Charles Herbert, ordinary people found themselves transformed by the war. They believed that they, too, should be able to participate in the political system that they were helping to create.

∽∾∾

In the hands of Revolutionary sailors, the flag became an emblem of liberty in all its political and social meanings: a rejection of British monarchy and hierarchical culture and an embrace of American democracy and egalitarianism, indicating a nation-state that had staked a claim for humanitarian values. The flag, and the patriotism it represented, was a radical force. But in the hot summer of 1787, as the rebellious colonies struggled with the very different challenge of forming a government, a conservatism came to the fore. As delegates crowded into Philadelphia to argue, compromise, and eventually craft the Constitution, their patriotism began to look very different from that of Charles Herbert.

On the docks of the Delaware River, dozens of flags fluttered from the rigging of American vessels; half a mile away, no flag waved over the Pennsylvania State House. Inside the hall, the delegates deliberated over how widely to extend the vote. Benjamin Franklin, who had been a sailor in his teens, was now an old man. As a diplomat in France, he had taken a special interest in the sailors in Old Mill Prison, advocating for better treatment and working for their freedom. When he finally secured their release, many had come to visit his French headquarters. He fed them, housed them, and gave them money. Now he stood before the Constitutional Convention, eager to convince his fellow delegates that sailors deserved the vote: "The revolutionary war is a glorious Testimony in favor of plebian Virtue—our military and naval men are sensible of this truth. I myself know that our Seamen who were Prisoners in England refused all the allurements that were made use of, to draw them from their allegiance to their country."[48]

English seamen, Franklin pointed out, had been quite ready to change their loyalties: an observation that dramatized the virtue of the American sailors. With their extensive sacrifice and their deep national loyalty, argued Franklin, these American sailors deserved to be part of the franchise.

Other delegates were ambivalent about sailors and the rest of the crowds in the port towns. The statesmen knew that waterfront actions had proved critical to the Revolution, providing the muscle and the threat behind the paper declarations from the Continental Congress. The ransacking of houses and the tarring and feathering that had been critical in overturning the British were also threatening: Who knew how far that rebellious spirit might be turned against the new republic? In the end, the Continental Congress kept the requirement that allowed only men with property to vote.

Down at the waterfront, the sailors who had been so central to the effectiveness of the American Revolution found themselves on the margins of the new political map. If they survived their time at sea, saved their earnings and bought property, they would be entitled to vote. For tens of thousands of sailors, this future was out of reach. Charles Herbert's prison vision of "a free country" with "just rights and privileges" in which he could participate was a dream that for sailors—as well as many other groups—would be long deferred.

The flag, too, stayed on the margins of the new republic. In the half century following the Revolution, it appeared only as a minor symbol. In paintings and drawings, it appeared as a decorative element framing the more favored national icons of the Goddess of Liberty and George Washington as Cincinnatus. But the early legacies of the flag remained: the extralegal tradition of popular resistance and a strong taste of saltwater egalitarianism that reminded all disenfranchised groups that the Revolution was yet unfinished.

# · ~2~

# FLAG OF NATIVISM
## *The Philadelphia Riots of 1844*

By the 1840s, the rowdy boys of the Revolution had become old men. The United States had also matured, proving its political and military viability. With the War of 1812, it had declared war with England over British interference with American trade and with England's continuing impressments of American soldiers. The war was seen as a second war of independence, and the American victory as a validation. Most importantly for the growing country, the decades between the Revolution and the 1840s had given the United States time to develop a geographically and culturally bounded sense of itself as a nation.

The country now found itself facing a new era of industrialization. Farmers still outnumbered city dwellers four to one, but a profound change had taken place in the cities. The small workshops of the turn of the century were losing ground. These had been easygoing places, often in the ground floor of a home, where masters sent messenger boys for beer and where journeymen learned the skills that would serve them when they became masters one day. In their place arose factories, large rooms where dozens of employees worked under the watchful eye of a foreman. These factories unleashed incredible productivity while transforming the way that both employers and employees approached work.

Philadelphia, along with New York and Boston, was one of the most industrialized urban communities in the country. The city center showed the prosperity brought about by the new economic system: The white marble façades of the government buildings shone in the sun, and the imposing Bank of the United States impressed visitors with its substance. Here, wealthy Quaker merchants sat and counted the gold coins they made from textile manufacturing and trade while elegant ladies rode carriages to the opera. But surrounding this broad and bright public city was a shadow city, where narrow streets slanted in diagonals and crisscrossed each other at odd angles. The shadows were literal, as three-story buildings crowded tightly against one another, rarely allowing the sun to peek into the alleys below. The shadows were also figurative, as hunger, drink, and never-ending poverty plagued the inhabitants.

This shadow city existed in the manufacturing districts that ringed Philadelphia proper: Kensington, Northern Liberties, and Spring Garden to the north; Southwark and Moyamensing to the south. In these districts, workers produced the textiles that made the merchants rich. The weavers, the poorest of the working poor, pushed shuttles through hand-looms in tottering back buildings while barely able to buy bread. Others, working in small factories from sunrise to sunset, dyed the fabric; still others cut it and sewed it. The unemployed hung around shipyards hoping for work, and gangs of young men congregated around grog shops and oyster cellars. It was a world of rough-and-ready characters, poised to fight.[1]

This Philadelphia teemed with strange and ungovernable enthusiasms. As in other American cities, the tremors of industrialization shook forth all kinds of reformers anxious to harness the unleashed forces of a transformed society. Traveling millennialists predicted the precise date of the end of the world, while their followers bought white ascension robes in which they planned to rise to heaven. Temperance speakers packed lecture halls with their titillating tales of the moral ruin and financial disaster brought on by Demon Rum. At the same time, the city's shadowy streets sheltered continuous bloody clashes between Philadelphia's ethnic groups. Riots and racial violence were commonplace. In one instance, striking white workers locked black coal heavers in a warehouse and threatened to burn them alive. And when Irish immigrants and native-born workers brought the flag onto the streets of Philadelphia, it became the centerpiece of the bloodiest street conflict of a bloody era.

The riots of 1844 gave voice to a type of patriotism that had been largely silent in the new nation: one based on ethnicity. They unfolded haphazardly, as Irish and native-born Americans responded to each other with increasing levels of violence. The initial appearance of the flag was almost accidental, but the public relations campaign that followed was tightly controlled: In the hands of a brilliant, ruthless orator named Lewis Levin, the flag became a polarizing icon. More than any other man, Levin was responsible for bringing the American flag into the hands and the lives of ordinary people and for giving it powerful anti-immigrant connotations. Many Americans were outraged by this exploitation, as they saw it, of their national symbol, but even so, by the time the riots ended, the flag had come to represent a patriotism that was white, Protestant, and native-born.

In early May 1844, skeptical Irishmen stood on the edges of a political meeting at Second and Master Streets and watched an American flag go up. Around them swirled the lively life of the Irish working-class neighborhood of Kensington. Carters transported bundles of cloth from shop to shop, navigating the narrow streets with horses that left steaming piles on the paving stones. Apprentices, sent by thirsty masters, ran for beer, dodging the neighborhood women with market baskets on their arms as they picked their way through the streets. Laborers hoisted shovels on their shoulders, headed to and coming from the new construction sites on Philadelphia's outskirts. From the surrounding three-story buildings came the clack, clack, clack of hundreds of hand-looms.[2]

The Irishmen watched the speaker on the wooden stage. They knew him by reputation, if not by sight: Samuel Kramer was the editor of the *Native American* newspaper and, with fellow editor, Lewis Levin, was one of several leaders in the new American Republican Party. The party advocated disenfranchisement of Irish immigrants and nativist control of politics. Kramer and Levin modulated their message depending on their audience: To Philadelphia's gentry, they spoke mildly of the need to acculturate the immigrants; to discontented workers, they preached anti-Catholicism. Here on the street of the Irish neighborhood, Kramer was not given to fine distinctions. The Catholics were after the Constitution, he declaimed; they "wanted to get the Constitution of the United States into their own hands" and sell it to the pope.[3]

The small band of American Republicans who gathered around Kramer's stage were strangers to the neighborhood, and many were uneasy, aware that they were in the midst of an Irish Catholic stronghold. Antebellum street politics were always rowdy, a kind of rough and drunken dance between the speakers and the crowd. Speakers preached, ranted, and impugned while audience members bellowed their approval with phrases like "Hit him again!" and "Hit him on the wooly side!" or inter-jected catcalls and threw rotten vegetables. Political passion mixed with whiskey often led from verbal blows to real ones.

An American flag hung on the stage behind Kramer. Its pres-ence here was strange and noteworthy—outside the waterfront, the flag in an antebellum city was a rarity. As the necessity for Revolutionary patriotism had faded, so had the fierce attach-ment to the American flag. In the first decades of the nineteenth century, flags were most often seen down at the wharf: with tri-color stripes, with an eagle appliquéd to the field, with mottos such as *liberty* or *virtue*, with stars and without. But on land, there were dozens of other patriotic symbols with more hold on the American imagination: the long and lanky Brother Jonathan, the cartoon personification of American revolutionaries; the Goddess of Liberty, who wore a laurel wreath in her hair and crushed the chains of tyranny under her feet; the rounded female figure of Columbia, carrying grain and exuding fertility and who personified the New World.[4]

The War of 1812 had marked a brief resurgence of flag celebra-tion. While the American troops who marched into Canada and defended New Orleans carried regimental flags, the navy and American forts flew the Stars and the Stripes. On a September night in 1814, in the midst of a fierce thunderstorm, lawyer and poet Francis Scott Key stood on a sloop in the Baltimore Harbor watch-ing British ships barrage Fort McHenry with bomb after bomb, fearing that the city would almost certainly fall with the fort. As the parade of fiery shells illuminated the still-standing American flag throughout the night, Key rejoiced to see its fifteen stars and fifteen stripes. His poem, "The Star-Spangled Banner," was distributed by broadsheet in Baltimore and then throughout the nation with accompanying music. The song contributed to a popular interest in the flag that lasted for the duration of the war, but faded with the signing of the Treaty of Ghent in 1815. By 1844, the memories of that celebration had been dimmed for thirty years.

High on the wooden stage, the American Republican flag announced the convictions of the men below it. Twenty-six appliquéd stars marched in white rows on its blue canton: one for each state in the growing country. This was typical of all U.S. flags. But the stripes—four white and five red, for a total of nine—marked this one as a nativist banner. The number referred, as mentioned earlier, to John Wilkes's forty-fifth edition of the North Briton newspaper, as well as to the nine states that had adopted the Constitution and the nine that had ratified it. It was one of the nativist movement's many coded symbols.[5]

With the flag as his backdrop, Kramer warmed to his topic. Catholics *could not* be faithful to both the pope and the Constitution, he claimed. They should have twenty-one years of residency, twenty-one years of separation from the Old World, twenty-one years from the moment they stepped on American streets until they were allowed in the voting booth. After all, he said, native-born Americans were steeped in national traditions for twenty-one years before *they* could vote.[6]

More Irishmen came to join the crowd around the American Republicans, emerging from nearby houses and drawn from the marketplace and surrounding streets. The sight of the nativists

holding a political meeting in the heavily Irish Catholic neighborhood was a startling one. The immigrants were intent on making a
new home for themselves in the way they saw fit and without any
direction from others. As Irishmen, they encountered fierce prejudice that was both religious and racial: They were Papists whose
Irish blood marked them as racially inferior. In the antebellum hierarchy of race, they were closer to free blacks than whites. Such
prejudice drew a tight circle around their community, and they
forged their own society within the larger city of Philadelphia. Integration had little appeal: The Irish did not want to see their
churches torn down, their priests turned out of doors, their political power dissolved, and their children dispersed. The nativists
epitomized the daily racism the Irish faced. To find them engaging
in street politics, in an Irish neighborhood no less, was an invitation to a fight.[7]

The Irish, now numbering several hundred, started to heckle.
One of the community leaders, a loom boss and naturalized citizen,
led the charge. "Come on down here, you old crocodile!" he
shouted out, addressing the speaker. "I am a better citizen than
you, for I am sworn to the country and you may turn Tory any
minute!" Another Irishman raised his voice, not to the men on the
stage, but to the crowd. The nativists, he announced, were "not
Americans speaking." Instead, their agenda emerged from "the
money of British Whigs!"[8] How could these immigrants who spoke
in the brogue of the old country claim to be *more* patriotic than the
men who referred to themselves as Americans? And yet they did.

The nativists responded by asking if any Irishman wanted to
come up and debate them. A voice among the Irish shouted "Go
on, boys!" The crowd surged forward, splintering wood and
knocking over the stage. The flag fell to the ground. In a flash of

boots, the nativists dashed for safe streets beyond. Having settled the issue, the Irish dismantled the stage and took it home for firewood. They could not have foreseen the devastation that the afternoon would set about.[9]

༺༗༡༾

In the 1820s and 1830s, a national Working Men's movement had sprung up in American cities. The movement promised all workingmen, regardless of where they were born, a special place in the national polity. The essential element of the American promise, these men proclaimed, was equal access to the rights of citizenship. As the masthead of the *Working Man's Advocate* proclaimed, "All children are entitled to equal education; all adults to equal property; and all mankind, to equal privileges."

The Working Men's movement emerged out of a new world in which rapid transportation connected cheap labor with distant markets. All across the eastern seaboard, the invisible hand of the market economy was reshaping the human landscape. Farmers planted cash crops for sale to faraway markets, and young men and women moved to the city to work as large-scale factories opened their gates. The familiar circles of household production were giving way to the widening sweep of a market economy. Workers could no longer count on climbing, rung by rung, from apprentice to journeyman to master. If they were lucky, factory workers worked from sunrise to sunset; severe depressions in a fluctuating economy meant that they might not even get work. All they could count on was uncertainty.

Speaking to packed lecture halls, the Working Men's advocates articulated their distinctive vision of American patriotism, a vision that echoed that of the Revolutionary sailors. Ships' carpenters and shoemakers stood on wooden stages and spoke of the essential part that common people had played in winning the Revolution. Most strikingly, the Working Men insisted that the true meaning of the Declaration of Independence had yet to be fulfilled. Stumping through nine cities, one trade union leader pointed out that the Bunker Hill monument, a granite obelisk commemorating the Revolution's first major military conflict, was still unfinished after many years. He called it "a most excellent emblem of our unfinished independence. There let it *stand* unfinished, until the time passes away when aristocrats talk about mercy to mechanics and laborers. There let it stand unfinished, until our rights are acknowledged."[10]

The movement reached its height in Philadelphia, as native-born and immigrant workers banded together against their employers. When unskilled Irish boatmen went on strike, highly skilled native-born craft workers walked off their jobs in sympathy. The moment was historic: Not only were workingmen acting in union across the trades, but the more privileged also engaged significant risks in allying themselves with poorer, less-skilled workers. The unity paid off. Philadelphia workers won concessions that their counterparts in New York or Boston could only dream of: a ten-hour work day, higher wages, job protection. In Philadelphia, more than anywhere else, workers were able to realize their vision of economic self-determination and personal empowerment through class unity.[11]

As heirs to the Working Men's movement, the heckling Irishmen of 1844 saw the nativists as class traitors and un-American at that. The insults these workingmen hurled—"may turn Tory any minute," "the money of British Whigs"—indicated the extent to which workers defined the Revolution as a class struggle.

Patriotism, for the workingmen, was a commitment to equality and opportunity, not a bloodline or a birth certificate. It meant subscription to the republican and democratic ideals of the American Revolution and a commitment to extending them to all Americans. And it was the workingmen's advocates, whether Irish or American-born, who were the rightful successors to the national tradition.

By 1844, the Working Men's movement still lived in the hearts and minds of older workers, but it was no longer a potent political force. A brutal depression in 1837 had shattered the economic coalition of native-born and Irish workingmen, and the groups had parted ways. As the Working Men's movement dissolved, so did the sense that the government was responsible to the country's working classes. White American workers looked earnestly for someone or something to blame, some way to salvage their sense of identity. Protestant evangelicalism, with its promise of self-help and redemption, provided a positive vision; moral crusades against alcohol and the baleful influence of foreigners gave that vision its counterweight. Under the influence of men like Lewis Levin, native-born Philadelphians began to imagine a country defined primarily by white ethnicity and Protestantism.

Lewis Levin was a charismatic orator with a questionable past. Originally from South Carolina, he had been run out of Mississippi after a duel and had moved four times before settling in Philadelphia. By the time he was forty, he had been a teacher, a lawyer, a lecturer, and a newspaper editor. Like so many others in the city, he was a confidence man, although he dealt not in cards but in the hearts of men. A contemporary described him as "one of the most brilliant and unscrupulous orators I have ever heard."[12]

Levin began his Philadelphia career as a temperance preacher. It was a shrewd choice. Temperance was the fastest-growing movement in the United States, and Philadelphia was its fastest-growing center: For every one man who had signed a temperance pledge in 1838, four stepped up to do it in 1844. Down at the Philadelphia waterfront, Levin was at the very heart of that movement. He preached to dockhands and stevedores, firing their imagination by torching a great bonfire of liquor barrels. He held thousands captive in waterfront churches. "Evil," he thundered, came from "the *Rum Shop*." Levin could see the hole in a worker's heart, and he spoke to it. If workers stayed dry and temperate, he promised, they could close the "fatal chasm" between themselves and their employers. They would no longer be "tools and machines"; they would win respect as human beings.[13]

By 1842, Levin had moved over to the growing nativist movement. After persuading a wealthy dock builder to front him some money, Levin set himself up as the editor of a nativist newspaper. Bending over the printer's type in the office of the *Daily Sun*, he traced out his messages with inky fingertips. He described the unsteady world the men inhabited in terms of concrete foes. His message resonated with the white working class. The Irish were "an ignorant and deluded rabble"; their priests were guilty of "Guy Fawkes plots and infernal machinations." Urgently, he pressed "the purity of the ballot box," the importance of "incorruptible" leaders, and the almost-religious need for "Americans" to organize in self-defense.[14]

Levin also made his case in secret organizing meetings. On certain evenings, there were signs of preparation at the Sign of the Ball temperance hall. The glass globe that hung out front would be lit. People arrived out of the gathering darkness, mostly alone or in groups of two. Shrouded figures filed to the door; low voices asked for passwords; fingers twisted into secret handshakes. The door opened, and they passed through. Inside, the hall was full with white, working-class men. The better-off were ships' carpenters, cordwainers, and shopkeepers—traditional trades of the wharves—while the poorer ones were laborers, unskilled men who hauled heavy loads and dug cellar holes. All were native-born.[15]

In the spring of 1844, the globe was lit more often; more and more figures arrived at the hall. These secret gatherings served as organizing meetings for the American Republican Party. Members spoke knowingly of a mysterious "Sam," possibly the character of Uncle Sam that had emerged out of the War of 1812. They began to display images of an American eagle, which also gained in popularity after that war, and especially of George Washington. They frequently repeated Washington's famous line "Put none but natives on watch tonight," and the blue canton of stars on their flags was sometimes replaced with his appliquéd image. Unlike any group before them, they brought the American flag onto their stage and raised it over the hall as a ritual opening to their meetings.[16]

From the front of the hall, Levin spoke about immigration, about temperance, and about moral values. Given the events of that spring, he must have also spoken about Catholicism. He would have called it "Popery," a word that inspired fear, conjuring up the strange incantations of Latin masses and the secrets of confessional boxes. Levin's listeners were well acquainted with Catholicism, or so they thought. Like all native-born Protestants, they had heard horror stories for years. Some people had almost certainly sat in a gaslit lecture hall, among a rapt and horrified audience, as Philadelphia's own former priest, the

Reverend William Hogan, told shocking stories from their very midst. Most had heard stories repeated from the wildly popular *Awful Disclosures of Maria Monk: Or The Hidden Secrets of Life in a Convent Exposed,* a lurid account of a Montreal nunnery, written by a woman who claimed to have been held captive there. The book described secret corridors linking monasteries and convents, with lecherous priests ravaging young nuns and convent sewers clogged with the bodies of their bastard babies.[17]

Levin must also have spoken about the Irish predilection for extralegal violence. Desperate and angry when earnings sank below the breaking point, Irish workers responded with the only tool they had: labor strikes to halt the flow of textiles and raise their wages. The employers, predictably, rounded up even hungrier men and women and hired them as strike breakers. Irish strikers attacked these scabs, breaking into their workshops, pouring acid on the cloth that they wove, and axing their hand-looms until they splintered. When the American Republican Party began to organize more publicly, the Irish showed a similar willingness to use force. They chased nativists voters away from the polls at the local elections in Spring Garden, another section of Philadelphia, shot out the glass at the Sign of the Ball, and threatened to burn down any building used to house an American Republican Party meeting. To the nativists, such violent words and actions seemed clear proof that the Irish were unable to manage the self-control necessary for democratic government.[18]

Finally, Levin would have spoken about the growing crisis in the schools over which Bible should be used. From 1838 on, schoolteachers had read daily passages from the King James

Bible, the Protestant standard, as part of a lesson plan. This practice was called into question when Philadelphia's bishop asked that Irish children be allowed to use their own Douay Bible, with its Catholic notes and comments. Failing that, the bishop argued, the Bible should be banished from the classroom altogether. Such a statement was sacrilege, and nativists exploded with outrage, forming the American Protestant Association in 1842. Take the Bible out of the hands of babes? Clearly, the Catholics were trying to undermine their traditions and lure their children to the iniquities of Popery. In Levin's skillful formulation, the Catholic Irish became the source of social unrest and moral wickedness, providing a more tangible and more satisfying enemy than the invisible hand. The American flag was an excellent banner under which to do battle.[19]

∽₀₀∽

After the Irish knocked down the stage at the American Republican meeting, the shaken nativists reconvened at a temperance hall, furious and insulted. They decided to return to the Irish neighborhood the following Monday: They needed to claim their right to free assembly as Americans in an American city.[20]

All weekend, the nativists conferred furiously about the events of the interrupted rally. To this they added all the accumulated insults, real and imagined, of the past years. They described how Irish weavers had beaten American citizens waiting to vote. They repeated the story of the newly arrived Irishman who had stood on the stage of Philadelphia's Chinese museum during a public meeting and proclaimed that if he was not given the rights of native-born Americans, he would seize those rights "with the bowie knife and the rifle." Irish priests, the nativists had heard, were stockpiling weapons in their churches. Together, these pieces added up to an image of a native-born community under siege, a country attacked from within.[21]

Party members pasted placards all over the city. Nativist newspapers put out a call to native-born citizens and their sympathizers, asking them to join a mass meeting. The nativists knew that Philadelphia was full of men who felt that their security, their livelihood, the very world they had always known, was being pulled from under them. And they knew that those men were angry and frustrated.[22]

On the afternoon of Monday, May 6, three thousand men crammed onto the same tiny lot in Irish Kensington, standing shoulder to shoulder and fist to fist. The sky was cloudy and ominous. The men looked up to the rebuilt stage where Lewis Levin waited with other American Republican Party members. A ritual flag-raising opened the meeting. Hands lifted the American flag upward and hung it against the stage, and the crowd burst out with three hearty cheers.[23]

The Irish, too, had gathered. Many stood sentinel in surrounding houses, and several dozen of the bravest Irishmen had staked out a place in the Nanny Goat Market just down Master Street. They felt their hackles rising. To them, the flag symbolized not a nation-state to which they belonged but a political party that excluded them.[24]

The first speaker sat down, and the second took his place. An Irish carter pushed his horse and cart through the crowd and dumped a load of manure in front of the stage. Another followed. The crowd grew restive: What kind of insult was this? Some men attending the rally lurched forward; others held them back. As the crowd pushed and pulled, fat drops of rain began to patter down. Then the clouds broke open. While three thousand men scrambled for cover, Levin and others hurriedly pulled the flag from the stage.[25]

Through the ropes of rain, the men saw the most obvious shelter: the long, rectangular, open-sided structure of Nanny Goat Market. And they ran, shouting and whooping, splashing through the wet street. They flooded into the market building, shaking and dripping with water as they came under its sheltering roof, crowding into stalls, surrounding the stage, massing into the open central area. "Keep the damned natives out of the market house," one of the Irishman shouted. "This ground don't belong to them, it's ours!" But the nativists were already there, and Levin climbed onto a stack of packing boxes and hung the American flag over the speaker's stand.[26]

The Irish felt the insult sear. The Nanny Goat Market was the center of Irish life. Under its roof, merchants sold vegetables, fish, milk, and meat from its rudimentary stalls. Irishwomen did their daily shopping and met their neighbors; men spat tobacco juice and stood in groups, discussing the news. The market stage, in particular, was the heart of Irish resistance and pride. On that stage, Irishmen had inspired one another to resist unfair wages; they had gathered for political meetings. They had even been known to chase back a posse and beat an arresting sheriff. And now a member of the American Republicans stood on the stage with the American flag.[27]

As Levin looked down, he saw the marketplace full of wet bodies, jammed in together. It smelled like rain and sweat. Men bellowed. An Irishman waved his muscular arms above the crowd, threatening to fight. A pushing contest developed, and two men fought their way through the sea of flesh. Levin stood on the market stage, in front of the flag, trying to command attention. "Fellow citizens," he shouted. "We have reached an important crisis—"[28]

A nativist in the crowd brandished a musket. An Irishman dared him to use it. The armed man fired. All of a sudden, it was mayhem. A Protestant Irishman tried to make peace and was shot in the face. Bodies jostled; elbows met elbows. The crowd spilled onto the street.[29]

The Irish watching from surrounding buildings were well armed for the event. Gunfire rattled out of the Irish fire station and the Irish houses on Cadwalader Street. When nativists ran out of the market to escape the shooting, they found themselves ambushed by Irishmen who tore paving stones up from the streets to hurl as weapons. Even the Irishwomen joined the rioting, straining their skirts with the weight of the stones as they bent to pick up ammunition and hand it to their men.[30]

What happened next would play a critical role in defining the American flag. A young nativist named George Shiffler had adopted the flag as his special responsibility. He was a tanner's apprentice, and though he was not himself a member of the American Republican Party, he was one of the young men who hung around the meetings. Shiffler must have taken the nativist flag from the market house and brought it into the streets, holding it high as a tangible symbol of the American Republican Party. In so doing, he became a target. Two or three times, the Irish grasped at the flag and tried to bring it down. Two or three times, Shiffler recaptured the flag and hoisted it. The last time, as he raised the flag above his head, Shiffler was shot in the chest: six slugs to the heart. Still clutching the flag, he slumped to the ground. As four men carried Shiffler to a nearby apothecary, where he would die, the fighting continued. A silver-haired man shouted, "On, on Americans. Liberty or Death!"[31]

Violence continued throughout the afternoon and into the night. One nativist leader raced home and returned with eighteen muskets for his compatriots. Now armed, they roared down Cadwalader Street, where most of the gunfire had come from. The nativists heaved bricks and rocks at the houses, breaking down doors and shattering windows. Young Irishmen built bonfires in the streets, firelight flickering over the bullet-ridden buildings and the tense crowds. Late in the evening, a crowd of nativists marched into the neighborhood and broke into homes, heaving the furniture into the street. They torched the fence of the Catholic seminary, stoned the caretaker, and exchanged fire with the Irish. Two more men were killed.[32]

But for the flag, the riots might have ended there, a bloody, violent event like so many other bloody, violent events on Philadelphia's streets during these years. But the dramatic story of Shiffler's death generated fresh anger and resentment. The riots crystallized around the flag. They were no longer about specific issues like schools, or drink, or which Bible to use. Now, these issues had found expression in a national symbol.

The flag had meant something to nativists before that afternoon. But in the wake of the two meetings in Kensington, the flag ceased to be a symbol solely marking a shared culture within a group; it became a badge identifying the group to an outside world. When that badge was deliberately attacked, the nativists' claim to it was magnified. The attack did something else. Symbolically, it turned the Irish into enemies not only of the nativists but also of the flag and so, by extension, the country.

The following day offered promise. The night before, nativists had attacked the seminary with fire; at 3:30 that afternoon, over three thousand of them assembled at a public meeting in the yard behind the old statehouse. The brick building behind the platform was the same hall in which the Declaration of Independence had been signed; the bell looking over their gathering was the Liberty Bell; the ground under their feet was Independence Square. There, at the very center of American nationhood, the American Republican Party staked its claim to national tradition.[33]

Lewis Levin and other party members gathered on the platform. Despite, or perhaps because of, his role in the previous day's events, Levin was not one of the listed speakers. He looked out at the men gathered in the crowd before him. Many were bona fide members of the American Republican Party. Many were not party members but were sympathetic. Some were even Orange Irish, Protestant Irishmen at odds with their Catholic countrymen. And in the raucous tradition of nineteenth-century street politics, some just wanted to be where the action was. The mayor and other political leaders were nowhere to be seen.

It could have been a moment for restraint: a moment to appeal to a peaceful political process rather than violent street traditions. And in part it was. Speakers condemned the previous day's riots, passing a series of resolutions urging a fund for the victim's families and redress through nonviolent means. They insisted that their primary concern was not racism but an important matter of principle: the right to free speech and assembly. Most of the speakers deprecated any attempt at revenge.

But two elements undercut that possibility. One nativist speaker recounted the previous day, event by humiliating event, in a speech that inflamed the crowd. And there was the flag, George Shiffler's own flag, which had been carefully rescued and brought to the meeting. For the men who gathered around it, the torn fabric was filled with resonance, conjuring up emotion-filled scenes of Irish violence and nativist patriotism.[34]

Restless men pushed up shirtsleeves and flexed forearms as the meeting turned into a call for yet another rally on the same lot in the Irish neighborhood. A final speaker pleaded for the crowd to go home. Some people did. Others tightened into a posse several hundred strong, filing into the streets, shouting, "Adjourn to Second and Master now!" and "Let's go up to Kensington!" As they marched in military fashion to the accompaniment of fife and drum, they lifted the torn and tattered flag. In front of it, they carried a black-rimmed banner reading "This is the flag which was trampled under foot by the Irish Papists." Their grim line led north on Second Street for a mile and a half, to the Irish neighborhood.[35]

Meanwhile, the Irish prepared. Some took out guns and braced themselves in dilapidated houses. Some filled carts with their possessions and pulled them through the streets, heading for refuge in Carmac's Woods, north of the city. Others took out glue pots and pasted the mastheads of the *Native American* newspaper to their doors, or smudged their fingers with charcoal as they inscribed the words "Native American" on makeshift wooden signs. And in many rooms, Irishwomen rummaged through their stashes of fabric, pulling out scraps of red, blue, and white. They took out their needles, their thread. Hurriedly, ears to the street outside, the women sewed. Stitch after stitch, the scraps of cloth became small, makeshift flags. With the crowd coming on, they hung the flags outside, attaching them to doorways, to windows, to whatever would hold them. Then they went back inside and prayed.[36]

As the nativists marched into Kensington, they broke down doors, kicked in windows, tossed beds and chairs into the street. When they saw one of the makeshift flags, the men roared with approval. The flag acted as a protective talisman, shielding the occupants from the rage of the crowd. At its sight, nativists moved on to the next house.[37]

The nativists did their worst on Cadwalader Street, where many Irish leaders lived. Most of the gunfire had come from these houses the day before. The street was occupied by dilapidated three-story houses of brick and wood, so here the attackers unleashed the scourge of nineteenth-century cities: fire. The flames raced through the old frame houses, leaped to the Irish fire station, engulfed the Nanny Goat Market, and forced people trapped in the buildings to emerge under nativist gunfire. In all, an entire block of buildings blazed, a flaming brand on the Irish neighborhood. Before leaving, the members of the American Republican Party paused to hoist Shiffler's torn and dirty flag over the scene.[38]

But the party had sparked violence that could not be contained. For another full day, men roamed the neighborhood, looking for trouble. Some were American Republican Party members; many were not. In the guise of searching for Irish weapons, they set fire to homes and shops. They broke windows and doors, splintered furniture, tossed books and papers out of doors, knifed featherbeds. Feathers skittered along the street and wafted upward in the flames. Boys drummed out a tattoo on an overturned stove. The crowd set fire to St. Michael's Catholic Church, the priest's residence, and the seminary. The mob swarmed downtown to the city's largest Catholic church, St. Augustine's on Fourth Street below Vine, where an observer described the attackers as "a busy multitude moving like disturbed bees in a hive." Mayor John Morin Scott tried to stop them, standing in the church entrance and pleading for forbearance. When he was done, his listeners shouted for him to step aside while a teenage boy climbed into the church cellar, cut a gas pipe, and set the building on fire. The church exploded into flames, and the crowd cheered as the steeple fell, sending sparks high into the night sky.[39]

Finally, three days after the riots had begun, Kensington lay still. Irish families, returning from the woods where they had fled, found blocks and blocks of fire-eaten buildings. People made their way around piles of broken detritus in the street. More than fifty houses, a fire station, the marketplace, three churches, and a seminary had burned down. Mourners walked somberly in funeral processions. Against this blackened, broken cityscape flickered strips of red, white, and blue cloth, the flags that the Irishwomen had hastily sewn to protect their houses. Hundreds of the handmade flags hung against the ruins of the charred district.[40]

Forced to come to terms with the terrible destruction of the Irish neighborhoods, Philadelphians pointed blame at the na-tivists. In the city's many newspapers, angry editors castigated the nativists, describing "the crumbled ruins of Kensington," "the blackened bones of the slaughtered," "the still smoking cin-ders," and the Irish "wandering houseless and homeless." Against this vivid portrait, the papers thundered:

> Look at these things, and if you have the courage, say—all this was done in the Republic of America! . . . This was done in the

name of the Bible! This was done to glorify the flag of the union! . . . Say this if ye dare, all who can truly boast of being not Americans by *birth* only, but Americans by nature![41]

Editors drew particular attention to the "mortifying" and "humiliating" vision of small flags flying amid the destruction. The American flag, they contended, was not the property of the American Republicans; it did not mean America for the Americans. Rather, it meant that "our laws afford equal and efficient protection to all." The outrage was palpable.[42]

The upper classes had previously tolerated the nativists but now turned against them. If the wealthier citizens had previously felt that the Irish represented a violent threat, they could now see that nativists were capable of far greater destruction. Merchant Thomas Cope wrote that the sound of the statehouse bell, which rung out to warn citizens of the city in flames, "remind[s] us of the awful tocsin of Revolutionary France." Another wealthy citizen, lawyer Sidney George Fisher, darkly predicted the death of civilization, which would be "destroyed by the eruption of the dark masses of ignorance and brutality which lie beneath it, like a volcano."[43]

One newspaper, the *Daily Sun*, stood unapologetic about the nativists' rampage. The *Sun* was Levin's paper. While Samuel Kramer's *Native American* declared that the riots had gone too far, Levin ignored the general violence and focused selectively on violence done by Irishmen to nativists. He spun the story of George Shiffler, emphasizing his heroic defense of the flag. Like Shiffler, Levin claimed, nativists merely asked for the right to assemble on American soil. The riots had been an Irish attack on that right. "We stand like persecuted martyrs," Levin proclaimed, "defending our lives and liberties."[44]

Levin's words may have misrepresented the riots, but they captured a deeper truth, one that resonated with the workers' feeling that their lives were under siege. The American Republican Party was poised to take advantage of the moment. During the months of May and June, the party held enormous open-air meetings nearly every night. Upward of ten thousand native-born men and women came out into the warm evenings to see their neighbors and listen to the stirring words of party leaders. Under the new green canopy of leaves, they watched the flag rise and felt the strong personal tug of ownership. Lewis Levin stood on the wooden stage and drew his audience to him with phrases that straightened the spine and boiled the blood. He described how they, the Americans, had been deprived of their rights to free assembly and to free speech. He retold the story of Shiffler, spinning and elaborating. He made Shiffler's valiant defense of the flag and the young man's untimely death, rather than the destruction heaped upon the Irish, the central story of the riots.[45]

The crowds treasured that story. They retold it to one another, on the waterfront, at home, and in political meetings on the street. It had everything: a young hero, a valiant cause, dark enemies, a talismanic banner. Mostly, it had explanatory power. This was the meaning of the riots: The Irish hated America and wanted to attack it. The young men at one firehouse took on the story as their identity, naming themselves the Shiffler Hose Company. Booksellers and printers brought the story into print, selling Shiffler sheet music and poetry. Women bought a lithograph depicting the young man sinking to his knees, one hand on his heart and the other clutching the flag. At the open-air meetings, the tune of "Auld Lang Syne" rose out of many throats, now with a new set of verses:

*Our Flag's insulted, friends are slain,*
*And must we quiet be?*
*No! No! we'll Rally round the Flag,*
*Which leads to Victory.*[46]

Meanwhile, nativist women sat down with their sewing baskets and pulled out lengths of silk cloth, an expensive luxury they had sacrificed to buy. With scissors, they carefully sheared long strips of red and white silk and snipped stars out of the white material to lay on silken blue squares. Needles stitched images and mottos onto the stripes: "Beware of Foreign Influence"; the Goddess of Liberty; a schoolhouse; an eagle. When they finally put away their needles and thread, just before the Fourth of July, hundreds of flags were ready to wave.[47]

That Independence Day, the nativists held an enormous parade. Even in an age of parades, it was grander than any other procession Philadelphia had ever seen. Participants began to fill the streets by 6:30 in the morning. As the hour for the parade came nearer, Arch Street filled with tens, then hundreds, then thousands of men and boys. Riders reined in their horses; musical bands lined up with their instruments; newly sewn flags and banners billowed. Lewis Levin stepped into the barouche that would carry him. For over five hours, five thousand marchers strode by in waves of silk banners, horses, flags, and music. They made their way through dense and cheering crowds: As many as one hundred thousand people, or a quarter of the city's population, swarmed the streets along the parade route.[48]

The flag was everywhere. Most prominently, a horse drew a simple car displaying a ragged flag with a sign identifying it as "the torn flag that was trampled on at Kensington." A silk banner showed Shiffler collapsing to the ground, one hand on his heart and the other gripping the flag. Another showed the Goddess of Liberty draped in the American flag, teaching a young boy from an open Bible. Everywhere, banners blazed with anti-immigrant words and images. George Washington's famous quote "Beware of Foreign Influence" appeared in no less than thirteen places.

This Independence Day parade was strikingly different from any that had preceded it. In fusing the story of Shiffler's death to the broader notion of American patriotism, nativists brought the flag openly into the public arena as *their* banner, a symbol of *their* nation, infused with *their* meaning. Theirs was both a massive claim to the flag on the part of a single group and a public equation of nativism and patriotism. Unlike the Revolutionary sailors, who had also claimed a national symbol as their own, the nativists did not use the flag to extend rights and liberties to a larger population. They used it to define the group—the native-born—whom they considered the rightful heirs to these privileges.

Nativism was particularly seductive because it recast concerns about an economic gap in ideological terms. Philadelphia's native-born workers needed to feel like whole human beings engaged in an important effort. Industrialization had belittled their work, casting them in the role of tools and machines. It was a dynamic that Karl Marx, writing across the ocean that same year, would diagnose as the alienation of labor. If native-born workers had tried to strike, employers would simply have gone down to the docks and hired men off the next incoming boat from Ireland.

Levin understood this crisis. Over the dark landscape of industrialization, he transposed the bright light of spiritual salvation. He cast his words in the familiar mold of spiritual struggle:

n 1846, and both Whigs and Democrats tried to claim it
844 elections. But by far the flag's most powerful conno-
n the Eastern cities, where the country's population was
rated, was as a nativist symbol. Nativist newspapers fea-
he image on their mastheads; nativist politicians waved
at their rallies. In their hands, the red, white, and blue
oudly: "America for the Americans." Nativists were so
ful in claiming the outward symbols of American patriot-
t others veered away from them: In Baltimore, one man
efused to speak at an Independence Day celebration be-
e feared that his participation would earn him a reputa-
a nativist. For the moment, the flag meant a white,
nt America that sought to vanquish, if not eliminate, the
nts who massed in its urban centers. It was only with the
ar in 1860 that these nativist connotations would be sub-
n an even more powerful set of nationalist ideas.[53]

purity versus degradation, temperance versus drunkenness, good versus evil. He placed the workers in an imaginative landscape where they *could* win. The flag served as a battle standard against the dark encroachment of a new industrial order.

Levin's success reveals much about the nature of patriotism. The Irish and the nativists held many values in common. Both drew on freedom, citing founding documents or concepts. A generation before, both groups had subscribed to the patriotism of the Working Men's movement. There was no inherent reason that the two groups should have found themselves on opposite sides of a patriotic divide. But as the American Republicans wooed native-born workers, the workers dropped their common cause with the Irish immigrants. They traded the patriotism of the workingman's struggle, with its strong egalitarianism, for the hierarchies of belonging offered by the nativists. Or, rather, they did not abandon egalitarianism entirely; they offered it only to a much smaller circle: native-born, white, Protestant workers.

These events marked nativism as a forerunner of a nationalist patriotism that would dominate American culture in the twentieth century. A form of nationalism, nativism was defined by loyalty—not to ideas but to a people or a government—and by a sense of union or belonging. The nationalist patriotism that arose during the Revolution and then the War of 1812 could encompasses citizens of many faiths and ethnicities, and these patriots saw their nation as coextensive with the people who populated it. But nativism, in defining Americanism in ethnic and religious terms, circumscribed the community of patriots more tightly than before. And it offered a compelling formulation to those it welcomed into its fold: By dividing the larger community, nativism offered a powerful sense of union to its adherents.

The flag, a key part of nativism's early attraction, was critical to the growth of the movement after George Shiffler's death.

∽∘∾

In Philadelphia that fall, nativist politicians overwhelmingly carried the 1844 elections, sending Lewis Levin triumphantly to Congress. They took control of the school board, the police force, and the licensing of taverns, as well as filling many of the city's patronage appointments. The Democrats were defeated, and Irish power eviscerated. Meanwhile, the Irish slowly rebuilt their neighborhood. The weavers, formerly fierce and uncompromising, were beaten down: Their wages were slashed after the riots, and when they finally held another strike two years later, it lacked the vehemence of their earlier ones.[49]

The middle and upper classes were alarmed at the riots: Another set had followed the Independence Day parade. Lawyers and merchants held a demonstration urging "law and order" in the statehouse yard. They pointed out the inadequacy of the existing system: Constables and night watchmen managed drunks and petty thieves, while in more serious situations, the constable alerted the sheriff, who in turn gathered a civilian posse, volunteer and unarmed, to find and confront any rioters. Such makeshift efforts could not contain the tumultuous urban forces of the 1840s. The result of their proposal for a city militia was the formation of one of the country's first professional police forces, in 1854.[50]

Up and down the East Coast, the Philadelphia riots galvanized the nativist movement. New York nativists asked Philadelphians to come to their city, hoping to carry Shiffler's flag in a parade through Central Park, but the mayor feared church burn-

ings and called off the plan. The power
mented by increasing fears of immigration
lowing 1845, nearly three million immi
numbers of Germans, escaping crop failur
displacement of the Industrial Revoluti
United States; they joined the Irish who
and disease during the potato famine of 18
ravaged Ireland's subsistence crop. Wh
moved westward, most found themselve
cities like Boston and New York, more th
was foreign-born.[51]

The American Republican Party died
the victim of a recovering economy and
much of its platform. But in the early 185
as the American Party, a name that differ
the new Republican Party while further u
to patriotic status. Most Americans came
Party as the Know-Nothings. The pa
through massive write-in campaigns tha
nents: Democratic candidates frequently
were being challenged until the votes cam
found themselves the losers. The Know
states in the 1854 elections and came
more; in the East, it replaced the Whigs
opposing the Democrats and gained 63
highly industrialized Massachusetts.[52]

In the wake of the Philadelphia riots,
bol as fully associated with the nativist
U.S. government. Commercial ships still
Mexican-American War marched under

battle
in the
tation
concen
tured t
the flag
spoke
success
ism tha
nearly
cause h
tion as
Protesta
immigr
Civil W
sumed

# ~3~

# FLAG OF WAR

## *Fort Sumter to the Emancipation Proclamation*

In late December 1860, a tiny company of Union soldiers—fewer than a hundred men—took Fort Sumter in a surprise operation. The following day, the men stood on the parade ground: soldiers formal in blue uniforms and workmen wearing their usual open-necked shirts and suspenders. All stood at attention and faced the flagpole, where the fort's new commander knelt. A chaplain gave thanks for a successful operation and prayed that the flag would soon wave over a united and happy country. The commander attached the flag to its halyards. Above, high on the brick ramparts, a handful of military musicians struck up "The Star-Spangled Banner." The soldiers and laborers watched in silence as the flag rose up the pole and unfurled over the fort. Thirty-three stars shimmered against a brilliant ultramarine background; thirteen red and white stripes stretched thirty-six feet in length. Then the men cheered three times for the Union and three times for the flag, "Huzzah! Huzzah! Huzzah!"—"Huzzah! Huzzah! Huzzah!" Their cries rose up over the high walls and reached across the waters.[1]

The place was South Carolina, just outside the capital city of Charleston. For two centuries, the South had built an economy on slaves laboring on cotton, rice, and indigo plantations. The North had moved away from slavery and toward industrialization. Since the Revolution, the two sections of the country, North and South, had maintained an uneasy balance of power. The nation's history was littered with compromises. The Three-Fifths Compromise, the Missouri Compromise of 1820, and the Compromise of 1850 each balanced the political interests of slave states and free states. But this equilibrium, always tenuous, was getting harder and harder to maintain. The steady flow of settlers toward the west threatened the country's stability: If Nebraska was admitted as a slave state, would there be a free state to offset its influence? The ruling principle of popular sovereignty, the ability of each territory to vote on slavery within its borders, threatened to tip the whole country toward slavery as Southerners moved west and brought their slaves.

No one knew when or how war would happen, and some still hoped that it would not. But tensions began to erupt in an increasingly dramatic set of events: the Fugitive Slave Act, the publication of Harriet Beecher Stowe's antislavery novel *Uncle Tom's Cabin* in 1852, and the Dred Scott decision in 1857, in which the Supreme Court ruled that Congress could not outlaw slavery in federal territories. They exploded in abolitionist John Brown's raid on Harper's Ferry in 1859, in which Brown and his followers seized a federal arsenal and attempted to arm slaves with the weapons; the attack ended in the death of seven people and eventually Brown's conviction and hanging. It was a deeply polarizing event.

The 1860 presidential campaign reflected the country's divisions. Instead of two candidates, there were four. The Democratic

Party had split into a Northern faction, led by Stephen Douglas, which argued for popular sovereignty, and a Southern faction, led by John Breckinridge, with a proslavery platform. The Constitutional Union Party, led by former Whig John Bell, carried the border states with its hopes for reconciling the Constitution and the Union. And the young Republican Party, led by Abraham Lincoln, argued for the necessary containment of slavery. The Republicans carried the North, but were anathema in the South. Slaveholding Southerners did not trust Lincoln. He was an abolitionist in disguise, they felt, and his presidency would inaugurate an era of slave uprisings and a world turned upside down. This fear was widespread. "I see poison in the wells of Texas—and fire for the houses in Alabama," wrote a Southern congressman. "How can we stand it? . . . *It is enough to risk disunion on.*" From Alabama to Georgia to South Carolina, white Southerners warned that Lincoln's election would precipitate secession. So when the votes were tallied and Lincoln emerged a minority winner, with only 40 percent, the country waited in suspense.[2]

Though no one knew where a conflict might begin, it was clear that federal forts in Southern states were potential flashpoints. Southerners watched as these garrisons, which had been built for their own protection, now threatened to become enemy fortifications within striking distance of their cities. With Lincoln as commander, the armed forces might well be used against the South. Northerners, too, were suspicious. Lincoln's inauguration was still more than two months away. They knew the deep Southern sympathies of President James Buchanan's secretary of war, John Floyd, and watched as he sent guns, cannons, armaments, and ammunition to Southern forts—in South Carolina alone, enough to equip seventeen thousand men. Floyd's orders were particularly troubling to Northerners since he sent no troops to man the arms: Instead they lay, virtually unguarded, in undefended garrisons. He seemed to be preparing the forts for a moment when Southern troops could walk in and aim their cannons northward. South Carolina was especially vulnerable. Not only did Charleston have four federal forts, but it was also home to many of the loudest secessionist voices.[3]

Charleston was the South's second-largest city after New Orleans, with just over forty thousand residents: roughly half white and half black. It lay low on the South Carolina coast, surrounded by swamps and wetlands, islands and channels. Built on a peninsula, the city extended a well-laid grid of streets south into the harbor. On the Battery, the city's southern tip, well-dressed ladies and gentlemen strolled along a broad promenade shaded by leafy trees and cooled by gardens. Slave boys leaned against the railing, looking out at the harbor. In the streets adjoining the Battery, large and beautiful mansions, painted in pastels, sheltered the town's elite white families. Midway up the peninsula, merchants and auctioneers bustled along busy Broad Street to the wharves on the city's east side. Farther north, the sheen of gentility gave way to the raw economic grind of gristmills, foundries, and furniture factories.[4]

In November and December 1860, Charleston's streets flashed with colored swaths of silk and cotton: flags, banners, sashes, and cockades. Many depicted the state's symbol in white on a dark blue background: the tall, straight trunk and feathery leaves of the palmetto tree with a crescent moon in the upper left corner. Other flags showed a similar silhouette in different colors: white against red, or green against white under a startling red star. Other images included crescent moons set in a circle of stars against a field of dark blue and bold red stars on a white background, a symbol of state's rights. Banners urged "Strike Now or Never." "We can scarcely pass through a street," wrote a reporter, "without finding additions to the banners, flags and ensigns that are given to the breeze."[5] The flags had appeared in response to the presidential election results: The colorful, constant protest to Lincoln's coming presidency was designed to keep the outrage at a peak. Palmetto flags fluttered over the wrought-iron balcony of the Mills House and the stone portico of city hall as speakers urged independence. When militiamen gathered to drill, they tied red sashes around their waists and pinned blue cockades to their hats: each embellishment a colorful tribute to the rebellion.

That November, immediately after Lincoln's election, the South Carolina General Assembly called for a special convention for the purpose of secession. The convention met in mid-December in Columbia, but moved to Charleston to avoid a smallpox outbreak. On the twentieth, the delegates met in the city's large Institute Hall to make a formal declaration of secession. Their measure declared that "the union now subsisting between South Carolina and other States, under the name of the 'United States of America,' is hereby dissolved." It passed by a roll call vote of 169 to 0.

The ordinance was signed in the evening with great ceremony. The hall was packed with white Charlestonians eager to witness the historic event. When a speaker announced, "The time for action has come," he was greeted by a rebel yell that shook the great hall. Ladies brandished their handkerchiefs, and men gave great whooping huzzahs. Church bells rang, and cannons boomed. Deep into the night, the city was filled with the leaping

flames of bonfires and the crack of small explosions. Militiamen
paraded through the city, their hundreds of boots hitting the
ground in time to the martial music of military bands. The deed
had been done.[6]

In the next few days, all eyes turned to the federal forts
around the city: Castle Pinckney just off the wharves, Forts Johnson and Moultrie on either side of the harbor, and Fort Sumter
strategically situated on an island where the harbor met the sea.
They were not highly manned. Just over one hundred Union soldiers lived in Moultrie, while Sumter and Pinckney were under
renovation and Johnson was used as a staging area for the
work. Before secession, these buildings had been irritants; now,
seen through the eyes of an independent state, they were illegal
occupations. Bands of men gestured and argued and debated
how best to storm the federal forts. Horses hauled cannons into
place; piles of ladders lay ready for breaching parapets. Two
thousand of the state's best sharpshooters cleaned their rifles
and watched Fort Moultrie, ready to fire if the garrison showed
signs of arming.[7]

∽o∾

On December 20, the day South Carolina seceded, Major Robert
Anderson stood in Fort Moultrie looking out at Fort Sumter in
the middle of the harbor. Anderson was a career military man
whose double row of buttons down his uniform marked him as
an officer. Still trim and handsome in his mid-fifties, he carried
himself erect. Everything about him, down to the silvering hair
cropped close to his head, bespoke his preference for order. He
was coolheaded and steady, firm in his faith and methodical in
his habits. His moral compasses, explained a relative, were the

Ten Commandments, the Constitution, and the book of army regulations.[8]

Anderson faced a tangle of loyalties as his country teetered on the verge of civil war. He had been selected for duty in Charleston partly because he was considered a good man to keep the hot spot out of trouble. But it was his divided loyalties, even more than his temperament, that made him an attractive commander for Fort Moultrie at that tense moment. A Northern-leaning general would have inflamed the Charleston crowds and invited attack; a Southern-leaning one might have turned the fort right over to them. But Anderson was tugged both South and North by a complex calculus of personal ties, convictions, and experience. Many of his strongest sympathies were Southern. He had grown up in Kentucky, where his big limestone house was surrounded by slave cabins, and he watched as nearby Louisville grew from an outpost town into a booming city on the strength of its slave trade. Attending West Point as a young man, he felt an immediate affinity with other Southerners there and formed strong friendships with Jefferson Davis, the man who would become president of the Confederacy, and other future secessionists. When he married, he chose a Southern bride, the daughter of a Georgia general and rice plantation owner. Yet Anderson also had a powerful connection to the Union. His father had fought in the Revolution, and that history was still only one generation away. Having joined the merchant marine at the time of the Stamp Act, his father was in Boston for the Tea Party, joined the army at the Declaration of Independence, fought in battles from Trenton to Monmouth, spent the winter at Valley Forge, served as aide to General Lafayette, and was finally captured and imprisoned in Charleston. Anderson's Union sentiments and

Southern sympathies reflected the ambivalence of the country as a whole in 1860.[9]

Like many Southerners of his era, Anderson believed slavery was sanctioned by the Bible. When the topic came up among the men at Fort Sumter, he would cite the relevant biblical passages to prove his point. And yet Anderson had little personal taste for slaveholding. When he inherited slaves from his father as a young man, he freed them. When he married, his wife's family offered him the opportunity of settling down to the life of a wealthy slave owner—Anderson might have ruled a five-thousand-acre rice plantation in Georgia, where the roses bloomed at Christmas—but he chose to continue his work as a professional soldier instead. He was not above participating in slavery (he seemed to have owned slaves and sold them in 1860) but it was not essential to the fabric of his life. Unlike Jefferson Davis and other Confederates, Anderson had little riding on the survival or downfall of slavery.[10]

More than anything, Anderson loved the Union. By 1860, he had spent his entire professional career, nearly forty years, in the service of the American military. As a cadet at West Point, he found himself in a meeting ground of North and South that proved congenial: It was a place he would return to repeatedly. In the Black Hawk War, the Seminole Wars, and the Mexican-American War, he had fought again and again on the side of the Union. For men who had lived their careers in the service of the United States, national patriotism often proved stronger than sectional loyalties. As one fellow Southerner and military man expressed it: "I am as I have always been a Union man—I know no North or South. . . . All that I know is my duty to flag & country under which I have served for the last 30 years."[11]

The military men who found themselves leaders in 1860 had a particularly strong connection to the flag, stronger than any developed by previous soldiers. They treated it with great ceremony and frequently spoke of their service in its terms. The Mexican-American War was the crux of this connection. The war, begun after Texas was annexed by the United States in 1845 and ended in early 1848 when the border between the two countries was established, saw the flag's coming of age. It was the first war in which soldiers carried the national flag rather than a regimental one into battle, and civilians seized on the banner as a popular symbol of the American cause. The war generated so much demand that the nation's first flag company incorporated and began machine-producing flags, though manufacturers still sewed the stars on by hand. The Stars and Stripes became a leitmotif of the war, and most of the Civil War generals, South and North, had fought under it in Mexico: Robert E. Lee, Stonewall Jackson, Ulysses S. Grant, William Sherman, and George McClellan.[12]

Robert Anderson was one of these men. When Anderson served as a colonel in the Black Hawk War, fighting the Sauk tribe in Illinois for their lands in 1832, he had fought under a regimental flag. The same was true when he waged war against the Seminoles from 1835 to 1842, forcing their relocation from Florida. But when Anderson made the long trek through Mexico in 1847, he and other soldiers marched under the national flag for the first time. For five long months, Anderson followed the flag, marching behind it from the beaches at Veracruz, inland through rocky mountain passes, and finally down into the lush Valley of Mexico. He followed the flag at dawn into the Battle of Molino del Ray, where he fell wounded and lost a quarter of his comrades. While Anderson's gunshot wound was cleaned and his shoulder bandaged, the American army rode on to the gates of Mexico City, right up to the halls of Montezuma. General Winfield Scott's appearance in the main square, resplendent on his charger, was a dramatic moment, complete with the flag flying in the sun. That flag became the symbol of conquest when the soldiers hauled the Mexican banner down from the citadel and the American flag rose over the city.[13]

But the flag under which the army men rode and fought also became a symbol of their collective experience. Each military man had his own private theater of war. For Jefferson Davis, it was the Battle of Buena Vista under the high peaks of northern Mexico; for Robert Anderson it was the unexpected Mexican fire at Molino del Ray. The one constant was the image of the flag: red stripes, white stripes, blue field, white stars, all in motion on a military standard. It was a connective visual tissue between soldiers at war, linking them not only across geography but across time. One captain in the war described the American flag with a deepening sense of history. The Stars and Stripes, he wrote, was "the most beautiful of all flags, dyed in the blood of our fore-fathers, and redyed in that of their sons upon the fierce battle-field . . . an emblem of American possession to the Sierra Madre!"[14] The flag's stars and stripes had become a repository of the nation's history.

In 1860, Americans were not nearly as polarized as they would become only one year later: Abolitionists and secessionists were still minorities, however vocal they might be. Like Anderson, most white Americans accepted slavery; like him, most believed in the Union. Lincoln may have claimed that a house divided could not stand, but many Americans saw no insoluble conflict between slavery and union. The United States had always been a slaveholding country; there was no reason it should not continue half slave and half free. South Carolina, Anderson told others privately, should not have made the attempt to break free from the Union: The state was like "a spoiled child that needed correction." His time as a soldier had taught him the costs of war. Thirteen years earlier, he had promised his wife not to go "a-soldiering" anymore. In a letter sent from Mexico, he exclaimed that "no more absurd scheme could be invented for settling national difficulties than the one we are now engaged in—killing each other to find out who is in the right!"[15]

As Anderson stood in Fort Moultrie on the day that South Carolina seceded, he wanted, above all else, to avoid provoking a war. He felt certain that a secessionist attack on Fort Moultrie, whether or not it were repelled, would precipitate war. And Fort Moultrie practically invited attack. It lay on the northeast side of the harbor, on the popular summer resort of Sullivan's Island. The fort's immediate surroundings were peaceable enough—the grand hotels and summer houses of the Southern gentry—but it stood only a few miles from the gathering city crowds in Charleston. The fort was indefensible. Long dunes of sand blown up against the fort allowed children to walk to the height of the fortification. Inside, fissures in the walls were so deep that men could pull themselves to the parapet by jamming hands and boots in the cracks and climbing. Wooden houses around the fort provided perfect cover for hostile sharpshooters. Adding to Anderson's frustration, secessionists rode out to the fort every day to watch him and his men at work. He and his men were trapped: in a rickety fort, under constant threat of attack, in the most volatile region of the country.

Fort Sumter, a garrison built on an island in the harbor, promised welcome protection. Though still under construction, it was in much better shape than Moultrie, and being in the middle of the harbor, it had perfect visibility: There was no cover for attackers. Hundreds of workmen there, many from the North, were mounting guns. With those guns, Sumter would be the ideal place from which to control the harbor. A move to Sumter, Anderson realized, would allow him to defend his men, and it would preempt an assault by the hotheaded Charleston mobs. "The clouds are threatening," Anderson had written to Washington in November, "and the storm may break upon us at any moment." Militiamen milled around Charleston, guns at the ready. They goaded one another with tales of Fort Moultrie's glorious past and the way their ancestors had held it during the Revolution. The city's rumor mills reported that four companies of Southern troops would soon attack the fort; whether or not the specifics were true, everyone considered some kind of attack a given. "We appreciate your position," Anderson was told by gentlemen in the city, as they armed against him. "It is a point of honor with you to hold the fort, but a political necessity obliges us to take it."[16]

Unwilling to sustain such an attack, Anderson resolved to move his men to Sumter. He waited as long as he dared, until the day after Christmas. Just after dusk, he announced the plan, giving the men only twenty minutes to ready themselves before departure. The maneuver was complex and perfectly executed. Schooners for supplies had been hired under another guise. Large rowboats carried the men. Three times they rowed back and forth, eluding the Charleston ships that patrolled the harbor. When they finally arrived, Anderson's men took possession of the fort from the surprised workmen. The soldiers put the Southern sympathizers among the workers on a boat for the mainland and welcomed the Union men into their ranks. And in the morning, Anderson and his men held their flag ceremony.

Anderson had intended the small ceremony to be a ritual of thanksgiving for himself and his men. By moving his men away from the secessionist crowds, he thought he had removed the possibility of an unintentional military clash. But when white Charlestonians stood on their promenade and saw the U.S. flag flying over the fort, they reacted with a howling sense of betrayal. Their own city was almost entirely decked out in Confederate banners, and to the secessionists looking out at Fort Sumter from the city's waterfront, Anderson's raising of the flag seemed an aggressive claim for Northern abolitionism. All the rising tension between North and South was condensed and encapsulated in Sumter's fluttering flag.[17]

When informed that Sumter was in Anderson's hands, the governor of South Carolina, Francis Pickens, countered quickly. Pickens informed the secession convention that he considered the move a violation of "the distinct understanding" between the president and South Carolina officials. Its inexorable effect, he announced, was "bringing on a state of war." On his orders, state militiamen seized Castle Pinckney, Fort Johnson, Fort Moultrie, and the federal arsenal in the city. One by one, the men ran palmetto flags up the poles at each of these forts, forming a circle around the harbor. In the city, they hauled the U.S. flags down from the post office and the customs house.[18]

Only one American flag flew in the midst of a widening circle of Southern flags. Atop the dark hulk of Fort Sumter, the Stars and Stripes fluttered like a matador's cloth in the pale December light.

In the years leading up to the Civil War, a variety of ideological battles had played out on the fabric of the flag itself. Many Americans sewed flags that represented not the number of states that *were* in the Union, but the number of states that they thought *should* be. The Hayes arctic expedition, departing Boston for the North Pole in 1860, flew a flag of eighteen stars, one for each of the states that was unquestionably loyal to the North. A Charleston captain, in 1856, flew a flag of fifteen stars to indicate the states that he thought would soon belong to the South. The inventor Samuel F. B. Morse responded to the Civil War by suggesting that the national flag be divided into two, split by a diagonal line from the top left to the lower right corner. Northern states could fly the upper half; Southern states would have the lower. At some later time, Morse pointed out, the two halves would hopefully be reunited. This was known as a peace flag, and such flags were flown both in the North and in the South, though in Massachusetts, crowds tarred and feathered the flyers of these flags.[19]

To abolitionists, the flag had been a long-standing irritant, a stark visual reminder of the distance between American ideals and American slavery. As early as the 1830s, British poet Thomas Campbell had used the flag as a critique of American hypocrisy, reenvisioning the flag's red stripes as bloody whip-markings on the back of a slave:

*Your banner's constellation types*
*White freedom with its stars.*
*But what's the meaning of the stripes?*
*They mean your negroes' scars.*

In the 1850s, other abolitionists took up the association between slavery and the flag. The *Liberator,* William Lloyd Garrison's abolitionist newspaper, incorporated the flag on its masthead: waving over a slave auction. Abolitionist flags proliferated, reflecting in their design the conviction that slaveholding states had no place in a country dedicated to freedom. The followers of John Brown sewed such a flag. Instead of thirty-three stars—one for every state—it bore only twenty, for the Northern states. Other fervent Northerners sewed similar flags, with different numbers of stars, depending on the maker's criteria: some flags carried stars for all those states that had not yet seceded; others included stars only for those states that were securely pledged to the Union.[20]

To Union sympathizers, the flag seemed increasingly a symbol of lawfulness and orderly government. Like Robert Anderson, they saw secessionism as hotheaded and anarchical; *Harper's Weekly* argued that the South's action threatened "the universal destruction . . . of all property [and] of all the guarantees of civil society." Northerners saw the South's secession as tantamount to ripping up the Constitution. The flag in Charleston Harbor was a protest against that lawlessness.[21]

But the government that the Unionists revered for its lawfulness seemed, to secessionists, to be a ruthless ideological and military power bent on conquering the South and destroying its institutions. For Southerners and secessionists, the Stars and Stripes was an enemy flag in the harbor. It threatened their most profound institution, indeed their whole way of life. Southerners feared the unleashing of slave power, either openly in armed insurrections like the one led by Nat Turner in Virginia three decades earlier, or quietly, with poison dropped in the soup tureen. As Thomas Jefferson had said so many years ago, "We have the wolf by the ears and we can neither hold him nor safely let him go." What would the South do if run by a government that was openly hostile to slavery? How could it exist? Slavery was the economic foundation of Southern civilization. All the cotton, the ships, the rice, the sugar cane that came out of the South had been touched in some way by slaves. Just as profoundly, slavery was essential to the social workings of Southern society: the gentility, the hospitality, the plantation life that white Southerners prided themselves on. For poorer white Southerners, slavery provided a profound marker of their relative worth: At least they were white, not black; at least they were free, not slave.

Immediately after Mississippi's secession in January 1861, Jefferson Davis made his final appearance as senator in a farewell speech on the floor of Congress. The speech reflected the newfound significance of the flag after the Union's taking Fort Sumter. Davis spoke wistfully of his attachment to the flag from his service in the Mexican-American War and described his sadness that the flag might no longer be "the common flag of the country." The banner, he said, was a "constellation" of the many stars—and states—that comprised the nation. The flag had signified "unity and confederation and community independence," ideals that appealed to Southerners and that were being promulgated through the Confederacy. However, Davis said, that flag no longer stood for those things. In one passage, he expressed a tender solicitude for the flag, contending that it should be folded away "as a sacred memento of the past." He identified one star as Mississippi's, declaring his desire "to tear it from the flag," ripping it out of the constellation. The confederacy, rather than the Union, was the true heir to its legacy.[22]

One of the most common symbols in the seceding Southern states was the Bonnie Blue flag. The single white star dominating a blue field was a visual manifestation of Davis's desire to take back his state's star. State symbols appeared as an assertion of local power in face of the Union threat: palmettos in South Carolina, white pelicans with spreading wings in Louisiana. Georgia's flag depicted the coiled rattlesnake of the Revolution with the words "Don't Tread on Me" and, to make its meaning clear, "State Rights." The very existence of these Southern flags redefined the meaning of the national flag and was a sharp reminder that the American flag was no longer the flag of a united country. The Confederate Congress would make that point explicit when it adopted the Confederate flag of Stars and Bars.[23]

∽∘∾

For four long months from December 1860 through March 1861, the time crept by. Every morning, the flag at Sumter was raised; every evening, it was lowered. Anderson had added some ceremony for the troops: A drummer beat a tattoo and a fifer played reveille.[24]

Inside the fort, Anderson's men worked to secure their position. They barricaded the great wooden gates with stone and mortar. They rigged a mine at the end of the wharf in case the enemy tried to land there. Food ran low and so did fuel; the two cooks had little to work with but salt pork and flour. There was no soap, few candles, and, worst of all, no tobacco. To official convoys that ferried back and forth to Charleston, the men had a parting request: "You haven't such a thing as a late newspaper about you, have you?"[25]

They were uneasy at what they saw from the parapet. When Anderson and his staff climbed the stairs and scanned the horizon with their spyglasses, they could see their former forts being armed in a ring around them. At Fort Moultrie to their east, they could see about six hundred black workers busy through the day and into the night, a strange and ominous sight to their Northern eyes. The fluttering colors around them underscored their isolation. "We saw nothing but uncouth state flags, representing palmettos, pelicans, and other strange devices," wrote one of Anderson's officers. "Our glasses in vain swept the horizon; the one flag we longed to see"—another American flag—"was not there."[26]

The strong Union men in the fort urged Anderson to do something. Destroy these forts, they pleaded, before the strongholds were used to destroy them. There was no sense in waiting: The enemy only grew stronger while their own supplies of wood and pork shrunk. But Anderson waited, convinced that to act would bring on a civil war. If he waited, the politicians in Washington would come up with a solution to avoid the crisis.

Outside Fort Sumter, political events unfolded. South Carolina had been out alone as a secessionist state; now it was joined by others. States that had wavered on the verge of secession saw the Union occupation of Fort Sumter as proof of the North's aggressive posture. Florida seceded on January 7, Mississippi on the ninth, Alabama on the eleventh, and Georgia on the nineteenth. By February, the whole picture was plain. "Fort Sumter in Anderson's hands united the cotton states," wrote a South Carolinian observer. Meanwhile, the country waited to see what would happen when Lincoln took office.[27]

In early February, Lincoln left his home in Springfield, Illinois, for the long train ride to Washington. His journey took him on a long loop east and then south toward the White House. Everywhere he stopped—at state capitols, train stations, hotels—he addressed the crowds. In Philadelphia, he held a flag ceremony that had been arranged by local supporters at Independence Hall. Although it was February, the morning was mild. A carriage drawn by four white horses brought Lincoln through the streets; he was escorted by veterans of the Mexican-American War carrying the flag they had carried twelve years before. Crowds waited outside as he spoke briefly in the historic hall; they then cheered him as he came out onto the platform. Lincoln's lanky frame waited beside the flagpole as a navy man rolled a flag for him, bending it onto the halyards. Then Lincoln grasped the ropes and raised the flag up to the height of the staff. All at once, it unfurled dramatically into the morning sun. Cannons boomed, bands played, and the crowd roared.[28]

Later that afternoon, Lincoln told the Pennsylvania legislature:

> I could not help hoping that there was, in the entire success of that beautiful ceremony, at least something of an omen of what is to come. . . . [I]n the whole of that proceeding I was a very humble instrument. I had not provided the flag; I had not made the arrangement for elevating it to its place; I had applied a very small portion even of my feeble strength in raising it. In the whole transaction I was in the hands of the people who had arranged it.[29]

He concluded: "If I can have the same generous co-operation of the people of this nation, I think the flag of our country may yet be kept flaunting gloriously." Lincoln's words underscored a subtle but important shift in the wake of Anderson and his troops holding Fort Sumter. Southerners responded to the flag of a *state*—what they saw as a hostile foreign power in their harbor. But Northerners increasingly saw the flag as representing the almost spiritual power of a *country,* a *nation.*[30]

March 4 was inauguration day, when James Buchanan handed power over to Lincoln. On the streets of Washington, well-dressed citizens mixed with hundreds of uniformed troops, who were stationed against an assassination attempt. At the White House, thirty thousand spectators gathered to watch. In his new black suit, Lincoln stood at a small table and gave his famous inaugural address. The speech offered a stirring vision of a country united by mystic chords of memory but gave few hints about the future of Fort Sumter. Lincoln was unforthcoming. He would "hold, occupy, and possess the property, and place belonging to the government," yet "there will be no invasion—no using of force against, or among the people anywhere." Addressing Southerners, he said:

> In *your* hands, my dissatisfied countrymen, and not in mine, is the momentous issue of civil war. The government will not assail *you.* You can have no conflict, without being yourselves the aggressors. *You* have no oath registered in Heaven to destroy the government, while *I* shall have the most solemn one to preserve, protect and defend it.[31]

The whole country, and especially the men in the fort, were about to find out what this might mean. "There stands Fort Sumter," wrote a Charlestonian observer, "and thereby hangs peace or war."[32]

The attack on Sumter began on April 12. Its immediate impetus was a message from Lincoln that a supply ship was coming to resupply the fort. Lincoln had been faced with a dilemma: Either appear to be the aggressor by sailing into the harbor, or appear weak and abandon his men by not sending anything at all. The president decided to defuse the situation by specifying that the ship would be unarmed and that it would contain only food for the hungry men. It was a brilliant tactical move. Charlestonians had to decide whether to let the supply ship arrive with impunity—impossible, given the political climate—or else attack a defenseless, unarmed ship carrying only supplies: a choice that left them immediately in the wrong.

The Southerners chose to attack the fort. The first cannons were fired at 4:30 a.m., as soon as the darkness paled enough for the gunners to make out the fort's silhouette against the sky. For a day and a half, the men in Sumter found themselves caught between fire from Fort Moultrie to the east and Fort Johnson to the west. Inside the fort, Robert Anderson told his men to keep off the unprotected upper balustrade; they shot from the lower tier instead.

In Charleston, men lined the wharf. Ladies tucked up their skirts and climbed to the rooftops. They watched as cannonballs arced back and forth between the forts, crashing into the fortifications and sending up clouds of smoke and debris. The secessionists took special aim at the flag. When they missed, their ammunition overshot the fort and dropped into the water beyond. One shot shattered the flagstaff and the flag tumbled down, but one of Anderson's men nailed it to a spar and raised it again.[33]

By the next day, April 13, the fighting was over. Anderson agreed to raise the white flag of surrender; there was no more point in fighting. He insisted, though, that he be able to salute the American flag before it came down.

The lowering of the Sumter flag was a moment of great triumph for the South: As the U.S. government was forced from the harbor, men and women poured into Charleston to watch. Crowds on the docks craned their necks toward the fort. In the harbor, hundreds of boats full of Southerners in their Sunday finery sailed out to watch. They heard a fifty-gun salute from within the fort. They heard the military drums and the band playing "Yankee Doodle." And then they saw the flag slowly lowered from its high position on the flagstaff.[34]

Charlestonians were giddy. Governor Pickens came out to address the crowds: "We have defeated their twenty millions," he announced with startling prematurity. "And we have made the proud flag of the Stars and Stripes, that never was lowered before to any nation on this earth—we have lowered it in humility before the Palmetto and the Confederate flags."[35]

∽o∾

The lowering of the flag at Fort Sumter was also the single most powerful event to unite the North. In the following week, tens of thousands of flags sprang up all over the North. Lincoln called for volunteers on April 15. Within days, whole regiments of Northerners stood ready to depart to the South—enlistments signed, bags packed, farewells made. "The feeling runs mountains high," wrote one young man, "thousands of men are offering their services where hundreds only are required."[36]

That feeling—"a thrilling and almost supernatural thing"— was particularly concentrated in New York. This, the largest city, was the first place where Anderson, his men, and the garrison flag were to arrive after Fort Sumter. On April 19, their boat steamed into the harbor. The "heroes of Sumter," as they were called, were greeted by an entire city in celebration. The nation had watched their fate for months. Their letters had been printed in the newspapers, and actors had played them on stage. Now they found themselves feted and cheered and even tossed in the air. "It was impossible for us," wrote one soldier, "to venture into the main streets without being ridden on the shoulders of men, and torn to pieces by handshaking."[37]

New Yorkers honored Anderson and his men by raising, hanging, waving, and wearing flags. Contemporaries estimated that one hundred thousand flags waved in the city. Ordinary people poured into shops, handing over fifty cents in exchange for a three-by-five-foot flag. Cart drivers decorated their horses with flags; carpenters hammered flagpoles onto buildings; merchants hung flagstaffs out second-, third-, and fourth-story windows. High on the rooftops, laborers stretched cords from cornice to cornice, suspending banners horizontally above the street. Two ship riggers raised an enormous flag on the steeple of Trinity Church, 240 feet above Broadway, as a crowd shouted in approval. "Broadway was almost hidden in a cloud of flaggery," one reporter wrote. "Nothing but red, white, and blue, red, white, and blue, greeted the eye, turn which way it would. Every window, every housetop, every awning, every stage, every railroad car, every hotel, every barroom, every liberty pole had its flag waving gaily, or rolled into graceful folds." On the street, every second man carried a flag or wore a cockade in his hat. Some women attended the festivities in red, white, and blue hoopskirts. Flagmen on the railroad put away their white cloths and used the Stars and Stripes instead. There were so many flags that the *New York World* coined a new term to describe the scene: "flag mania."[38]

The flag had become the central symbol of pro-Union feeling. Those who were suspected of Southern sympathies, or even luke-warm support for the North, were given the chance to manifest their loyalty through flags. Crowds gathered ominously outside certain businesses whose owners reportedly supported the South. Merchants promptly responded, displaying flags in self-defense. On April 15, the day Lincoln called for volunteers, a mob chased the Democratic publisher of the *New York Herald* up the street and threatened his building. When he hung two flags out the window, the crowd dispersed. Two days later, a similar crowd threatened the *Journal of Commerce*, which was suspected of Southern sympathies; again, the publishers hung a flag out the window, and the crowd cheered, waved their hats, and moved on up Wall Street. The incidents echoed the violent swath through Kensington made by the nativist rioters only seventeen years before.[39]

What is perhaps most interesting, however, is that in each of these cases, the crowds required *symbolic* support of the Union more than *actual* support. They did not require a change of heart. Neither publisher was dragged onto the sidewalk below and forced to repudiate old beliefs or proclaim the righteousness of the Union cause. The flag was enough. It marked not physical but ideological territory. Its symbolic display was not agreement but acquiescence, an acknowledgement of the rightness of over-whelming popular feeling.

On Saturday, April 20, people flowed into Union Square from all directions, holding flags and wearing them in their hats. The square's three and a half acres filled with people until between fifty thousand and one hundred thousand stood crowded to-gether. Observers were stunned at the numbers of people, nearly one out of every eight of the city's inhabitants. It was, one said, "the most immense and astonishing demonstration ever seen." Above the milling people, the immense bronze equestrian statue of George Washington towered against the sky. With great ceremony, Robert Anderson carried the flag of Sumter to the statue. Grasping the flagpole, he placed it in Washington's bronze hands so that it appeared that Washington himself had taken up the cause of Sumter and was leading the Northern troops. Orators spoke, bands played, people cheered. "Rally to the star-spangled banner," urged one speaker, "so long as a single stripe can be discovered, or a single star shall shimmer from the surrounding darkness."[40]

In the midst of such powerful ceremony, the flag took on a religious dimension. At a similar flag raising in Boston, "enthusiasm," as one witness said, "knew no bounds":

Men, women and children seethed in a fervid excitement. "God bless it!" uttered my father in tender and devout tone as he sat beside me in the carriage, leaning heavily forward on his staff with clasped hands. And following the direction of his streaming eyes, and those of the thousands surrounding us, I saw the dear banner of my country, rising higher and higher to the top of the flagstaff, fling out fold after fold to the damp air, and float proudly over the hallowed edifice. Oh, the roar that rang out from ten thousand throats! Old men, with white hair and tearful faces, lifted their hats to the national ensign, and reverently saluted it. Young men greeted it with fierce and wild hurrahs, talking the while in terse Saxon of the traitors of the Confederate States, who had dragged in the dirt this flag of their country, never before dishonored.

I had never seen anything like this before. I had never dreamed that New England, slow to wrath, could be fired with so warlike a spirit. Never before had the national flag signified anything to me. But as I saw it now, kissing the skies, all that it symbolized as representative of government and emblematic of national majesty became clear to my mental vision. . . . It was this holy flag that had been insulted.[41]

The federal banner that had flown over Sumter had been transformed. Once a symbol meaningful almost solely to the nation's young soldiers, it had become a symbol of national majesty. The rising collective passion of the North made it a "holy flag," a symbol of something so powerful and spiritually resonant that the flag too absorbed those qualities. While nativists in the 1840s had invested the flag with Protestant righteousness, this was something else entirely. The flag had become a religious object—an icon—in itself, capable of bringing those who claimed it to a place of spiritual union, where ten thousand throats roared in concert. This passionate ecstasy and its sense of belonging marked the full fruition of nationalist patriotism.

∽∘∾

In 1861, among both Northerners and Southerners, the flag signified union: one nation, North and South, governed by the rule of law. It invoked the geographic reach of the country, the legal structure of the Constitution, and past wars. It did not speak to slavery. Almost all Northerners saw the war as a battle for union, and it was national unity that most volunteers signed up to defend. A few Northerners were abolitionists, but most were not willing to make emancipation a defining issue. Many stated emphatically they were willing to fight for their country but not for the slaves.

While the flag had resonance across the population, it was particularly powerful for soldiers. The flag was both a symbol of their mission and a daily presence in their lives. In military drills, they saluted it; on long marches, they followed it; in battle, it provided a landmark in the tangle of bodies and the clouds of smoke. They made the flag their own with dozens of popular flag songs: "Defend the Stars and Stripes," "The Red, White, and Blue of '61," and "The Starry Flag," among others. On the days of marching through dusty countryside, soldiers used flag songs to synchronize their strides and to pass the time. "The Stars and Stripes" provided a rousing cadence, perfect for swinging arms and stamping feet:

> Their *flag is but a rag—*
> *Ours is the* true *one;*
> *Up with the Stars and Stripes—*
> *Down with the new one!*[42]

When Union soldiers forded the Potomac in the summer of 1861, they sang flag songs to get them through the difficult venture. One regiment fortified itself with patriotism, plunging into the waters to the chorus of "Red, White, and Blue." The next regiment, when its turn came, launched into "The Star-Spangled Banner."[43]

Many soldiers spoke of their vision for their country in terms of the flag. A soldier dying from two bullets through his lungs wrote: "I hope that from Heaven I may see the glorious old flag wave again over the undivided Union I have loved so well."

Those Northerners who became prisoners of war, much like the Revolutionary sailors before them, found the flag to be a consolation. Flags appeared among inmates at the notorious Andersonville stronghold in Georgia and at the Libby Prison in Richmond, Virginia. When Yankee inmates imprisoned in Andersonville heard news of Union victories, they gathered to sing flag songs. At Libby, on Independence Day 1863, prisoners used shirts of red, white, and blue to stitch together a makeshift flag.[44]

Yet, as Northern soldiers marched through the South and saw slavery firsthand, they began to connect their nationalism to abolition. At first, their abolitionism was primed by their disgust at Southern society. They were shocked by the social effects of slavery: the laziness, miscegenation, and immorality they saw, the way it affected both whites and blacks. Many described slavery as a withering blight. Others began to see it as an untenable threat to the Union, opposing it not for the slaves' sake but for the Union's sake. "I am no abolitionist," wrote one Ohio soldier to his family at home, "in fact I despise the word." But his observations led him to oppose slavery: "As long as slavery exists . . . there will be no permanent peace for America. . . . [H]ence I am in favor of killing slavery." His brutal metaphor reflected a larger sense that Northerners were fighting not simply to persuade the South to return, but also for the death of the old South.[45]

It took Lincoln's Emancipation Proclamation, first tendered after the bloody Union victory at Antietam in September 1862, and definitively reissued on January 1, 1863, to redefine the purpose of the war. The Emancipation Proclamation declared that "all persons held as slaves" in Confederate states were "then, thenceforward, and forever free." In theory, the proclamation was a military measure; it abolished slavery on grounds of expediency as a necessary step toward winning the war rather than as a moral issue. This was a reflection of military reality. Lincoln had realized that the North could not win without a dramatic change in policy. But in effect, the proclamation was a much broader statement, for the first time putting slavery explicitly at the center of the conflict. At the same time, it enabled the enrollment of black troops in the Union army, a measure that, while it had tactical value, also asserted the humanity and manhood of former slaves. To make a man a soldier was to acknowledge his fitness for civic duty.

Northern soldiers differed widely in their reactions. Some felt betrayed. "[Men] say it has turned into a 'nigger war,'" wrote one New York captain, "and all are anxious to return to their homes for it was to preserve the Union that they volunteered." A German immigrant was dismayed: "I don't want to fire another shot for the negroes, and I wish that all the abolitionists were in hell." Others were delighted. "Thank God," wrote a New York private, "the contest is now between Slavery & freedom & every honest man knows what he is fighting for." When the men looked up at their battle flag now, each saw his own meanings inscribed there.[46]

As conditions improved dramatically for Union troops in the spring and summer of 1863, Northern soldiers became increasingly supportive of the Emancipation Proclamation. In the west, General Ulysses Grant's capture of Vicksburg gave the Mississippi River to the Union forces, and in the east, General George Meade's victory at Gettysburg turned Confederate forces south again, both within days of the Fourth of July. Northern soldiers became more amenable to Lincoln's leadership and credited the proclamation as a way to weaken the South. Every slave who left a plantation, they reasoned, pulled a white Confederate out of combat to go back and work the land. One private, previously opposed to abolitionism, wrote that he supported the proclamation "if by so doing it will help put down the rebellion, for I hold that nothing should stand in the way of the Union—niggers, nor anything else." Another concurred: "I have always until lately been opposed to abraham linkins proclamation," wrote a Pennsylvania private in May 1863, "but I have lately been convinced that it was just the thing that was neded to weaken the strength of the rebels."[47]

The proclamation's military virtues allowed Northern whites, especially soldiers, to come to peace with its social implications. It added much-needed black troops at a time when the army was in desperate need of men and recruitment had stagnated. By the end of the war, nearly 180,000 African American soldiers were fighting for the Union. Moreover, black troops proved their bravery at battles like Milliken's Bend, just north of Vicksburg, when two new regiments of black soldiers repulsed a Southern brigade from a Union garrison. That battle, reported Assistant Secretary of War Charles A. Dana, had profound social effects: "The bravery of the blacks completely revolutionized the sentiment of the army with regard to the employment of negro troops. I heard prominent officers who formerly in private had sneered at the idea of negroes fighting express themselves after that as heartily in favor of it." In other battles, black soldiers marched into combat under the American flag.[48]

In the 1864 presidential election, Lincoln won 55 percent of the popular vote and fully 78 percent of the soldier vote. Out of military and psychological necessity, the logic of Lincoln's war required that the flag of the Union become the flag of antislavery.

The flag that the soldiers followed in the last battles of the war, as General William Tecumseh Sherman marched through Georgia to the sea, brought emancipation in its wake. It accomplished an unusual feat, fusing the impulse of nationalist patriotism, with its emphasis on Union and belonging, to humanitarian patriotism, with its emphasis on individual liberty.

On one cover of *Harper's Weekly* in 1867, the flag appeared as part of an image that would never have been seen before the war. The drawing featured a dignified, white-haired African American man, with patches on his trousers and tools in his pocket: clearly a former slave. Behind him stretched a line of other respectable-looking black men, one dressed as a businessman, one as a soldier, each with squared shoulders and upraised head. The former slave stretched out his hand to deposit a ballot in a container, while light illuminated his head and an American flag draped protectively over the scene. The drawing was titled "The First Vote." It was precisely what South Carolinians in 1861 had feared when they had looked darkly into the harbor at the federal flag waving over Fort Sumter.

# ~4~

# FLAG OF CAPITALISM
## Mark Hanna and the Election of 1896

The 1890s marked a watershed decade in American history. On one side lay the past: a countryside dominated by agriculture, dotted with small towns and Protestant churches, with the infinite promise to settlers of western lands. On the other side lay the future: the growth of large cities that were filled with factories to make goods and shops to sell them in and populated by large numbers of foreign-born. Immigration, urbanization, and industrialization were changing the landscape. The skyscraper was the new triumph of American architecture, but for each one that went up, there were dozens of squat tenement buildings crowded with families.

Chicago exemplified rapid urban growth. In the thirty years since the Civil War, the country's North-South division had been modified by a Western orientation as that region became a more powerful economic force. Chicago was the great Midwestern city. It was the link between the great urban centers of the East and the Great Plains and mountains of the West. The city boasted six railway stations, and a thousand trains rolled in every day. Railroad cars from the West brought lumber, grain, and cattle into the city, where they were processed and then loaded back onto the cars as planks and flour and cuts of beef. Observers called it "the most American of cities."[1]

Like all American cities in this period, Chicago wrestled with the extremes of wealth and poverty. In the city's central Loop district, skyscrapers and department stores promised a future full of possibility and lovely things. Elegant ladies shopped along the "Ladies' Half Mile" on State Street, crowding up to Marshall Field's counters in search of kid gloves and embroidered handkerchiefs. Nearby, in the Board of Trade Building, their husbands made and lost fortunes under stained-glass skylights and cathedral ceilings. Carriages waited outside to drive the businessmen north along Lake Shore Drive to the mansions that looked out over Lake Michigan. But just outside the tightly concentrated Loop was a different world, filled with the working people who made up the bulk of the city's population. At Hull House, on Halstead Street, reformer Jane Addams found herself living among immigrant women who sewed in sweatshops and men who carried coal. To the south of the city were the Union Stock Yards, where acres of animals were slaughtered every day, bludgeoned by sledgehammers and dissected on an assembly line. The stench of rotting meat permeated miles of desperate shacks at the back of the yards. This was the city that Upton Sinclair would make famous in *The Jungle*.[2]

The Midwest and the Great Plains were the golden key to American electoral politics at the century's end. The East belonged to the Republicans; the South and the Rocky Mountains belonged to the Democrats. Party strategists knew that the presidential election would be won in the cornfields and the farmers' kitchens of the great Midwestern sweep. Illinois, Indiana, Iowa, Michigan, Ohio, and Wisconsin were rich prizes, boasting fully one-quarter of the country's population. In the fourteen elections from 1860 to 1912, the Republicans chose a presidential candidate from Ohio, Illinois, and Indiana in every case but two. Both Republicans and Democrats set up their campaign headquarters in Chicago, and Republicans set up a satellite office in New York to bring in money.[3]

The Republican candidate for president in 1896, William McKinley, was the most well-known politician in the Midwest. His home state of Ohio was a political powerhouse, and he had spent the previous several years stumping up and down the region in anticipation of a presidential run. Graying at the temples, with a square face, a sharp nose, and tufted eyebrows, he looked like Napoléon to his admirers. McKinley was a Midwesterner through and through, with a deep distrust of the East and especially of Eastern politicians. He did not read and did not travel, but he loved singing parties around the piano and especially the old favorite hymn "Nearer, My God, to Thee." Above all, McKinley was an unpretentious man, an affable and well-loved politician with the ability to frame popular sentiment in familiar and comforting words. By 1896, he had served a long run in Congress, and when he lost in the Democratic sweep of 1890, he was elected governor of Ohio the following year. He had been talked of for the presidency as early as 1888, had found a groundswell of support in 1892, but both times played the cautious course. When the election of 1896 came, he was ready.[4]

William Jennings Bryan was the youngest candidate ever to emerge for the presidency. At thirty-six, he was boyish, with a dimpled chin, strong nose, and curling hair that crept back from his forehead. He was a prize-winning public speaker; at the same time, he had a strong moralistic streak, drinking sarsaparilla instead of whiskey. He had contemplated a career as a Baptist minister. Like McKinley, Bryan was a Midwesterner. He had been raised in a small town in Illinois, then lived in Chicago in the early 1880s while he studied law, and finally set up practice in Lincoln, Nebraska. There he found himself drawn into politics, speaking frequently on behalf of the Democratic Party. His electrifying "Cross of Gold" speech at the Democratic Convention in 1896 propelled him to sudden candidacy.[5]

The defining campaign issue was the economy. The depression of 1894 had been devastating; it was the worst economic crisis the country had ever experienced. The New York Stock Exchange fell by 60 percent, hundreds of banks and thousands of businesses failed, and two to three million men—one out of six Americans—were unemployed during the terrible winter of 1893–1894. Thousands roamed the streets, homeless. Children were sent out by despairing parents to steal food and fuel to keep their families alive. There was no government assistance: only the breadlines and soup kitchens of private charities.[6]

The experience radicalized Americans. At its convention in Chicago, the American Federation of Labor declared: "The right to work is the right to live" and called for government intervention. "When the private employers cannot or will not give work," it claimed, "the municipality, State or Nation must." In the West, unemployed men began to march in what became known as "industrial armies." These were unemployed men, frequently war veterans, who banded together in a quasi-military fashion to march behind a flag toward Washington, D.C. Calling themselves "a petition in boots," they asked for jobs, payment of their veterans' benefits, and unemployment relief.[7]

Even some who did have jobs went on strike as they faced deep cuts in pay. Conflicts between bosses and workers descended into violence, which intensified as the federal government sent troops to break the strikes. In 1894, in the depths of the depression, the Pullman railway car company cut workers' wages five separate times while paying nearly $3 million in dividends to its stockholders. When thousands of workers petitioned, the company president refused to listen and fired three members of the delegation that came to speak to him. Rebuffed, the workers turned to Eugene Debs, the founder of the American Railway Union. Debs organized a strike in which his railroad workers refused to move Pullman train cars. Beginning on June 26, the strike involved more than a quarter-million workers and halted rail traffic throughout the country. A special federal prosecutor, formerly a lawyer for the railway companies, was appointed to deal with the situation. He called an injunction against the strike—an injunction that barred union leaders from participating and threatened all strikers with the loss of their jobs. When news of this injunction reached Chicago, workers rioted, tipping over train cars and stopping rail traffic. The U.S. Army entered the city's suburbs on July 4, causing a major uprising as strikers fought back: windows shattered, train cars overturned, buildings torched, and twelve people killed. After a week, the strike was broken. The workers were blacklisted, and Debs was sent to jail. To industrialists, the Pullman strike dramatized a threat to law and order; to workers, it showed the extent to which American society had drifted from its humanitarian mooring.[8]

All these economic concerns coalesced into a single, defining issue in the presidential campaign: the showdown between McKinley's gold standard and Bryan's silver standard. If the gold standard were adopted, the country's currency would be backed by gold bullion in the banks, a result desired by the Eastern bankers, who wanted assurance behind their loans and feared inflation. If the country adopted the silver, with sixteen silver dollars equaling one gold dollar, more money would be put in circulation. This solution was favored by farmers and workers, who believed there was an insufficient money supply and that greedy Eastern bankers were at the root of the problem.

But gold versus silver was, above all, a passionate debate about an American society in upheaval. When McKinley advocated the gold standard, he described it as "sound money" and emphasized its stability. Manufacturers saw government's most important role as protecting business, and they feared the volatility of financial markets and the uprisings that they had seen during the Pullman strike. Their solution was not redistribution of wealth but an invocation of law and order. McKinley saw his role as supporting the existing capitalist system, while adding a tariff to protect American manufacturers. He preached a united America, insisting that his countrymen had no significant social classes and that it was divisive to speak that way. "In America," he said, "we spurn all class distinctions. We are all equal citizens and equal in privilege and opportunity."[9]

When William Jennings Bryan described free silver in his campaign speeches, he offered a different American vision: one that was shaped by a Jeffersonian belief in the people and a Jacksonian distrust of privilege. He saw a country threatened by financial interests—what he and Debs called "the Money Power." His silver policy would put money back in the hands of the people, and he proposed a graduated income tax to lessen the burden on farmers and workers. "The principles upon which Democracy rests are as everlasting as the hills," he said, "but ... they must be applied to new conditions as they arise." He made it clear that the concentration of money was the new and threatening force in American society. Silver became a reference point for a whole host of economic, social, and even religious values.[10]

It was during the presidential election of 1896 that the Republican Party turned definitively from the party of abolition during the Civil War to the party of big business. As a consequence, the party raised and spent unprecedented amounts of money: twice as much as in the previous presidential election. The Democratic candidate also broke with tradition by traveling around the country, bringing his message directly to voters, rather than staying at home. And it was this election in which the flag entered American peacetime culture as a symbol of the combined forces of capitalism, nationalism, and the Republican Party.[11]

∾∽

For a long time after the Civil War, the flag had been too volatile a symbol to use, too closely associated with the Northern triumph and Southern defeat. When it was used, occasionally in the 1860s and 1870s, it was trotted out by Republican politicians who called on the memory of the Civil War to paint Democrats as disloyal to the Union and gain political advantage. (Contemporary commentators called this practice "waving the bloody shirt.") But slowly, as veterans aged and the memory of the Civil War receded, the flag once again became a national symbol for white Americans. The centennial celebration in 1876, in which the flag flew from floats and in parades to highlight the country's united Revolutionary history, was instrumental. So was the Rutherford Hayes election, which marked the end of Reconstruction as the North pulled troops out of Southern states. As the North revoked its interest in protecting former slaves, Southern whites lowered their resistance to the nation.

Veterans' organizations of the late 1880s also reinvigorated the flag, putting new emphasis on it while disentangling it from its abolitionist meanings. Twenty years after the war, 350,000 old soldiers were members of the Grand Army of the Republic, combining patriotic activity with political advocacy on veterans' issues. They did not talk about slavery. Unlike veterans of any other war, they held Blue-Gray reunions in which former Union and Confederate soldiers met to reminisce about battles in which they had tried to kill each other. And as old soldiers retreated from an emphasis on abolitionism, they reshaped their interpretations of the Civil War. They talked about bravery, heroism, and personal sacrifice. As one Union veteran explained, "wars come to husk off the invidious surroundings of place and circumstance, and show us the real grain of manhood in everyone's nature." These were the themes that felt deeply pressing as the veterans looked around and saw the selfishness and greed of the Gilded Age. To these men, the flag began to stand for a kind of protest against the cult of individual gain; it became an affirmation of responsibility, sacrifice, and shared values.[12]

These developments were not unique to the United States. All across Europe, nationalism was taking hold. The massive changes in economic structure, social structure, and communications led to the consolidation of new nation-states like Italy and

Germany. In existing countries, like Britain and Ireland, a host of new "traditions" appeared: recovered folk songs, national anthems, and flags helped build a sense of shared nationhood among people who had never met.

In the United States, the nationalist flag promised a way to integrate the waves of immigrants entering American society. Public schools began to hold elaborate ceremonies including patriotic poems, the singing of national songs, and salutes to the American flag. Ministers earnestly urged Polish-, Greek-, and Russian-born schoolchildren to find union under the flag:

> [W]hatever nation you belong to by birth, whatever tongue your mother taught you, whatever your color or your race, no matter, there is only one flag. . . . Now let us come and gather under its blessed folds. Let us be tangled in the stars and covered with the stripes.[13]

The first man to promote the flag as a tool for integrating immigrants was a conservative New York City school auditor named George Balch. In the late 1880s, as Balch visited classrooms, he was struck by the instructive possibilities of the flag. A West Point graduate and a Christian, Balch saw the flag as a way to inculcate the qualities that he deemed most essential for citizenship: obedience, respect, diligence, punctuality, neatness, and cheerfulness. He developed a whole series of classroom exercises around the flag, including the first pledge: "We give our Heads!—and our Hearts!—to God! and our Country! One Country! One Language! One Flag." In 1890, Balch published an influential book called *Methods for Teaching Patriotism in the Public Schools*. The book promoted flag rituals in classrooms and suggested a system of patriotic rewards, including the election of a class standard bearer and small flags to be worn as badges. Balch also encouraged the celebration of Flag Day on June 14, the anniversary of Congress's adoption of the Flag Resolution. The ceremonies spread outward to New Jersey, Chicago, and San Francisco and were enacted by teachers and other groups, such as the Grand Army of the Republic and the Sons and Daughters of the American Revolution. In cities, the rituals were often focused on immigrant children, but they also found a powerful reception in small towns across the country.[14]

A man with very different political principles soon picked up on Balch's flag advocacy. Francis Bellamy was a Christian socialist and former Baptist minister who had been forced out of his church for his radical beliefs. Jesus, he insisted, "was emphatically the poor man's friend." His cousin Edward Bellamy had written the book *Looking Backward,* a socialist critique of American society. Both men believed that socialism was most likely to make a foothold in the United States through nationalism. Francis Bellamy's version of patriotism was egalitarian, a natural extension of his Christian socialism. He compared American society to a sand heap, saying that American liberty had been perverted into freedom for "great corporations to oppress the people . . . for the atoms on top of the sand heap to press down harder and harder on the atoms below." He offered a vision of American liberty that incorporated equality and fraternity, ideas that, "when applied to the nation, mean . . . that we are not a sand heap, but a family."[15]

Bellamy was hired by the country's foremost children's magazine, the *Youth's Companion,* to plan a children's patriotic campaign for the upcoming Columbian Exposition. He conceived of a pledge of allegiance as a way to pay tribute to the nation's history. He found Balch's pledge "pretty childish" and too military in its orientation. Asking himself about our purpose as a nation, he contemplated including the French Revolutionary slogan of "liberty, equality, fraternity," which he had often incorporated into his speeches; these ideas captured his vision of the brotherhood of Christian socialism. But Bellamy chose instead the line "with liberty and justice for all." It was a choice, he figured, that could apply to either a socialistic or an individualistic nation.[16]

Why were both Balch and Bellamy, two men with such different visions, drawn to the flag? With the great tide of immigration, the flag appeared as a powerful symbol of American allegiance: one that might include foreigners who were willing to adopt the mores of their new country, and one that might assist these newcomers on the road to assimilation. If immigrants were going to vote—and they were already doing so in large numbers— then men like Balch wanted to pull them into the body politic, ensuring a continuity of values. Men like Bellamy saw an opportunity to democratize national culture, fostering a spirit of idealism amid the money-grubbing of the robber barons. The flag offered a vision that was at once humanitarian and nationalist, combining an emphasis on extending the franchise with the rhetoric of family and an evocation of oneness.

The first performance of the Pledge of Allegiance on Columbus Day, in 1893, included millions of children in schools across the country, but the centerpiece was in Chicago, where the Public School Celebration provided a dramatic opening to the Columbian Exposition. Across the city, schools were decorated in flags and bunting, and crowds gathered to watch the children perform their exercises. Old veterans of the Grand Army of the Republic presided over the ceremonies. A speaker read a proclamation from the president. Then the flag was slowly raised up the flagpole in front of the crowd. The principal gave a signal, and the schoolchildren recited the pledge in small, unified voices. It was the first time it had been heard in public:

> I pledge allegiance to my Flag and the Republic for which it stands: one Nation indivisible, with Liberty and Justice for all.

When the children came to the words "to my flag," all the children raised their right arms in salute, then dropped them to their sides. Then the band struck up, and the whole school, teachers and children and audience, sang "America." Nearly identical programs took place in over a hundred thousand schools across the nation, a vision of a unified nation, pledging allegiance to shared values. In short order, the pledge became standard in many schools, taking advantage of the elasticity of the flag's symbolism that could encompass both the militarism of George Balch and the Christian socialism of Francis Bellamy.[17]

The symbolism was also expansive enough to serve a growing sector of American society: companies looking for a powerful marketing tool. Even as children soberly saluted flags in their classrooms, whiskey manufacturers painted flags on their barrels, and sausage-makers printed their labels on giveaway flags. Some dry-goods producers began turning out flag-themed textiles: handkerchiefs, pillow covers, door mats, and more. A dozen companies registered trademarks incorporating the flag; many others simply used the banner as an eye-catching image.

Chicago was full of these commercial flags. The front of Marshall Field's department store was festooned with waving flags that beckoned shoppers. In the streets, horses plodded along, pulling flag-bedecked furniture vans and laundry wagons. Flags waved from saloons, lemonade stands, fireworks stores, and Salvation Army headquarters, as well as manufacturers of all sorts: tent makers, soap makers, piano makers, breweries. The flag even appeared as costumery in the boxing rings and entertainment halls: prizefighters wore flag sashes around their trunks, minstrels wore tight-fitting coats fashioned out of flags, and circus clowns decked themselves out in red and white stripes and blue and white stars. It was difficult to walk around the city or go out in the evening without encountering the flag in some commercial setting.[18]

In response, a small but vocal group formed a flag protection movement. Veterans, reformers, and members of patriotic groups like the Daughters of the American Revolution were dismayed to see their beloved symbol prostrated for dollars. They had harsh words for the advertisers who wrapped their goods in the flag—"mountebanks of every description," "selfish mercenary hucksters," and "sordid business sharks"—and for the capitalist impulse that produced them: "the leperized taint of private gain." At the most basic level, the flag protectionists argued, these advertisers were "not true Americans in fact or in spirit." The movement tried to shame advertisers with such words, but it also took more practical steps, lobbying congressional representatives for flag desecration laws. The protectionists succeeded in passing laws in many states, but were blocked in Congress by powerful senators supported by the business interests the movement abhorred. One senator, according to a colleague, "hoped the American people would continue to wrap hams in the flag, not to teach patriotism, but to teach ham eaters to eat American hams." The flag, it was clear, was good for business.[19]

∽∘∾

The man who would do the most to politicize the flag in the nineteenth century was also the most important figure in the 1896 campaign. Mark Hanna was McKinley's campaign manager, a Midwestern industrialist who established the dynamics of the modern presidential race with this election. His critics charged him as having "a cash-register conscience." He even looked like a caricature of a capitalist: bulky and wide with a square, fleshy face. He ran the presidential race with an efficiency learned from long years running a variety of businesses, raising more money than had ever been raised and spending more money than had ever been spent. It was Hanna who effectively claimed patriotism and the flag for the Republican Party.[20]

Hanna was shaped by his experiences as a wealthy man in a society that rewarded wealthy men. Like John D. Rockefeller, another young man from Cleveland, he seized on the possibilities offered by the growing Midwestern towns and increasing railway connections. Beginning in his father's grocery business, Hanna established himself as a traveling salesman and then married the daughter of a coal and iron merchant just when coal and iron were becoming indispensable for the nation's growing railroads. Soon, he owned a bank, a newspaper, an opera house, and a streetcar business. He managed these affairs from his office high above Cleveland's busy waterfront, where he worked long hours in his shirtsleeves, writing letters and receiving delegations of his employees.[21]

Hanna shared the ethos of his generation of industrialists, in its belief of the survival of the fittest. Darwinian evolutionary theory had inspired social Darwinism: the belief, popular in the late nineteenth century, that society rewarded its fittest members and condemned the others to expiration. Government's role was not to help the most vulnerable members of the society but rather to assist businesses in their growth. "He believed in monopoly more honestly than most men believed in religion," wrote one observer, and Hanna translated those convictions to the political sphere. He was convinced that business needed more involvement in the party system in order to influence legislation. In 1880, he founded a Business Man's Republican Campaign Club in Cleveland, which held a torchlight parade in support of its candidate and raised money for each campaign. The idea spawned similar clubs in other cities. Over the course of the 1880s, Hanna played a key role as the Republican Party became increasingly aligned with the agenda of big business.[22]

Hanna had met McKinley in the mid-1870s and admired him immediately. He spent a good deal of his own money on McKinley's campaign, and he was good at raising funds from businessmen like himself. When McKinley found himself deeply in debt, it was Hanna who arranged to bail him out with $130,000. Cartoonists seized on this relationship, portraying Hanna as the power behind McKinley. In the Democratic-leaning Hearst newspapers, Hanna appeared as a big-bellied man in a checked suit, chomping on a cigar, dollar signs all around, with a tiny McKinley strapped on to his belt for the ride. Hanna was never shy about the role of money in politics. He did his share of patronage assignments, paid bribes where he had to, and did not seem to mind the dirty work. He once shocked the guests at a dinner party by announcing that political questions in a democracy were essentially questions of money. The statement marked Hanna as the harbinger of a new political order.[23]

In Chicago's gilded Auditorium Building, Hanna set up the first mass-advertising political campaign in America's history. A staff of between fifty and sixty worked tirelessly. Pollsters tested public opinion in key areas, measuring the responses to different initiatives. Specially staffed bureaus appealed to different groups: a women's department, a German department, a "Colored bureau," and a traveling salesman's department. Writers composed nearly three hundred pamphlets, which translators interpreted into every language spoken in the United States; they wrote news bulletins that went into local newspapers, which were often published unedited. In all, the campaign produced 250 million copies of pamphlets and sent trainloads of publishing materials out in all directions. Theodore Roosevelt would remark in disgust, "He has advertised McKinley as if he were a patent medicine."[24]

To pay for all this activity, Hanna rode the trains between Wall Street and Chicago, canvassing the wealthy men of the nation and bringing their contributions back to campaign headquarters. The money came from corporations that feared what might happen if Bryan won. Standard Oil and J. P. Morgan each contributed $250,000, the equivalent of about $6 million today. Altogether the four meatpacking houses of Chicago gave $400,000—roughly $10 million today. A railroad company gave him fifty $1,000 bills, which he carried in an envelope on the train. Banks contributed, too, dipping into their reserves to write checks.[25]

While the Chicago headquarters turned New York money into campaign propaganda, McKinley waged a "front porch" campaign at his home in Canton, Ohio. Every day, he received trainloads of visitors who came on a kind of pilgrimage to his house—apparently unbidden, but often organized by major employers and Republican campaign committees. McKinley received them standing on the porch hung with trumpet vines under a swath of red, white, and blue bunting. Soon, the grass on the lawn was trodden into an earthen floor, and McKinley's picket fence disappeared in the hands of souvenir hunters. But all his speeches were reported in the newspapers, and the people who came went home and told hundreds more about their experience.[26]

By contrast, Bryan had very little money. He decided to take his campaign to the people, riding a train car from west to east and back again. While he lacked the party organization and financial support of the Republicans, he was a charismatic speaker whose repeated calls to "the people" were powerful.

Both Republicans and Democrats cast their candidate as the heir to an American patriotic tradition and their opponent as a threat to that tradition. McKinley claimed that Bryan's program threatened the foundations of Americanism:

> My countrymen, the most un-American of all appeals observable in this campaign is the one which seeks to array labor against capital, employer against employed. It is most unpatriotic and is fraught with the greatest peril to all concerned. We are all political equals here—equal in privilege and opportunity, dependent on each other, and the prosperity of one is the prosperity of the other.

McKinley's supporters went further. A letter writer to the *New York Times* claimed that "the Republican form of Government is on trial here," and predicted anarchy if McKinley were to lose. "Within six months of Bryan's election mobs would be rushing up and down our streets howling for bread." Teddy Roosevelt, campaigning for McKinley, compared Bryan, Debs, and others to Maximilien Robespierre, the radical French Revolution leader who guillotined thousands of his enemies during the Reign of Terror.[27]

Bryan rarely used the word *patriotism*, but his speeches frequently invoked the themes of liberty, Thomas Jefferson, and the Constitution. He and his supporters consistently described a democracy threatened by oligarchy. In the words of one Wisconsin Democrat: "The fight today is, in my judgment, whether there shall be a republic or not. Whether a few men of wealth shall govern this land or the people." Eugene Debs, who campaigned for Bryan, articulated this perspective the most fully, teasing out its possibilities. For Debs, American patriotism was best embodied in a dedication to liberty, a rejection of despotism, and a commitment to the principles of the Declaration of Independence.[28]

By early September, Hanna knew the Republicans were in trouble. Despite Bryan's lack of money and organizational structure, he was a compelling opponent. He appeared to be winning votes in the Midwest and poised to take certain key states. The newspapers predicted doom in McKinley's own state: "McKinley will lose Ohio!" the headlines announced. There was trouble in the financial markets, and gold became scarcer, further flaming the passion for silver. It was then that Mark Hanna turned to the flag.[29]

The flag had been part of the campaign all along, in the usual tradition of late-nineteenth-century politics. Campaign managers had invested heavily in bunting, the light woolen fabric used to make flags. Half-moons of the red, white, and blue fabric draped from McKinley's front porch. Like other presidential candidates since Ulysses S. Grant, McKinley and Bryan had their portraits superimposed onto American flags; these flags were then waved by their supporters at campaign rallies and strung over the streets in small towns. The only early sign that this campaign would feature the flag in a different way was a button that McKinley supporters wore during the Republican nominating convention: Instead of a McKinley portrait or slogan, it showed only an American flag. Hanna would take that tiny emblem and enlarge the association a thousand times before the campaign was through.[30]

Hanna's capture of the flag began as a defensive strategy, a redirection from the economic focus on the gold standard, which was doing McKinley little good. Hanna started with an appeal to Civil War veterans by emphasizing McKinley's military service, a strategic choice in a decade when veterans formed a large and well-organized voting bloc. As a commissary sergeant, McKinley had driven his mule wagon straight into the bloody battle of Antietam to serve his soldiers with food and hot coffee. This story, told and retold, was a profound political asset, casting McKinley as a war hero. Hanna's crafting extended to subtle details: Even the candidate's title of general, rather than the equally appropriate senator or governor, evoked his military past.[31]

Old Union soldiers had by this time come to view the flag as a symbol of the idealism that had driven many of them to fight. "The flag is to us what the cross was to the Christian apostles, what the cross on the sword was to the knightly crusader," a veteran proclaimed in a flag presentation to a school. "Loyalty to the colors, whether to victory or defeat, whether to life or unto death—these are the marks of the true believer."[32] The flag was everything that industrial society was not: It symbolized a purer, more idealized set of human motivations. It was, in short, ripe for political redefinition.

Hanna created the Patriotic Heroes Brigade, a special campaign of Union generals, organized to appeal directly to wavering veterans. The men led a railway campaign through ten Western states, stopping in scores of towns every day and speaking to a million voters by the end of their trip. The train was a dramatic sight; the newspapers called it "the greatest train of its character ever seen in the United States." The engine and passenger cars were swathed by thousands of yards of bunting. A flatcar carried a working cannon and two large flagpoles with fluttering flags. As the train stopped in front of the crowds in each town, an old Civil War bugler came out on the platform and played taps. Then the aging generals came out and addressed the crowds. They did not stop with a simple endorsement of McKinley. Their message was stronger: The country faced a crisis as grave as the Civil War had been. The threat to the Union embodied by Bryan and Debs was as powerful as that formerly posed by the Confederacy. A banner hanging from the side of train served as a constant reminder of this message: "1896 is as vitally important as 1861." True patriotism meant a vote for McKinley and the forces of order.[33]

Meanwhile, McKinley emphasized the flag in his speeches from his front porch in Canton. Like the Patriotic Heroes Brigade, McKinley drew powerful parallels between past and present. He folded the old patriotism of the Civil War in with his new vision of patriotism, casting both as a defense of national unity and national order against threats from outside:

> Let us settle once for all that this government is one of honor and of law and that neither the seeds of repudiation nor lawlessness can find root in our soil or live beneath our flag. That represents all our aims, all our policies, all our purposes. It is the banner of every patriot; it is, thank God, today the flag of every section of our common country. No flag ever triumphed over it. It was never degraded or defeated and will not now be when more patriotic men are guarding it than ever before in our history.[34]

In speech after speech, McKinley used the flag as the figure of a united America. Using the Civil War history of the flag as a way to marginalize the social critiques of 1896, he implicitly cast the strikes of starving workingmen as an organized national threat similar in magnitude to that of the Confederate army.

Hanna's coup de grâce, however, was the creation of a special Republican Flag Day. He himself called this the "great climax" of the campaign. Working with state and local Republican committees, Hanna organized special Flag Day celebrations in the nation's largest cities. Millionaires, influential businessmen, and industrialists all prepared for the marches and announced to their employees that the workers, too, were expected to march. The Republican National Committee had purchased millions of campaign flags, which the committee sent all over the country. The McKinley campaign purchased additional paraphernalia, including buttons, hats, and horns. On October 31, the last Saturday before the election, several hundred thousand people turned out to celebrate both the Republican candidate and the flag. From his front porch, McKinley told a crowd of twenty-five thousand that the American flag was "a holy banner": "No flag represents as much as it does; it represents liberty, it represents equality, it represents opportunity, it represents possibilities for American manhood obtainable in no other land beneath the sun."[35]

There were Flag Day parades in major cities from east to west: Baltimore, Boston, Milwaukee, St. Louis, Cincinnati, and Detroit. In Boston, thousands of employers marched alongside their employees; in San Francisco, the parade lasted four hours. In Chicago, the campaign put on a huge civic celebration in the Auditorium Building. In each seat was a tiny American flag, which the crowds picked up and waved.[36]

The most incredible news came from New York City, where the Business Men's Sound Money Association sponsored a parade that took more than seven hours to pass. Fully 103,000 men marched down Broadway, each one wearing a yellow chrysanthemum in his lapel to show his support of the gold standard, and each one carrying a flag on a staff over his shoulder like a rifle. For every marcher, there were seven witnesses: three-quarters of a million people cheering in the streets. The effect was overwhelming. As the McKinley-sympathetic *New York Tribune* described the scene:

> The flag was everywhere. It flaunted from every window; it waved from every portico; it flew from every roof; it floated over almost every street, and many times in every block. The marching thousands trampled between walls of human faces that were almost entirely folded in the stripes and dotted with

the stars, while every man in the whole vast line carried a flag of his own which he held aloft.[37]

Like nativist Lewis Levin before him, Mark Hanna's clever use of flag symbolism effectively appropriated the banner as an emblem not only of the nation but also of the Republican Party. His strategy was somewhat risky: The flag protection movement activists might have decried it as self-serving and un-American, and Democrats certainly did. But in fact, Flag Day paid off beautifully. The many elaborate public celebrations forged a visual link between American patriotism and the Republican agenda. By the end of the day, there was no question that the flag stood for the gold standard and for capitalism.

Bryan and the Democrats were caught off guard. They attempted to counter the Republican Flag Day by urging Democrats to put out their flags as well. The flag, they urged, "should be displayed prominently, both for love of the Stars and Stripes as well as a rebuke to those who would prostitute the flag of our country to ...base political uses." Bryan supporters were instructed to join the Flag Day demonstrations, but to do so in honor of the flag rather than McKinley, and to show pictures of Bryan to make their loyalties clear. As the head of the Democratic campaign told a crowd of Chicagoans, "[We] still believe that the American flag is an emblem of American liberty and not the trade-mark of a political party that would make the rights of the citizen the subject of barter and sale." This tactic was most successful in St. Louis, where the Democratic Flag Day parade was almost as big as the Republican one.[38]

Many Bryan supporters were simply too angry at Hanna's use of the banner. In an unprecedented display of violence, Democrats and Populists ripped, trampled, and burned Republican flags—those bearing McKinley's likeness—from New York to California. In Iowa, they shot at a McKinley flag. In Florida, someone ripped down a McKinley banner from over a city street. In Missouri, a parade of pro-silver horsemen torched a Sound Money banner. In St. Louis, Bryan supporters grabbed a flag from a veteran marching in a parade with the Old Soldiers' McKinley League. In Indiana, a judge pulled down a Republican flag hung in his courthouse, saying that it was not the national emblem and had no place in his courtroom. At a silver meeting in Chicago, a speaker urged the crowd to tear down the large Republican flags outside a prominent city club. He then took a McKinley flag, called it a "rag," and dropped it on the floor.[39]

In one of the most widely reported incidents, a Bryan rally in Missouri was interrupted by the arrival of a McKinley train of campaign workers. The McKinley people distributed literature, which the Bryanites instantly turned into a bonfire. One of the McKinley operatives had a five-year-old daughter, who stepped onto the rear platform of the train, singing sound-money songs and waving a flag. A Bryan supporter reached for the flag and wrested it away from the girl and her father and then threw it into the flames, at which point the Bryan supporters gave a great cheer. These incidents made very poor press for Democrats and Populists. "How They Hate the Flag!" proclaimed the headlines.[40]

Strange and threatening, this behavior confirmed preconceptions that such "agitators" were unable to govern themselves. The situation was made even more confusing by the partisan nature of the flags. Were Republican flags national flags, or were they political advertisements? Hanna's Flag Day had conflated the two meanings, and it left Bryan supporters with no effective symbolic way of disengaging them. The violence that Populists and Democrats wreaked on McKinley flags may have been emotionally satisfying, but it was politically devastating.

∾∘∾

McKinley won the election. As a contemporary newspaper noted, the election of 1896 witnessed the Republican accession of "the monopoly of patriotism"; it gave the party "a sort of divine right to the flag." The icon that had been a symbol of the North and the Union was now reincarnated as a symbol of the Republican Party, sound money, and the status quo.[41]

The flag desecrations, and the larger pool of anger and violence that they suggested, shifted the agenda of the flag protection movement. Where earlier flag protectors had felt the flag threatened by partisanship and greed endemic to Anglo-Americans' own order, now they saw threats to the flag as coming from radical and immigrant constituencies. And in an America that was still reeling from the events of 1893 and 1894, attacks on the flag came to symbolize, with Mark Hanna's concerted help, attacks on the social order.

The Republican manipulation of the flag took advantage of deep economic insecurity and a society in flux, as had the nativist campaign in 1844. Both Levin and Hanna diverted attention from economic issues and recast the country's divisions along spiritual and moral lines. Both provoked, wittingly or unwittingly, attacks on the flag; both used these attacks to consolidate their claim on the flag's political meaning. Both paid lip service to humanitarianism, but claimed, through the logic of nationalism, that their opponents were unpatriotic and un-American.

And both established a new political landscape, one in which cultural issues formed the axis of social division.

The nationalism set in place by Hanna and McKinley had a strong political edge: This was the patriotism behind sentiments such as "My country right or wrong." There had been glimpses of such nationalist patriotism before, but never had it dominated the culture of peacetime. Within twenty years it would intensify to a fever pitch.

# ~5~

# FLAG OF RACE

## *The Ku Klux Klan*

William Joseph Simmons stood six feet two, sported wild red hair, and favored striped trousers. He was a born-again Christian with a taste for bourbon who kept cloves and mints handy to cover the smell of alcohol on his breath. Thirty-five years old in 1915, he was old enough to remember the 1896 election but young enough to be part of the generation that succeeded it. Simmons had fought in the Spanish-American War, toured Alabama and Florida on horseback as a Methodist circuit rider, taught history, and become a garter salesman. Like so many others of his generation, Simmons moved from the small world in which he was born into the larger one of geographical mobility and bigger cities. Leaving his tiny hometown of Harpersville, Alabama, to fight in the Spanish-American War, he then migrated through a series of towns until he made his way to growing Birmingham and then finally to the booming city of Atlanta.[1]

Simmons had come to Atlanta as the district manager of the Woodmen of the World, a smaller companion to the Elks and the Moose and hundreds of similar organizations designed to rebuild small-town culture in big-city environments by offering clubhouses and social networks. Part of the new world of fraternal organizations, Simmons wore lapels and vests that glittered with lodge pins signifying his membership in twelve organizations, including the Masons and the Odd Fellows. He was in charge of organizing Woodsmen membership, a job that suited his hail-fellow-well-met style.[2]

Atlanta was rapidly becoming the largest city in the South, and it boasted the features of a new world: hotels and restaurants and department stores. The city was growing—from 150,000 residents in 1910 to more than 200,000 in 1920. On Peachtree Street, the city's main thoroughfare, the old and new were evident together: The old, high Victorian buildings, built of brick and marble, that lined the street were being outmoded as new "elevator buildings" of eleven stories and taller began to push upward on the skyline. Streetcars clanged by, two and three in quick succession, thronged by shiny black Model T cars. The city had a new baseball team and had just attracted the regional branch of the Federal Reserve Bank and Emory College.

But growing cities had fragmented families and frayed their ties, as sons and daughters grew up and moved away from their hometowns. The urban areas had brought large numbers of people into daily contact: whites and blacks, native-born and immigrants. There had been strides in legislation to protect workers—an increasing number of child labor laws and a recent acceptance of an eight-hour workday—but wages were meager and it was difficult to keep a family together.

Only months after he arrived in Atlanta, Simmons was standing on a street corner when a touring car veered off the road and struck him. He spent three months in bed recovering from the car accident, during which time he mapped out a plan for a new organization, one based on the Reconstruction Klan. The Klan had been founded in 1865 by former Confederates as a way to promote white supremacy in the wake of the Civil War and federal occupation of the South. The Klan was conceived as an "invisible army," a loose network of men who perpetrated violence and intimidation through a series of nighttime visitations, whippings, and murders. With the end of Reconstruction and the withdrawal of U.S. troops, this early Klan disappeared. It was no longer necessary. Absent federal involvement, Southern states imposed legal means like segregation, poll taxes, and literacy tests to ensure white supremacy.[3]

But in Simmons's eyes, the Klan was a romantic aspect of the old South. Stories of it played a large part in his memories of his youth. Simmons's father had been an officer in the organization, and the young boy's nurse and other family servants had told him stories of Klan exploits that both terrified and excited him. "I was always fascinated by Klan stories," he explained later. "My old Negro mammy, Aunt Viney, and her husband, used to tell us children about how the old Reconstruction Klansmen used to frighten the darkies. 'Why, dat Klansman was shore twelve foot high,' I heard Aunt Viney say to Uncle Simon. 'Go 'long with you, Viney,' said Uncle Simon. 'Dat Klansman was twenty foot tall, on his hawse!'"[4]

Simmons's stylized memory of his youth was bound up with the problems that confronted his generation in the early twentieth century. The combination proved extremely powerful. Who, in the anonymity of the city, did not long to be seen as twenty feet tall?

Lying in bed, consulting a copy of the 1867 Reconstruction Klan prescript, Simmons worked out an elaborate set of structures for his new Klan. It would be, he thought, the ultimate fraternal society: "It is altogether original, weird, mystical, and of a high class," he wrote. "It unfolds a spiritual philosophy that has to do with the very fundamentals of life and living, here and hereafter." He asked a friend whether the Ku Klux Klan might work as a locker club, one of the Atlanta institutions where gentlemen could keep liquor despite nationwide Prohibition. "What do you think of it, Walter?" he asked. "The name I mean. For a locker club. Will they join?" His friend was doubtful. "Naw," he replied, "they all want to be animals." But Simmons's personal vision connected with two important historical events that year to form a volatile combination.[5]

The first occasion was the movie release of D. W. Griffith's *Birth of a Nation*. The film event of the decade, it portrayed Reconstruction Klansmen as modern-day knights saving white citizens from vicious blacks. It was filled with chase scenes and dramatic confrontations: Lascivious black men cornered virtuous white women while white-clad Klansmen galloped to the rescue with flaming crosses. The drama of the plot was enhanced by the newness of the film experience. Audiences sat in the dark, clutching their seats, while the images flickered larger than life on the screen; Wagner's "Ride of the Valkyries" enhanced the suspense. The film's triumphant conclusion—a parade of the Klansmen heroes and white citizens cheering them for restoring law and order—was an invitation to those who sought opportunities for heroism.[6]

At the same time, a sensational murder case tapped into fears about the perils of the modern world. In the Atlanta suburb of Marietta, the body of fourteen-year-old Mary Phagan was found raped and murdered in the basement of the pencil factory where she had worked. Suspicion quickly settled on Leo Frank, the Jewish factory owner who had emigrated from New York. Frank was later exonerated, but the case proved culturally significant. His triple outsider status—as Jew, as agent of industrialization, and as big-city man—made him a symbolic villain who represented dynamics much larger than the case itself. Like *Birth of a Nation*, the Frank case dramatized the threats to a small-town, white, Protestant culture that found itself losing cultural dominance in an industrialized America. In conjunction with the film, the case inspired vigilante action. A group of twenty-five men calling themselves the Knights of Mary Phagan abducted Frank from prison, lynched him, and burned a celebratory cross on Stone Mountain.[7]

Simmons worried that the popularity of Griffith's film would lead to rival Klans, so he sent out invitations to friends and associates, asking them to join him in resurrecting a historical fraternal association. On a cold November night in 1915, Simmons greeted thirty-four men at the Piedmont Hotel in Atlanta. His friends expected a comfortable room, a banquet, brandy, and after-dinner speeches. Instead, Simmons presented them with a rented sightseeing bus and a plan to hold a mysterious ceremony on top of Stone Mountain. More than half the men rebelled. "Jesus, Doc," said one friend, "I can't climb Stone Mountain in the daytime. Can't you revive the ancient glories in the flatlands?" But the emotion over Mary Phagan's murder was high, and sixteen of the men climbed into the bus.[8]

At the base of Stone Mountain, the men switched on electric flashlights and stared up the trail. As Simmons described it:

> Down at the bottom of the mountain there's a spring of sparkling cold water. I stopped at the spring and took some of

the water in my old army canteen and stopped to make a few remarks on purity and honor. Then we struggled to the top. . . . Each pilgrim, when nearing the crest, gathered a granite boulder, and on the summit of Stone Mountain the sixteen boulders were built into an altar.[9]

The flashlights cast pools of light over an eerie landscape: bare granite underfoot, pools of water pocked the surface, big rocks strewn everywhere. After the men built the makeshift altar, Simmons directed their attention to a cross of pine boards, soaked in kerosene, which he had carried up the mountain earlier that day. They hoisted the wooden cross on top of the altar and stood back. Simmons described what happened next:

> I put the canteen of water on the stones with a few remarks. My father had once given me an old American flag, which had been carried in the Mexican War, I had brought it with me. I laid it across the altar, with some more remarks. Next I placed a Bible on the altar, explaining my reasons for doing. . . . Suddenly I struck a match and lighted the cross. Everyone was amazed.

As the firelight flashed over the sixteen faces, onto the stones, and across the flag's white stars and red stripes, Simmons administered the oath of the reborn Ku Klux Klan.[10]

Simmons focused on the ritual rather than political elements of the society he hoped to build. The Bible signified spirituality; the spring water symbolized purity; the burning cross came directly from *Birth of a Nation*. The American flag was Simmons's addition. He brought the flag that night for reasons he had only half articulated. He brought it because, like the Bible and the pure spring water, it was a ritual object. He brought it because it spoke to him of history, both personal and national. He brought it because he imagined his reconstituted Klan as a patriotic society.

Early Klan members shared Simmons's passion for drama. Before the Atlanta premier of *Birth of a Nation* in December 1915, a group of them dressed up in sheets, took their rifles, and mounted their horses. In a flurry of white sheets and pounding hooves, they galloped down Peachtree Street. Right in front of the Atlanta Theater, they stopped and fired a rifle salute, making a powerful impression on the line of moviegoers waiting to see the film.[11]

സ๛

World War I led up to nationalist patriotism run amok. For a year before the United States entered the hostilities, Americans held "preparedness parades": flag-filled events replete with marching bands and rows of patriotic citizens. Schools and communities held pageants featuring flags, marching, songs, and drills. In case anyone missed these events, they were shown as newsreels in the new moving-picture houses. The physical appearance of the flag reflected this nationalist uniformity, as forty-eight stars marched in six even rows across the blue field of the canton. The design was symmetrical, orderly, and military in its precision: All measurements were standardized, down to the width of the stripes and the diameter of the stars.[12]

When President Woodrow Wilson walked into a special session of Congress on April 2, 1917, to request a declaration of war, he found a hall full of congressmen wearing flag pins on their chests. These were the hawks, who had distributed the flag ahead of time as a symbol of war and patriotism. The congressmen who opposed intervention wore lapels that seemed conspicuously bare. Wilson's message invoked humanitarian principles: "We shall fight for the things which we have always carried nearest our hearts—for democracy, for the right of those who submit to authority to have a voice in their own governments." But it was accompanied by the threat of unprecedented political crackdown. "If there should be disloyalty," he warned, "it will be dealt with with a firm hand of stern repression." It was not an idle threat. In 1917, Congress passed the Espionage Act, which allowed for censorship of the press. The following year, the legislators passed the Sedition Act, which prohibited criticism of the government and the flag. Nine states passed laws making criticism of the war illegal; fifteen outlawed syndicalism.[13]

A special propaganda office set up by the government, the Committee on Public Information (CPI), provided a steady output of war news. The CPI's Division of News writers filled more than twenty thousand newspaper columns each week with official news emphasizing American heroism and German atrocity. The Division of Pictorial Publicity created appealing and inflammatory propaganda posters: In one, a German soldier stands menacingly over a defenseless woman and baby, underscored by the words "Germans are barbarians." The Division of Films worked with Hollywood directors to dramatize the war in popular cinema, bringing out films entitled *To Hell with the Kaiser*, *Wolves of Kultur*, and *The Kaiser: Beast of Berlin*.[14]

The war effort criminalized political dissent and labor activism; it habituated Americans to the loss of their civil liberties. In 1920, looking back at the war era, Senator Hiram Johnson was struck by the deep impression it had made: "The war has set back the people for a generation. They have bowed to a hundred repressive acts." Immigrants who were suspected of disloyalty were interned in three camps for "enemy aliens" in Georgia and Utah; over four thousand were held there, behind barbed wire, during the war. The Justice Department compiled lists of all suspicious foreigners and attempted to register all Germans. These programs were a point of pride for the administration. In 1918, the attorney general was pleased to announce: "It is safe to say that never in its history has this country been so thoroughly policed."[15]

Many citizens, including Simmons and his Klansmen, participated willingly. Seventy-five thousand volunteers, known as Four Minute Men, provided short, patriotic talks to audiences in churches, movie theaters, and fraternal lodges. Together they gave more than seven million speeches with titles like "Why We Are Fighting," "Unmasking German Propaganda," and "Where Did You Get Your Facts?" President Wilson's attorney general set up private auxiliaries to the Justice Department, voluntary domestic groups who volunteered their time in exchange for quasi-official status. The most famous such group, the American Protective League, comprised 250,000 business and professional men who reported to public officials any pro-German statements that reached their ears.[16]

As the Klan absorbed the political culture of World War I, Simmons began to see his organization as an important civic adjunct to Wilson's domestic strategy. He was a member of the Citizens' Bureau of Investigation, an organization much like the American Protective League but whose members were shop owners instead of professionals. Under his direction, Klansmen denounced a shipyard strike in Mobile, Alabama, and hunted down young men who had avoided the draft. The Klansmen harassed the prostitutes who gathered around military bases. The Klan's most frequent activity was threatening Wobblies, members of the International Workers of the World, who organized strikes and openly criticized the war effort as being driven by a money machine. In the Klan's eyes, this was un-American. A Klan parade in 1918 through the streets of Atlanta featured one hundred Klansmen in robes urging the onlookers to buy war bonds and shouting warnings to any spies to leave town. Simmons ordered Klan members not to reveal their identity so they could act more effectively as spies. As he remembered later, "I issued a decree during the war submerging membership in the Klan. Our secret service work made this imperative. I ordered members to keep their membership in the Klan a secret from everybody, except each other." In Simmons's eyes, Klansmen were a cross between medieval knights and government secret agents.[17]

The flag played a special role in this patriotic lockdown. World War I was the first major war since the election of 1896, and the flag culture built by Mark Hanna and the Republican party intensified sharply with American entry into the war. Demand for flags doubled. In flag factories, rows and rows of seamstresses bent over dozens of sewing machines, fingers guiding thousands of yards of wool bunting under the needle. Individuals bought so many flags that the price was driven upward 300 percent over the course of one year. President Wilson declared the "Star-Spangled Banner" the official anthem of the army and navy; professional baseball leagues hired bands to play the song at the beginning of games. Several states passed flag salute laws, requiring schoolchildren to participate in flag ceremonies at least once a week.[18]

The flag no longer symbolized the inviolable values of the nation; it had become one of those values. The Sedition Act had specifically outlawed "any disloyal profane, scurrilous, or abusive language" about the flag. In Kansas, the state supreme court ruled that disrespectful language "will not, cannot, be used by any man in any place concerning our flag, if he has any respect for it. The man who uses such language concerning it, either in jest or in argument, does not have that respect for it that should be found in the breast of every citizen of the United States." The Kansas law required only a fine, but some legislation was far more punitive. Texas passed a law in 1918 that raised the penalty for flag desecration from thirty days in jail to twenty-five years.[19]

Ordinary citizens became vigilantes, using the flag as a litmus test for American patriotism. German Americans were surrounded by crowds and forced to fly a flag, kiss a flag, or sing the "Star-Spangled Banner." In Kansas, a German-speaking Mennonite man was captured by five carloads of men and taken from his farm into town, where a mob tried to force him to buy liberty bonds and salute the American flag. When he refused, the mob covered him with yellow paint and tried to lynch him; though he was rescued, he was arrested under the Espionage Act for desecrating the flag. In Illinois, five hundred people kidnapped a German American socialist, stripped him, and dragged him down the street barefoot, wrapped in a large flag that he was forced to kiss as he went. When police put him in jail to protect him, the mob broke in, abducted him, and hanged him from a tree.[20]

Critics of American capitalism were pursued just as virulently. Members of the International Workers of the World, in particular, were frequently harassed; some were castrated and hung. In Montana, one Wobbly was cornered by a crowd who tried to force him to kiss an American flag. He refused. "What is this thing anyway?" he told them defiantly. "Nothing but a piece of cotton with a little paint on it and some other marks in the corner there. I will not kiss that thing. It might be covered with microbes." Brought before a court, he was convicted of sedition and sentenced to ten to twenty years at hard labor. The judge, bound to the verdict by mandatory sentencing laws, censured the mob for its fanaticism, questioned its patriotism, and quoted playwright George Bernard Shaw's statement that American courts in World War I were "stark, staring, raving mad."[21]

Vigilante patriotism reached back through the Civil War mobs in New York all the way to the rowdy-boys of the Stamp Act rebellion, who forced the stamp collector out of office. From the nativists onward, crowds had forced individuals to embrace the flag as a proxy for their country The ideal of belonging to a community, so fundamental to nationalist patriotism, was realized in flag-waving crowds who roamed the streets identifying as the nation's enemies those who refused to join. Whereas the Civil War ultimately used nationalist patriotism in pursuit of humanitarian values, the Great War used nationalist patriotism for nationalism's sake alone. There were more vigilante incidents than ever, and the flag became an increasingly violent sign of opposition to those whom some citizens considered outsiders.

The end of the war in 1918 brought widespread change. Large numbers of veterans were returning from the war. The Great Migration of Southern blacks to Northern cities had changed the face of those cities. At the same time, massive immigration continued. These altered demographics led to social upheaval, and in 1919 alone, there were twenty-five race riots in American cities and more than thirty-five hundred strikes. In the culture created by the war, the government felt justified in continuing its persecution of outsiders. The Palmer Raids targeted organizations deemed subversive by the government, breaking into and ransacking offices in a number of different cities, arresting aliens with membership in the Communist Party, and deporting many of them without due process. The war may have been over, but the anxieties that had fueled it were not.[22]

Meanwhile, the Klan's mission again shifted, tapping into the increasingly violent national mood. In 1920, Simmons hired a duo of professional advertisers, a slim former newspaperman named Edward Clarke and an auburn-haired widow named Bessie Tyler. Between them, they had raised money for the War Fund campaigns, solicited for fraternal organizations and the Anti-Saloon League, and run a highly successful Harvest Festival in Atlanta, complete with a Better Babies parade. Clarke and Tyler had learned a great deal about what motivated people to join organizations and to give money. Under their leadership, the Klan became an organization that tapped into the fear and distrust that had been so carefully cultivated during the war.[23]

Clarke and Tyler portrayed the Klan as the country's only hope for salvation against the evil forces of Jews, Catholics, African Americans, and immigrants. As imperial wizard, Simmons adapted quickly to this new strategy of using the visual language of patriotism. He posed for photographers in front of the Liberty Bell in Philadelphia, kneeling in front of the sacred object. But his language was increasingly violent. Before beginning a speech to Georgia Klansmen, he silently laid out two guns on the table and then stabbed a bowie knife between them: "Now let the Niggers, Catholics, Jews, and all others who disdain my imperial wizardry come on."[24]

Clarke and Tyler sent more than a thousand foot soldiers all over the country. These men, known as kleagles, tailored their message to whomever they were speaking, channeling local anxieties about race, religion, immigration, labor unions, and alcohol. In the North, the kleagles focused their rhetoric against Catholics. In the South, the Klansmen stoked racism. In cities heavily populated by immigrants, the target was "aliens." In each case, the Klan identified a set of villains and let fear do the recruiting.[25]

In late 1920, the night riding began. Hooded Klansmen abducted and beat victims who offended their sense of social order: a doctor who performed abortions, a black dentist, a man who spoke German, a divorcé, a white lawyer who represented black clients. A black bellhop in Dallas was branded with acid on the forehead with "KKK." In Tenha, Texas, a woman suspected of adultery was abducted from the hotel where she worked, stripped naked, and tarred and feathered. In Miami, an Episcopal archdeacon was whipped and tarred and feathered for preaching "racial equality." The Klan specialized in intimidation, putting out warnings against striking black cotton workers in Corsicana, Texas, to force them back into the fields. A Socialist speaker was dragged from her platform and driven to the edge of town, where she was ejected from the car and warned that the next time would be worse. By September 1921, Klansmen had been responsible for at least 150 instances of intimidation, including four murders, forty-one whippings, and twenty-seven tar-and-featherings.[26]

By then, nearly one hundred thousand Americans had donned white robes and stood anxiously waiting to be inducted into the mysterious hierarchy of "kludds" and "klexters." When the klokard—the officer who administered the oath—asked them, "Are you a native-born white, Gentile American citizen?" they answered with a proud yes. A year later, membership had grown tenfold to more than a million; within three years, it would swell to four million.[27]

At the same time, the flag was the increasingly public face of the Klan, the tangible symbol of the patriotism the group avowed. Visitors to the imperial wizard's office in Atlanta found Simmons at a desk in front of a large American flag. The flag formed part of the closing ceremony at the klaverns' monthly meetings as members bowed their heads before it. White-clad horsemen bore it proudly at the head of Klan parades. The flag and the cross together provided the central symbols for nighttime cross burnings and daytime corn roasts. Klansmen included the flag in the formal photographs of their klaverns. They frequently brought it to church and bestowed it on the congregations. Sometimes their cloaked and hooded figures appeared at the back of white churches in the midst of Sunday morning service, holding folded flags. Wordlessly, mysteriously, they moved through the congregation to the altar, where they silently lay the flags and offerings of money. These ceremonies illustrated the Klan's assumption of a special patriotic status—the flag was theirs to bestow.[28]

For those outside the Klan, the flag raised the question of how the group fit into the national polity: Were members un-American or especially American? Klansmen had harassed people during the war, but always with the putative sanction of the government. This vigilante violence was new and horrifying. In 1921, with the help of a former kleagle, the *New York World* ran an exposé that chronicled an account of Klan violence: "It would be impossible to imagine an attitude more essentially lawless. Ku Kluxism as conceived, incorporated, propagated and practiced has become a menace to the peace and security of every section of the United States. Its evil and vicious possibilities are boundless."[29]

The Klan's 1924 manual laid out its stance clearly: "The military form of government must and will be preserved for the sake of true, patriotic Americanism, because it is the only form of government that gives any guarantee of success." Even more striking was the startling absence of the rhetoric of freedom and democracy in their organizational rhetoric: "We must avoid the fate of the other organizations that have split on the rock of democracy." Given such statements, Klan critics had little trouble painting the Klan as un-American.[30]

But there was plenty of evidence that the Klan *was* American, or at least that Americans were willing to claim it. Congressional hearings that were intended to discredit the Klan unwittingly advertised it to a willing country: Following the hearings, membership skyrocketed. Cultural critic H. L. Mencken contended that the Klan's version of patriotism was merely that of the rest of the country, taken to its logical extreme:

Not a single solitary sound reason has yet been advanced for putting the Ku Klux Klan out of business. If the Klan is against the Jews, so are half of the good hotels of the Republic and three-quarters of the good clubs. If the Klan is against the foreign-born or the hyphenated citizen, so is the National Institute of Arts and Letters. If the Klan is against the Negro, so are all of the States south of the Mason-Dixon line. If the Klan is for damnation and persecution, so is the Methodist Church. . . . If the Klan constitutes itself a censor of private morals, so does the Congress of the United States. If the Klan lynches a Moor for raping someone's daughter, so would you or I.

The point was driven home when President Warren Harding became a Klansmen that year, sworn in by Simmons in the Green Room of the White House.[31]

Like the nativists before them, Klan members came from the margins of society, yet they claimed the flag with such fervor, and so clearly on the heels of government policy, that it was hard for others to oppose their claim. The Klan epitomized the way in which the nationalist brand of patriotism sought to unite a white country divided along class lines and defuse the economic critiques of socialists and labor activists, but the Ku Klux Klan flag became defined by war in a way that the nativists' flag had not. The Klan claimed the flag before they knew what it meant to them; only over the course of World War I did it became infused with the superpatriotism of the Wilson administration. Their flag, unlike the earlier Philadelphia flag, had strong policy implications. Those who supported it recognized that; so did those who opposed it. The many citizens who refused to kiss the flag refused because the flag had become inextricable from the crushing policies of a repressive state.

This Klan-government alliance seemed to be borne out in the Klan's 1925 march in Washington. It was August, and the capital was suffering from ninety-degree heat. Busloads of Klansmen arrived to participate in the march. Thirty thousand Klan members marched through the streets in broad daylight, line after intimidating line of white-robed figures stretching more than a dozen abreast. Right under the Capitol dome they marched, raising American flags high above their ranks. The members' faces, usually shrouded by long hoods, were bare by order of the imperial wizard: an uncovering that made the Klansmen less mysterious but more terrifyingly like government men. It was a display of power and also of legitimacy. Like Lewis Levin's Independence Day parade, the Klan's presence in Washington seemed to symbolize state sanction for its activities and its version of patriotism.

But by this time, the Klan was already crumpling under the weight of ethics problems. It had made a name for itself as the defenders of national honor, but few of the primary figures were capable of sustaining that honor. Sitting under a large American flag in his inner-sanctum Atlanta office and swigging bourbon, William Simmons was an unlikely imperial wizard for a society that advocated Prohibition.[32] The two Klan promoters, Edward Clarke and Bessie Tyler, were arrested in 1916 in a bawdy house wearing only their underclothes: a shocking affair by early-twentieth-century standards, especially given the Klan's emphasis on the purity of womanhood. In Indiana, the most powerful Klan stronghold, Grand Dragon David Curtis Stephenson kidnapped and raped the young woman he wanted to marry. After he mutilated her by biting her all over her body, she committed suicide by swallowing mercuric chloride tablets. The case raised chilling echoes of the Mary Phagan case. This time, the Klansman was not the chivalrous knight riding to the rescue.[33]

In 1926, Klan membership dropped rapidly as corruption appeared in the political as well as moral spheres. From prison, the Indiana grand dragon documented the Klan's corruption of politics. On the state level, his information indicted the mayor of Indianapolis, the entire city council, the governor, and the chair of the state Republican Party. On the national level, the informant gave evidence of campaign fraud and willful deception of rank-and-file members. Klan members, especially those in the North, were horrified. Six hundred Klansmen from New Haven tendered their resignations in language that turned the Klan's own rhetoric against itself: "[The Klan] has become a travesty on patriotism and a blasphemous caricature professing Protestantism. . . . Real Americans must be awakened and made to use every effort to stamp out this slimy serpent that threatens the very life of our Nation."[34]

Many members simply refused to pay dues. From its peak of four million members in 1924, the Klan lost nearly 99 percent of its members. In 1930, only forty-five thousand were left, mostly in the South.[35]

The Klan typified the nationalist, racialist wave of patriotism that reached its height around World War I. Other groups were more mainstream, holding similar ideas of patriotism but distancing themselves from the Klan's extralegal activities. It was these groups—the American Legion, the Sons and Daughters of the American Revolution, the Boy Scouts, and representatives of the army and navy—that came together to form the Flag Code in 1923. Like the newly standardized design of the flag itself, the code provided a uniform set of guidelines for the treatment of the flag: how it should be hung, displayed, pledged to, and otherwise respected. Its urgency came not from the aftermath of the war but from the great 1920s rush of immigrants who were changing the face of the country—one of the threats most felt by the KKK. Even as the Klan itself faded from influence, its nationalist American vision persisted in the codification of the flag.

# ~6~

# FLAG OF EQUALITY

## *The Civil Rights Movement*

In 1925, the same year that Klansmen flooded the nation's capitol, Medgar Evers was born in Decatur, Mississippi. Mississippi was the most segregated state in the Union, as well as one of the poorest, with a strong tradition of local sheriffs' complicity in antiblack violence. The Constitution did not hold here: There was no right to vote or equal protection under the law. For Evers and other black Mississippians, the American flag was hardly a benign symbol. It represented the federal government that sanctioned segregation and the Klan that enforced it through burnings, rapes, and lynchings.

Decatur was a small town in the sand-clay hill area of the state, populated by poor farmers. It was one of the few areas where whites outnumbered blacks. Segregation was so powerful that blacks weren't even allowed to drive into town on Saturday nights. Evers's father owned his own house and was one of the few black men who wouldn't step off the sidewalk to let whites pass. He frequently told his children, "My family *will* be able to walk on the sidewalk. [Whites] will treat them with dignity. They will be able to register to vote."[1]

Young Evers learned quickly about the realities of life as a black male in Mississippi. In the years between 1880 and 1940, white Mississippians had lynched nearly six hundred black men, a rate of ten lynchings per year. Nearly everyone knew someone who had been lynched, and the Evers family was no exception. When Evers was in his teens, a close friend of his father's was killed and strung up in a nearby pasture. For a year afterward, the man's clothes lay under the tree. Month after month, as Evers passed through the pasture, he was drawn to the clothes. When he asked his father why the man had been lynched, his father only answered, "Because he was colored, son."[2]

In 1941, the United States entered World War II. Medgar was sixteen. Within a year, he had dropped out of school to enlist in the army with his older brother Charles. Black soldiers were being recruited, and the brothers decided to leave the segregation and fear of rural Mississippi for the possibilities abroad. They could make decent money in the army. They had other motivations, too. Like other black recruits, they were cynical about the American government that they would fight for, and Charles later described their pact: The two of them would use their time in the army to learn how to kill white people.[3]

World War II enveloped the country. Nearly every draft-age young man served: eighteen million all told, with ten million serving overseas. Twenty-five million workers bought war bonds out of their regular paychecks. Once again, the flag played a huge role in war culture. Four hundred magazines coordinated to feature the flag on their covers in July 1942, the first Independence Day after Pearl Harbor. Recruiting posters urged prospective sailors to "Follow the Flag." "Are you a girl with a Star-Spangled heart?" the posters asked WAC recruits. When the famous photograph of the flag raising came out of Iwo Jima, an artist's rendering was immediately printed as a liberty bond poster and the photographed marines were pulled from action and brought home for a promotional tour. Moviegoers regularly sang "The Star-Spangled Banner" in theaters before the show began. Baseball parks picked up the earlier practice of playing the anthem and transformed it into a more collective experience, so all spectators joined in the singing before each game.[4]

Yet newsreels of celebrations in Hitler's Germany, documenting massive stadiums full of flags, patriotic adulation of the führer, and the militarization of Hitler youth warned Americans about the excesses of patriotism. As early as 1933, comedian Will Rogers drew a connection between the Nazis and the Klan: "Papers all state Hitler is trying to copy Mussolini. Looks to me like it's the Ku Klux that he is copying. He don't want to be emperor, he wants to be kleagle." While the Klan was no longer respectable, there were plenty of other disconcerting similarities between American patriotic rituals and the public demonstrations of the Third Reich. Hitler's straight-armed salute was nearly identical to the straight-armed salute given by American schoolchildren during the Pledge of Allegiance. The parallel was sufficiently striking that President Roosevelt eliminated the salute in the Flag Code of 1942, replacing it with the gesture of hand over heart. American flag sales increased roughly 20 percent during World War II, a far cry from the 100 percent increase during World War I.[5]

The war also highlighted the contradictions between the U.S. role as harbinger of democracy abroad and racial oppressor at home. If Hitler's Germany was characterized by anti-Semitism, what did American segregation say about the United States?

When a group of black soldiers was asked what to do with Hitler if he were captured alive, their answer made the connection clear: "Paint him black and sentence him to life in Mississippi." The oppression of African Americans, anti-Semitism, the internment of Japanese Americans, all of which had rarely been questioned by white Americans, now seemed eerily close to Nazi conduct. The war prompted, as Medgar Evers later described it, "a kind of national soul-searching. . . . While fighting a war against forces proclaiming a doctrine of racial superiority, it became increasingly difficult to justify racial discrimination at home."[6]

The war had a transformative effect on black U.S. soldiers, many of whom traveled out of their home communities for the first time. It was particularly profound for the hundreds of thousands of black soldiers from the South: eighty-five thousand from Mississippi alone. Their experience gave them a new and wider context in which to understand segregation. As one black college student pointed out: "The Army jim-crows us. The Navy lets us serve only as messmen. The Red Cross refuses our blood. Employers and labor unions shut us out. Lynchings continue. We are disenfranchised, jim-crowed, spat upon. What more could Hitler do than that?"[7]

The black soldiers' experience training in other parts of the United States and serving in other countries was not only demoralizing, but also eye-opening. It dramatized the peculiarity of Southern racial culture and gave birth to a particular kind of patriotism among the generation of black soldiers who served in World War II.

While Charles Evers was sent to the Pacific theater, Medgar's unit followed the invasion of Normandy and was stationed in France. The segregation of his unit was familiar—white officers and black privates—but other experiences radically expanded the boundaries of his world. He was armed and trained. One of the white lieutenants encouraged him to better himself. He became friendly with a French farm family and developed a romance with the family's daughter. This black-and-white romance seemed sweet and normal in France; at home, in Mississippi, it would have been unthinkable. For Evers and other black veterans of World War II, these experiences were proof positive that discrimination was not an inevitable result of racial difference.[8]

When the war ended in 1945, black veterans returned home to their families and their towns, ready to insist on fulfilling the promise of the humanitarian patriotism they had been fighting for. Medgar and Charles Evers were among them. Their war experience had convinced them that Mississippi, too, needed some democracy. The Civil War hopes for suffrage were effectively dead in the water; the Klan had harassed and intimidated black voters for years. Voter registration numbers were dismal: Of Mississippi's 350,000 African Americans of voting age, only 5,000 were even registered—less than 2 percent. Their hometown of Decatur was even worse, with 900 white voters on the rolls and no black voters registered.[9]

What had become of the humanitarian impulse to enfranchise all Americans? The *First Vote* painting from the Civil War era had shown the American flag floating protectively over an African American voter, an image that now seemed hopelessly dated and naïve. The legacy of the war, though, opened a few fissures in the white-dominated voting establishment. The U.S. Supreme Court had recently outlawed the all-white primary. The election of 1946 would be the first in which blacks would be eligible to vote in the primaries in Mississippi. And the Mississippi legislature had passed a law exempting all returning soldiers from the poll tax. With four other black veterans, Medgar and Charles Evers decided it was time to test American democracy.

The courthouse in Decatur was a Greek Revival building with broad stone steps leading up to large columns. A few weeks before the election, the six young men walked inside and were able to register by surprising the clerk. Word got around quickly, though, and soon the Evers family began to get nightly visits. Whites and other blacks urged the young men's parents to keep them from voting. It did not help that Mississippi's Senator Theodore Bilbo, a white race-baiter, used the election to announce, "The best way to keep a nigger from the polls on election day is to visit him the night before." On July 2, Evers's twenty-first birthday, the six young men walked to the courthouse to vote. A crowd of about twenty young white men stood waiting, holding rifles and shotguns. These men had grown up together and played together; now they stood eyeing one another in an armed standoff on the courthouse steps. The sheriff watched. It was clear that attempting to vote would lead to violence and possibly death. Finally Medgar said, "Come on, Charlie, let's go. We'll get them next time." As he recalled later: "We split up and went home without voting. Around town, Negroes said we had been whipped, beaten up, and run out of town. Well, in a way we were whipped, I guess, but I made up my mind then that it would not be like that again—at least not for me."[10]

∞∞

Returning veterans formed the backbone of civil rights organizations in the South. In Mississippi in the 1950s, all three of the state's most influential civil rights workers had fought in World War II. In addition, James Meredith, the man who would integrate the University of Mississippi, was a veteran of the Korean War. These men had faced death. Many had been part of the defeat of Hitler, and some had seen parts of the world not disfigured by racial oppression. Their experiences both opened them to the hope of civil rights work and steeled them to its dangers.

For an African American wanting empowerment in the 1950s, the National Association for the Advancement of Colored People (NAACP) was the organization to join. Founded in 1909, it was the oldest and most influential agent of civil rights activity and it focused its efforts on the gains that could be won through the legal system. In Washington, the NAACP lobbied for federal antilynching legislation and worked for change through the courts. In the states, the organization encouraged voter registration and represented citizens challenging state segregation laws. It was the NAACP that was responsible for pushing *Brown v. Board of Education*, the case that tested school segregation, all the way to the Supreme Court. In Mississippi, membership had grown with the return of the veterans—ten new branches were formed in 1945 through 1947—although publicly acknowledging a connection with the organization was dangerous. Members were careful about identifying themselves and took care to vary their meeting places.[11]

Medgar Evers became the NAACP's first staff organizer in Mississippi in 1954.[12] He and his wife, Myrlie, whom he had married three years earlier, worked together in a two-room office in a big brick building in the black section of Jackson. Myrlie fielded calls from the national NAACP headquarters, the local press, and black Mississippians seeking help. Medgar drove around the state in his blue Oldsmobile, a gun in the trunk, speaking to groups of parents and urging them to petition for integrated schools in light of the *Brown* decision. He stood on the sidewalks of town, encouraging black citizens to register to vote. When the office telephone rang with news of a black Mississippian murdered or beaten or raped, he investigated. He was involved in every major civil rights development in Mississippi between 1954 and the end of his life. When, on a dare by his friends, fourteen-year-old Emmett Till talked fresh to a white woman and was murdered in 1955, Evers convinced Till's relatives to testify at the trial and publicized the case for the Northern media. When James Meredith enrolled in 1962 as the first black student at the University of Mississippi, Evers committed NAACP legal support and served as a friend and adviser through the harassment and riots that followed. These cases made national news; most others he was involved in did not.[13]

When he was called upon to speak, Evers frequently used his service in World War II to highlight American traditions of democracy and the pressing need to extend them to African Americans. "For two and one half years," he said, "I endangered my life as many other Negro Americans, on the far-away battlefields, to safeguard America and Democracy, only to return to our native country and be denied the basic things for which we fought." At heart, he argued, Americanism was a commitment to democracy. He excoriated segregationist powers as undemocratic, drawing analogies between white Southern power structures and Nazi Germany. The White Citizens' Councils that met openly and used economic pressure to suppress integration were in essence, he said, fascist groups. Police brutality against blacks was so horrifying that "only in Nazi Germany has such inhuman cruelty been equaled."[14]

Evers was not a patriot in the usual mold. As a young man, especially, he had harbored violent fantasies of revenge, and when his first son was born, Evers gave him the middle name Kenyatta in honor of the Kenyan Mau Mau leader who killed British colonials. But like many veterans and NAACP members, Evers gradually reframed his civil rights work in terms of broader American traditions. While black preachers spoke about civil rights primarily as a Christian issue, community organizers like Evers usually spoke about it as an American issue. Particularly after the *Brown* case, their civil rights speeches centered on the Declaration of Independence and the promise inherent in the Constitution. While Evers made some appeals to the church, his speeches were filled with references to Tom Paine and the founding documents. Abraham Lincoln was one of his favorite sources. As political events made the flag less palatable to segregationist groups, Evers was well placed to take advantage of the situation.[15]

∽∾∾

Outside civil rights organizations in the 1950s, Americanism, if not the flag, was heavily defined by Senator Joseph McCarthy's anti-Communist program. In the South, the flag still stood for a state that sanctioned lynching and segregation. In 1954, in response to the *Brown v. Board of Education* decision, the Ku Klux Klan started a renascence. At the same time, the White Citizens' Councils, known as the "uptown Klan" or the "country club Klan," organized. The councils grew quickly, gaining three hundred thousand members across the South and eighty thousand in Mississippi within a few years. As Medgar and Myrlie Evers set up the NAACP offices in Jackson, the White Citizens' Council set up their offices across town.[16]

Like the Klan, the White Citizens' Councils saw themselves as upholders of the American way. They embraced the American flag, placing it alongside the Confederate flag on their road signs and insignia. Council members saw American patriotism and segregation as highly complementary in 1954. Council members decried the *Brown* decision as "socialistic" and vowed to "stand together forever firm against communism and mongrelization." *Brown* had been a renegade case, they were sure, and it was only a matter of time until it was overturned. As Mississippi Senator James Eastland announced, "The South will not abide by nor obey this legislative decision of a political court. . . . We will take whatever steps are necessary to retain segregation in education. . . . We are about to embark on a great crusade to restore Americanism." Integration, as Eastland implied, was un-American.[17]

But as the 1950s progressed, Supreme Court decisions and other federal actions caused the segregationists to turn increasingly to the Confederate flag. When President Dwight Eisenhower sent troops with helmets and guns to enforce integration in Little Rock, Arkansas, in 1957, it was clear that the federal government was willing to put some weight behind integration. Subsequent events bore out the pattern: When Washington got involved, it was usually on the side of civil rights. For civil rights workers, that involvement was often far too little and disappointingly late; for segregationists, it was bald-faced interference.

Many white Southerners came to see the South almost as another country, one that was yet again under attack by the North. As White Citizens' Council founder Robert Patterson declared, "Sir, this is not the United States. This is Sunflower County, Mississippi." The Confederate flag summoned up the cult of the Lost Cause and Southern independence, and it was soon taken up by segregationist crowds as the primary symbol of white resistance.

After 1959, American flags disappeared entirely from segregationist gatherings, replaced by a red field of Confederate Xs.[18]

At the very moment that the segregationists were letting go of the American flag, rank-and-file civil rights activists began to claim it. Few African Americans had felt much affection for the flag, but the appearance of the Confederate flags meant that the American flag was suddenly an available symbol. The first people to seize this opportunity were not the seasoned civil rights organizers but the generation of college students who were beginning to resist segregation.

The American flag first appeared as a civil rights banner at the all-black North Carolina A&T State University. In 1960, four A&T students sat in their dormitory lambasting segregation and defying one another to do something about it. Together they decided they would go to Woolworth's, one of Greensboro's segregated downtown lunch counters, and ask to be served. At 4:30 p.m. on February 2, wearing ties and dress pants, the students walked into the store. They bought small items and then sat down at four of the shiny swivel stools along the lunch counter. Each requested a cup of coffee. One of the waitresses told them to go away, pointing to the segregated end, but the store manager told the waitresses to ignore them, so the students sat on the stools until the store closed at 5 p.m. The experience was a revelation. "It came to me all of a sudden," one of the four students described, "maybe they can't do anything to us. Maybe we can keep it up." The students went back to campus and recruited others for the next day.[19]

For the first several days, the protest was quiet and peaceful. Well-dressed black students sat quietly on the stools at the counter, some carrying Bibles and ending their protests with a prayer. The second day, thirty A&T students came; the third day, around sixty. Local papers began reporting the story, and crowds of whites began to gather under the striped awning outside. Most spectators were young men and boys, some drawn out of curiosity and some looking for a fight. They were the kind of men known as "roughs": One newspaper editor described "a ragtail rabble, slack-jawed, black-jacketed, grinning fit to kill." Their numbers grew, too. As the week progressed, the white boys started to bring Confederate battle flags, first one or two at a time, then many. The white crowds hovered outside the plate-glass windows, brandishing their flags and getting angrier and angrier at the protesters inside.[20]

Confrontation brewed for nearly a week. Hundreds of black students participated in the sit-ins: More than 90 percent of A&T students either sat in or participated in the accompanying boycott. The entire campus was energized. So was the growing number of white youths on the sidewalk. They swore at the protesters, threatened them, and waved their Confederate flags. Some came into the store and tried to hold seats for white patrons. Finally, at the end of the week, nearly three hundred white people pushed into the lunch area, pressing up against stools and counters, and filling the aisles. One youth set fire to a black student's coat. The white folks brought their symbols with them. Some carried full-size Confederate flags; others brought miniature ones, which they stuck into their cigarettes.[21]

Recognizing the imminent danger, the protesting students sent a message back to A&T for reinforcements. Soon, the A&T football team appeared at the door. They were large and imposing young men, and they made an impressive sight in their blue letter jackets. "Here comes the wrecking crew," cracked a white man. But the students did not seem like a wrecking crew. The uniformity of their blue letter jackets and their evident coordination invoked the discipline of a military unit. And in their hands they held a symbol that reinforced that image. In opposition to the Confederate flags that bobbed above the white heads, these black football players held small American flags.[22]

The players formed a flying-wedge formation. Sweeping aside the crowd, the lead players pressed through toward the lunch counter while the others fanned out to create a safe passageway. The protesters moved quickly from the stools to the door, protected by their classmates. The rowdies were taken aback by this display of coordinated black masculinity and power. "Who do you think you are?" a white man snapped. Flags in hand, the players did not hesitate. "We are the Union Army," they replied. Then a tall black man led an impromptu parade through the aisles of the store, holding the American flag high.[23]

The sit-ins spread rapidly. As fast as newspaper stories reported the Greensboro situation, students in other Southern communities decided to emulate the A&T students. Within a week after the first sit-ins, similar protests had been held throughout North Carolina, in Winston-Salem, in Durham, in Raleigh, and in five other cities and towns. By the end of the month, students had held sit-ins across seven states, in more than thirty cities and towns from Virginia to Alabama. Many protesters did not use the flag: For them, the power of the sit-ins was enough. But students in Raleigh, like their A&T predecessors, brought the American flag as well.[24]

Both in Greensboro and in Raleigh, students had thought out the symbolism of their actions, placing it in a specifically American context. Their flags had been bought ahead of time. Faced

with opposition from people waving Confederate flags, they realized that the resonance of the Civil War could be inverted. The
U.S. flag conjured up a host of far broader meanings, too. It
tapped into a long tradition of democratic practice, of inclusion,
and of righteous protest. It made the case that the sit-ins were a
continuation of those political traditions and thus eminently
American. Even President John F. Kennedy supported this inter-
pretation when later that spring, he said that the American way
has always been to stand up for what you believe, even if standing up sometimes means sitting down.[25]

∽○∽

Medgar Evers took the developing tradition of a civil rights flag
and brought it center stage, using flags to give a complex issue
direct, emotional appeal. In the spring of 1963, he was caught up
in the midst of the Jackson student movement—a movement that
recalled the Greensboro protests. For five months, black high
school and college students had led a boycott of downtown
shops and then began stepping up the boycott with protests. Ar-
riving in cars near the downtown area, they carried picket signs
in paper bags. Police stood guard in the boycotted area, and journalists watched. When the students arrived in the right spot, they
quickly pulled out their signs and formed a picket line. Police immediately arrested them. Often, the signs were confiscated, but
one time, at least, they were not, and as the students were driven
off in police cars, the youth pressed their signs to the glass windows for passersby to see.[26]

Signs were a staple of the civil rights movement. They came in
all kinds: cardboard and wood, sandwich-boarded or taped to a
stick, hand-lettered or printed. Their messages were clear and suc-

cinct: "I am a man." "NAACP." "Freedom Now." They spoke to passersby directly and to a much larger audience indirectly. When picketers were arrested, television footage and newspaper photographers brought those signs directly into thousands of living rooms.[27] Yet, a Jackson ordinance made picketing illegal. When students disobeyed by carrying signs as they walked on Capitol Street, police took the signs as quickly as possible.

As Flag Day approached, Evers considered this problem. What if the protesters carried American flags instead of signs? Evers had little faith in the enlightenment of the Jackson police force, but he doubted that the police would seize the flags. There was certainly no law against carrying an American flag. He figured there was a good chance the flag bearers might not even be arrested.[28]

As the student movement quickly intensified, the national media moved in, hailing Jackson as the next Birmingham. Protests proliferated with four, six, dozens of members. On May 28, three black Tougaloo College students and one professor staged a sit-in at Woolworth's, asking for service at the lunch counter. An angry white crowd smeared ketchup and mustard over their heads, slugged the men, and shook salt shakers over their wounds. At the black high schools, students filed out on the lawn and sang civil rights songs in direct defiance of their principals; the teenagers were attacked by police dogs and clubbed. Thousands of people rallied to mass meetings that rotated every night among Jackson's black churches.[29]

The high school students wanted to hold a mass demonstration, and Evers decided that this was the moment to introduce the flag. His wife, Myrlie, remembers the march being planned "like a military campaign" with great care and precision. Evers bought American flags and talked demonstration strategy deep into the night. The march was planned for May 31, the last day of classes. The night before, students dominated the nightly rally. In a crowded church, one young man, a high school junior, stood at the pulpit. He and other students would "march to freedom tomorrow." Addressing the fears of the older generation, he said, "To our parents, we say: 'We wish you'd come along with us, but if you won't, at least don't try to stop us.'" No one knew what would happen. "Bring your toothbrushes," said one speaker gaily, "because you're going straight to jail."[30]

The Farish Street Church was the gathering place the next day. It was strategically placed in the black part of town but close to the railroad tracks that separated it from Jackson's white downtown district. That afternoon, just after school had let out for the summer, the students walked through the church's doors, laughing, elated, nervous, determined. The oldest were in high school; the youngest were in elementary school. In the church, Evers, fellow civil rights organizer John Salter, and student leaders held a prayer session. They gave a workshop on nonviolent resistance. The minister passed the collection plate to gather knives and anything else police might construe as weapons. Student leaders spoke briefly: "Let's march!"[31]

When they were ready, more than six hundred students lined up in pairs. Evers handed them American flags. Two by two, the students emerged from the church's great swinging doors and stepped onto the sidewalk. They turned right toward Capitol Street, marching toward the downtown district. Each pair moved shoulder to shoulder, following the one before, so that the long line showed discipline and pride. They sang freedom songs. The hot May sun shone on the red and white stripes of their flags. Evers and Salter watched proudly from the sidewalk.

What happened next made the national news. As Salter described:

> Down a block in the direction of Capitol Street were hundreds and hundreds of law officers. They stretched from the buildings on one side of the street straight across to the buildings on the other side, rank after rank after rank of them. Their blue helmets, their clubs, their guns glinted in the hot sunlight. Behind this solid wall were large numbers of state highway patrolmen, recognizable in their brown helmets, and behind them were sheriff's deputies. And behind all of this were city garbage trucks.

The entire weight of Mississippi law enforcement was lined up to stop the students. Those at the head marched directly into the line of police.[32]

Officers reached out and grabbed hold of the students, trying to seize their flags. The marcher at the head of the line refused to give his up, clutching it tightly in his fist. Police beat him to the ground. As other students came forward, officers prodded them with rifle butts. They seized arms, legs, flags. They beat the students with nightsticks and clubs. They wrenched the flags out of the students' hands and flung them under their boots, a hasty blur of red, white, and blue thrown to the ground.[33]

The students were pushed back through the lines of officers, from blue helmets to brown helmets and into the paddy wagons. When all the wagons were full, officers pushed students into the garbage trucks. The large vehicles stank in the hot sun. At the back of the march, students waited patiently, stepping up in pairs to be arrested. Flies buzzed in the garbage trucks, and many students inside were nauseated from the rotting stench. Others sang freedom songs, enraging the police officers, who beat on the sides of the trucks in response. One by one, the mammoth trucks started their engines and drove off to a temporary prison site that police had set up at the Mississippi State Fairgrounds, a mass enclosure that was ringed with barbed wire and that looked for all the world like a concentration camp. The police turned their attention to the spectators. They ordered all blacks off the street.[34]

Medgar Evers watched grimly. "Just like Nazi Germany," he said. He pointed to officers marching in a platoon formation away from the scene. "Look at those storm troopers." As the street cleared of people, the road surface came into view. Along the ground, in the dust and the dirt, American flags lay trampled and broken. One woman picked up a flag. Holding it in her hand, she started to cry.[35]

The march garnered the attention of national journalists. The carrying of the flags was a telling detail that served to reinforce the image of the protesters as sympathetic and civic minded. The *New York Times* put a highly supportive story on the front page. Its headline was implicitly editorial: "Jackson Police Jail 600 Negro Children." The reporter described the riot guns, the dogs, and the officers' nightsticks. He quoted Evers's comments about Nazi Germany. The children, he emphasized, were both young and orderly; they were "singing and waving American flags." Two days later, another *New York Times* report featured a photograph of the Jackson police chief taking American flags from protesters.[36]

With Flag Day only two weeks away, Jackson demonstrators started to incorporate flags into every event. The day after the youth march, a hundred marchers carrying American flags were again arrested and thrown into garbage trucks. Two days later, the chief of police confiscated flags from six downtown picketers. A day after that, nine students carrying flags and wearing NAACP T-shirts were arrested. All of a sudden, flags were the hallmark of Jackson protests.[37]

Since 1954, activists had spilled many words on the Declaration, the Constitution, and the nation's history, showing that integration was the most truly American legacy. The flag made these themes explicit and visceral. American nationhood, it argued, was not the story of a white nation: Instead, it was the story of equality and democracy.

Conservative white Jacksonians were taken aback by this use of the flag. They had tagged civil rights activists as "agitators" and "communists": labels that set the protesters safely outside the boundaries of American society. But now the demonstrators' use of the flag put segregationists on the patriotic defensive. Conservative Southerners might wave the Confederate flag as a symbol of opposition, but they were certainly unwilling to cede the American flag to blacks. Police officers made repeated arrests of black Jacksonians waving flags even on Flag Day, when black ministers took flags in hand and walked down Jackson streets. The preachers wanted, they said grimly, to see if blacks could carry flags on Flag Day. They got their answer when they were arrested for violating a city ordinance that banned picketing and walking in groups.[38]

The use of the flag as an antisegregation symbol suggested that segregation was anti-American. The *Jackson Clarion-Ledger* ran a Flag Day editorial urging white Mississippians to display the flag. The piece pointed out that some Northerners had used the South's embrace of the Confederate flag as a way to question the South's regional patriotism. Readers were urged to counter claims that white Mississippians were "deficient" in "patriotism and love for Old Glory." Flying the flag, the article argued, would be "evidence of pride in our American heritage."[39]

The most powerful consequence of the civil rights flag was the impact it had on the marchers themselves. Activists began to see the flag as an untapped source of strength. As one of the Jackson organizers described it, the flag was a source of "inner sustenance," "almost as an icon or a religious symbol." Protesters realized that the flag had the potential to exude their intention, their sense of possibility, their American dream. After so many years of belonging to white Americans, it could be *their* flag.[40]

∽◦∾

The flag did not protect Medgar Evers. He was murdered less than two weeks after the Jackson march, shot in his driveway at night by a White Citizens' Council member. But Evers's use of the American flag provided a powerful legacy.

At the March on Washington that summer, Martin Luther King Jr. framed his call to justice as a uniquely American one. The patriotic vision he described included Jefferson, Lincoln, and the Declaration of Independence—all standards of the American patriotic tradition. As King stood there in front of the television cameras, the American flags behind him provided a visual reinforcement of the case he made. King's speech stood in clear distinction to Nation of Islam leader Elijah Mohammed's references to "white devils" and Malcolm X's threats of violence. The flag offered an implicit promise: As long as African Americans were included in the citizenship guaranteed by the American Revolution, there would be no race revolution.

In 1965, *Life* magazine published a photo essay of a civil rights march from Selma, Alabama, to Montgomery, the state capital. A prior march had been halted by state troopers with billy clubs; this one was protected by a federal judge, who ruled that the state could not stop the protesters. *Life* was one of the most popular magazines in the country, and when its hundreds of thousands of white readers flipped open the magazine, they saw images of the civil rights movement that counteracted the fear and unfamiliarity that they sometimes must have felt. There was the silhouette of a line of marchers coming over the hill, flags billowing above them. There was a sober young man, watching the camera with a serious face and standing against the backdrop of an enormous flag. These images allowed civil rights organizers to touch white citizens in a way that communicated a shared set of values. The flag provided a lexicon that connected them: a way for patriots to recognize each other across racial and cultural divides. It allowed black Americans to see themselves as full citizens, and it facilitated the willingness of white Americans to extend the rights of citizenship to that larger circle. The common ground of patriotism allowed both black and white to see themselves as American.

# ~7~

# FLAG OF CLASS

## *The Hard Hat Riot and the Vietnam War*

The flag had barely been claimed by the civil rights movement when another event—the Vietnam War—shifted its meanings yet again. Always an ambiguous symbol, the flag was particularly elastic in the late 1960s. A sizable minority of protesters in the Vietnam antiwar movement carried the Stars and Stripes to early antiwar gatherings. The flag signified their belief that protest was an American tradition, that the strength of democratic opposition would change the course of government policy. "Our way *is* the American way," it seemed to say.

On a chilly Saturday in mid-April 1967, an ocean of people gathered in the large grassy field known as Sheep Meadow at the southern end of New York's Central Park. Major public figures were there: Martin Luther King Jr. had recently broken his silence about the Vietnam War, and Benjamin Spock, the famous pediatrician and author, had been urging young men to resist the draft. Civil rights activist and Black Panther Stokely Carmichael had also come out against the war. Whole families attended, as did students with long hair, students in tweed coats, women in stockings and pumps, nuns in their habits, and veterans with medals on their uniforms. Between 300,000 and 400,000 Americans turned out in the largest antiwar protest the country had ever seen.

Opposition to the war had first gained momentum when Lyndon Johnson bombed North Vietnam in early 1965, shortly after being reelected on an antiwar platform. That year, hundreds of young men began to refuse induction into the service, and two Americans lit themselves on fire to protest the war. By 1967, roughly 40 percent of the population thought that the war was wrong and that American troops should withdraw.[1]

The wide range of opposition to the war was reflected in the forest of signs and flags that people carried. Some set their protest against the backdrop of patriotism with American flags. As one woman told a reporter:

> We want to criticize this war because we think it's wrong but we want to do it in the framework of loyalty. I hope this demonstration won't encourage the North Vietnamese. . . . Maybe the President's right and we don't know what we're talking about. Maybe we shouldn't be protesting. . . . Oh, but this war.[2]

This deep ambivalence was experienced by many in the crowd. Four out of ten were protesting for the first time, and they found themselves in an unfamiliar bind, wanting to be loyal to the United States yet unable to tolerate U.S. policy.

Other protesters cared little about the appearance of loyalty. They eschewed the American flag, instead waving symbols that rebuked American foreign policy. One protester carried an American flag with a Nazi swastika superimposed. Far more common were flags showing horizontal red and blue fields superimposed by a gold star: the colors of the North Vietnamese. Some protesters carried these as a sign of solidarity with the Vietnamese people; others felt their blood rising at the sight of the enemy flag in American hands. Some hand-lettered signs read simply "Peace" or "Love." One pointedly read, "No Vietnamese Ever Called Me 'Nigger.'"[3]

Slightly apart from the main protest, a group of sixty young men huddled on a rocky outcropping. A hand-lettered sign hung against the leafless trees: "Draft Card Burning Here." While a few war resisters had burned their draft cards as early as 1965, this was to be the first collective action. Journalists crowded in, circling the young men with cameras and heavy television equipment. Spectators stood around as the protesters linked arms to form a protective circle. Then the young men took out cigarette lighters and held the yellow flames to their white cards. They raised the burning rectangles above the crowd. "Resist! Resist!" called the onlookers, as the men dropped the scorched cards into a Maxwell House coffee can.[4]

On the periphery of that protest, several young men staged their own event. Instead of draft cards, they set fire to a large American flag on a long pole. As they held the burning flag high in the air, people clustered around and watched silently.[5]

The next day, residents of major cities opened their Sunday newspapers to an image that many had never even imagined. The *Washington Star* featured its photo of the flag burning on the front page; the *New York Daily News* spread its shot over two inner pages. Overnight, congressional representatives and senators were besieged by constituents who wanted to know why it had been allowed and what could be done to stop it. Veterans of Foreign Wars commander Andy Borg spoke for many when he said that he was "sick and tired of the American flag being burned, stomped upon, torn apart and vilified by communist-inspired peaceniks and others." New Jersey Congressman Dominick Daniel, who had served four terms, said that he had never heard constituents so unified on an issue. Within days, Congress had begun debating the issue, although only the American Civil Liberties Union and a couple of law professors testified against the bill. Representatives wasted no time aligning themselves with public opinion. "Which is the greater contribution to the security of freedom," asked Tennessee Congressman Dan Kuykendall in the debate, "the inspiring photo of the Marines at Iwo Jima or the shameful pictures of unshaven beatniks burning that same flag in Central Park?" The measure passed on a voice vote, and President Johnson signed the first federal flag desecration bill into law on July 4, 1968.[6]

⌀

Why was there so much outrage? Only a handful of Americans had ever burned a flag. Mississippians had burned one in 1861, as a response to Lincoln's decision to fight secession, and on Mark Hanna's Flag Day in 1896, some William Jennings Bryan followers had seized and burned a McKinley flag. There had been other, nonburning desecrations during World Wars I and II. Since the mid-1960s, there had been several dozen incidents nationwide. Flags had been burned as part of an experimental theater production in the East Village, as a classroom demonstration by a schoolteacher making a point about symbolism, and as a street protest by a black World War II veteran outraged by news reports of James Meredith's assassination—reports that turned out to be false. These were individual acts of symbolic protest largely hidden away in theaters and classrooms.[7]

On the other hand, many Americans had participated in the rituals of nationalist culture. Since the 1890s, the flag had been treated as something to revere. Schoolchildren said the Pledge of Allegiance every morning. At baseball games, the entire ballpark rose and held hand over heart for the singing of "The Star-Spangled Banner." There was a proper way to fold the flag and a proper way to dispose of an old one.

These flag rituals were becoming increasingly meaningful in the working-class communities that bore the brunt of the war. In the 1960s, it was class far more than any other factor that determined whether a young man would go to war. Eighty percent of the soldiers serving in Vietnam had a high school degree or less. Few could afford college, and the military looked like a good option compared with the low-paying jobs available right out of high school. With draft exemptions disappearing at the end of the decade, most of their peers were headed into the service. Many had little exposure to the debates about American policy. As one veteran said, "It never occurred to me that America would go to war without a good reason."[8]

For blue-collar communities, the American flag symbolized a collective pride in military service. Whether or not working-class men wanted to go to Vietnam, many expected to do military service of some kind. "My grandfather went in 1917, my father went in 1942," said one veteran. "It was my turn." Military service was not simply one option among others. In many families, to serve was to be inducted into manhood, taking one's proper place in the family and community. Avoiding that service seemed cowardly and childish. In these families and communities, the flag stood for duty and honor.[9]

Flags also bore the weight of grief, with increasing frequency. By early 1968, there had been 120,000 American casualties. As the bodies came home from Vietnam, military flags covered caskets and then lay folded in the homes of mourning parents. Tiny flags waved from the fenders of cars in funeral processions. On the day of a military funeral, towns hung out their flags along the main street as a way to honor the dead: Residents knew, when the flags went up, that another boy had been killed in Vietnam. The practice had a ripple effect in blue-collar communities, as homeowners put out their flags as a gesture of respect and solidarity. Flags on the streets marked a town in collective mourning.[10]

In these communities, flags did not speak to the rightness or wrongness of government policy. In fact, as American casualties mounted, blue-collar workers turned increasingly against the war, more so than white-collar professionals. By 1970, some 61 percent of those who had not been to college advocated for immediate withdrawal, compared with only 47 percent of college graduates. Labor leaders criticized the war for being unethical. They also pointed to the money it diverted away from American domestic policy needs. The United Auto Workers pulled out of the AFL-CIO on the basis of the larger organization's support for the war.[11]

Much working-class opposition was based on a desire to stop American boys from being killed. When blue-collar people talked about the war, they were concerned, first and foremost, with the American servicemen over there. Almost always, there was someone they knew, a family member or a neighborhood kid. Every death hit close to home. After watching a military funeral parade through his small town, flags on the car fenders, a

World War II veteran expressed his anger and disbelief: "For Christ's sake how long are they going to let that slaughter go on over there? The whole goddamn country of South Vietnam is not worth the life of one American boy, no matter what the hell our politicians try to tell us."[12]

Although blue-collar opposition to the war shared some similarities with middle-class protest, the two groups watched each other with suspicion. Blue-collar workers were changing their political allegiances in the face of the Democratic Party's turn to the New Left. For decades, these workers had been Democrats. The party had embraced the unions, the unions had embraced the party, and the Democratic platform reflected a set of working-class priorities. But in the late 1960s, the party began to focus on cultural rather than explicitly economic issues: civil rights, women's liberation, and the Vietnam War. Desegregation through school busing, in particular, polarized poorer white people against blacks. As George Meany, president of the AFL-CIO and a supporter of Nixon's war policy, said, "The Democratic Party has disintegrated—it is not the so-called liberal party that it was a few years ago. It almost has got to be the party of the extremists." As working people began to feel that their cultural values were no longer reflected in the party platform, they became swing voters.[13]

Most working-class people felt alienated by the student protesters, who seemed to care more about the Vietnamese than they did about American soldiers. One mother who had lost her son in Vietnam articulated this position with heartbreaking clarity. Both she and her husband, a firefighter, felt that their boy had died in vain. Both wanted the war ended. At first, the mother had considered antiwar protesters possible allies, but she soon reconsidered:

I told [my husband] I thought they want the war to end, so no more Ralphs will die, but he says no, they never stop and think about Ralph and his kind of people, and I'm inclined to agree. They *say* they do, but I listen to them, I watch them; since Ralph died I listen and I watch as carefully as I can. Their hearts are with other people, not their own American people, the ordinary kind of person in this country....

I'm against this war, too—the way a mother is, whose sons are in the army, who has lost a son fighting in it. The world hears those demonstrators making their noise. The world doesn't hear me, and it doesn't hear a single person I know.[14]

The mother's opposition to the war was an opposition born of grief, not anger. It was the kind that would never burn an American flag.

کهکه

The workers were not the only ones to feel a deep passion about the flag and about patriotism. The antiwar activists, too, felt that power. In the early years, flags were often seen at antiwar events. The protests came right on the heels of the civil rights movement, and the flag seemed a more potent symbol of democracy than it had previously in the century. Many activists were involved in both causes.

In the long tradition of humanitarian patriotism, many organizers had faith that the war would be stopped if only their fellow citizens understood what was going on. As children in the 1940s and 1950s, they had pledged allegiance to their classroom flags every morning, invoking "one nation, indivisible" and its goal of "liberty and justice for all." They had listened on the street and at Sunday dinner as their parents and neighbors talked about World War II. When they thought of war, it was that war, the Good War. The invasion of Vietnam stood in direct opposition to those values, and they felt hopeful that once the contrast was revealed, the country would right itself.

Initially, few people knew about what was happening in Vietnam. So in the spring of 1965, students organized over a hundred teach-ins at colleges and universities. These were all-day and all-night affairs, attended by thousands, where students and faculty explained the events in Vietnam and the history of American involvement. "I saw that we could really have an impact," said one of the organizers of the Berkeley teach-in. "It seemed as though we could reach a wide range of people.... The teach-in definitely was a very hopeful event."[15]

The protests spread in 1966 and 1967. Twenty thousand marched in New York City on March 26, 1966; less than two months later, on May 15, ten thousand gathered in Washington, D.C. On January 4, 1967, between twenty thousand and thirty thousand protested in San Francisco. During a Stop the Draft Week that October, more than a thousand men returned their draft cards. On October 21, 1967, a massive demonstration at the Lincoln Memorial became a march on the Pentagon, as over thirty thousand protesters surrounded the building. There were protests in London, in Spain, and in other European countries.

But as resistance spread and policies stayed the same, it became apparent that American democracy was either corrupt or broken. A Gallup poll in June 1967 revealed that more than 56 percent of Americans thought that the government was losing the war or at an impasse. The Johnson administration suffered such a credibility problem that CBS anchor Walter Cronkite announced on broadcast television: "We have been too often disappointed by the optimism of the American leaders, both in Vietnam and Washington, to have faith any longer in the silver linings they find in the darkest clouds."[16]

There seemed to be hope in 1968, when Johnson announced that he would not run for reelection and troop levels in Vietnam stabilized, but Nixon's presidency, beginning in 1969, continued the war. The activists' dedicated attempts to stop the war by persuasion and democratic means were not working: fatigue-clad soldiers kept being deployed to Vietnam, and flag-draped coffins kept coming home. The flag was carried deep into Vietnam, flown over base camps in the jungle, and painted on the back of the air force planes that bombed the villages. For a long time, the activists had relied on the promise of the American political dream and the tradition of dissent. Now, with years of organizing behind them and no visible change in policy, they felt betrayed by that dream. Humanitarian patriotism seemed an impossible naïveté.

The flag's increasing volatility became clear at the stormy 1968 Democratic Convention in Chicago. It was late August, and thousands of protesters sat on the ground, radiating out from the band shell in Grant Park, listening to speeches against the draft. American flags, if there were any, were far outnumbered by the Vietnamese flag and protest signs. To the left of the stage stood a flagpole bearing the American flag. An eighteen-year-old wearing an army helmet climbed up the pole's base to seize the flag's halyards, lowering it to half-staff because, he later explained, the authorities had "killed democracy." Many felt it was an appropriate gesture of mourning. "People started to yell to lower it to half-mast," a witness said. Others urged him to lower it all the way to the ground, shouting, "Tear down the flag!" The boy tied the flag at half-mast and was grabbed by police officers, who took him away to a squad car.[17]

The incident enraged the crowd. A group of young men approached the pole, untied the halyards, and lowered the flag to the ground. A few women started crying. A witness described the crowd's response as "non-approval": "Most people felt lowering the flag to half-mast was symbolic, a form of protesting the actions in and outside of the convention. But to take the flag down was not acceptable." The young men quickly tied a red cloth to the ropes and raised it to the top of the pole, a gesture interpreted as raising the red flag of revolution. The police moved in, and there followed two days of terrible rioting and brutality.[18]

By 1969, it was clear that the government was pursuing its Vietnam policy in the face of every humanitarian and democratic instinct. News of war atrocities were everywhere. On the front pages, the words "My Lai Massacre" evoked the mass murder of unarmed citizens by American troops. Blue-collar workers turned increasingly against the war, openly questioning whether it could be won and criticizing it for injustice and for the money it diverted from domestic issues. On October 15, 1969, more than two million people turned out across the country for Vietnam Moratorium Day.

Deliberate gestures against the flag became increasingly popular and increasingly public. The early flag burners had been drifters and anarchists, people on the radical fringes outside the antiwar movement. But increasingly, and especially after the publicized burning in Central Park, flag desecration became part of the symbolic rhetoric. A University of Wisconsin student cut the ropes on an American flag during a protest against Dow Chemical in October 1967. A year later, Yippie leader Abbie Hoffman wore a flag shirt to testify before the House Un-American Activities Committee. At Nixon's inaugural in January 1969, demonstrators burned dozens of small American flags. Protesters burned flags in San Francisco and Chicago, and at the University of Virginia, and a young man set fire to a small flag that he waved at the president's motorcade.[19]

Some activists continued to carry the flag to marches, but, recognizing its military connotations, modified its design. They superimposed symbols on it, painting a black peace sign across the banner or replacing the field of stars with hearts. Some inscribed a slogan: "To Want Peace Is American." "Make Love Not War— The New American Revolutionaries." Such additions were a visually dramatic articulation of the conflict between the two strands of American patriotism. They did not always convince— the peace sign, like the flag, had become a polarizing symbol— but they made their meaning clear.[20]

Most peace demonstrators found themselves unwilling to carry the American flag. Activist Todd Gitlin described his sense of betrayal as the American government continued its course, despite the protests: "I was implicated because the terrible war was wrapped in my flag—or what had been my flag. The American flag did not feel like my flag, even though I could recognize—in the abstract—that it made sense for others to wave it in the antiwar cause." Painfully aware of the gap between their hopes and their realities, many activists began to see the flag as a visual reminder of that chasm. The flag, which had been a symbol of democracy, now seemed more of a symbol of empire and even of genocide. As Gitlin wrote:

I did argue against waving the North Vietnamese flag or burning the Stars and Stripes. But the hatred of a bad war, in what
was evidently a pattern of bad wars—though none so bad as
Vietnam—turned us inside out. It inflamed our hearts. You can
hate your country in such a way that the hatred becomes fundamental. A hatred so clear and intense comes to feel like a
cleansing flame.[21]

All the long-held assumptions on which Americans had been
raised now appeared false. The U.S. Army was acting like an imperial power, greedy for land and natural resources. Large-scale
protests were having no impact on foreign policy. The government
seemed to belong to the U.S. military, not American citizens.[22]

Yet the antiwar activists did not relinquish the flag lightly.
Like the segregationists a decade earlier, they were alienated by a
seemingly irreversible pattern of federal action that took them by
surprise. In each case, the American vision they thought they
shared was destroyed; in each case, they watched as the rift between their vision and government policy widened and deepened. In each case, they felt a profound sense of betrayal that
caused them to reach for other flags and other symbols and to
push away the American flag.

The image of the burning flag cleaved down the middle of the
American population, estranging groups that might have been al-
lied. The large population of those troubled by the war were sev-
ered into two camps: those who saw the flag primarily as a
symbol of sacrifice and honor, and those who saw it as a symbol
of a government that had betrayed its people and American
ideals. The stage was set for the event that would come to be
known as the Hard Hat Riot.

In the spring of 1970, New York was in the midst of a build-ing boom. All over Lower Manhattan, cranes lifted reddish spires of steel onto the skeletons of new buildings. The Twin Towers were creeping upward to the sky, hives of activity as nearly five thousand workers laid steel, built elevators, ran wires, and connected plumbing. Signs of construction activity were everywhere: massive foundation holes, yellow hard hats, huge steel beams.[23]

The steady hum of building activity belied the stress and strain of a nation in shock. In late April, President Nixon had in-vaded Cambodia without consulting Congress. It was an ex-tremely unpopular move, and it had briefly united the country in opposition to Nixon. More than half of all Americans polled thought the invasion was unconstitutional; nearly half believed that Nixon had lied. Hundreds of thousands turned out for a march at the nation's capital on May 8. Students held a national strike, many of them closing campuses for the rest of the semes-ter. At Kent State College, where students set fire to an ROTC building, the National Guard shot into a crowd sixty-one times on May 4, killing four students and wounding nine others.[24]

Campuses exploded in response to the Kent State news. More than a hundred major demonstrations were held on campuses per day, and five hundred schools canceled classes for periods ranging from days to the rest of the school year. Students burned or bombed ROTC buildings at thirty campuses. At more than twenty schools, there were armed standoffs between students and police or national guard forces. Many Americans found that their dismay at the Kent State shootings was quickly superseded by a greater shock over the students' violent response. Night after night on American television, viewers saw the burned shells of ROTC buildings and the mayhem of student rioting. College students took over administrative buildings, shut down their schools, and burned down banks. The world felt out of control.[25]

On Whitehall Street at the southern tip of Manhattan, construction workers had erected an American flag on their job site, as was common practice. But in those volatile early days of May, the flag served as a flashpoint for all kinds of emotions. When seven hundred medical students gathered on May 6 to protest Kent State in nearby Battery Park, one of them ripped down the Whitehall flag.[26]

The workers were irate. "The steelworkers piled out of the building and pitched into them," said a fellow worker. "Several [students] were beaten up, though nothing much about it got into the papers." After returning to the building site, the steelworkers kept talking about the incident. As one worker reported later, "A lot of them feel strongly about the situation, no doubt about that. Their attitude was that not enough was being done about these goddamn kids."[27]

The next day, a group of workers went to an antiwar protest on Wall Street during their lunch hour. There was a shoving match, but no one was hurt, and the workers got back to the job right after their lunch hour ended. But the conflict left the men unsatisfied. "After they came back," their coworker reported, "they kept talking, kept psyching themselves up. They weren't satisfied they'd done enough, and the word began to go around that the next day they would really do it up right. The word circulated on all the jobs in the area. It was a planned thing."[28]

There was a strong class element to the antagonism. Construction workers, even young men, always used the term "kids" to describe students, the word illustrating their sense that the students were merely playing around. Even those who hadn't served in the military knew the realities of a difficult, dirty, dangerous life. In many ways, blue-collar work paralleled the dangers of war because manual labor held out a very real chance of being killed or injured. In 1968, more than fourteen thousand workers died in industrial accidents in the United States, nearly the same number as American soldiers killed in Vietnam. Construction work was especially dangerous: One out of fifteen ironworkers would be killed within ten years. Thus, even when the workers were not much older than the students, the laborers were men who had watched friends die on the job, falling twenty stories from iron scaffolding to the street.[29]

As word spread of the workers' plans to attack more protesters, New York's powerful Building and Construction Trades Council got involved. On one job site, the contractor offered the men cash bonuses to participate. On others, union bosses told the men they must participate. "[The bosses] came back," said one worker, "and said that everyone had to go out Friday—all the workers from the World Trade Center, the U.S. Steel building, and 2 Manhattan Plaza—and break some heads." These directives were unusual, but not entirely unprecedented. Peter Brennan, the head of the union, had a history of using his men to rough up war protesters. He also had a history of using workers with American flags to push for political advantage.[30]

Friday, May 8, would have been a volatile day under any circumstances. The day had been set aside by New York's mayor and city council to commemorate the Kent State massacre. As a tribute to the four dead students, the city hall flag hung at half-staff in the cool, rainy morning. The gesture inflamed many veterans, who felt that the students didn't deserve it. No flag at city hall had been lowered for their buddies killed in the line of duty. Adding insult to injury, antiwar demonstrations were planned all over the city. It was a good day to go "break some heads."[31]

Around noon, just as the construction workers were punching out for lunch, the sky began to brighten and the air became humid. On Wall Street, Federal Hall sat like a misplaced Greek temple amid the tall buildings. A scheduled protest was under way, and a speaker stood on the steps addressing a crowd of about a thousand people. "You brought down one president," he told them, "and you'll bring down another." The crowd, mostly students, was peaceful. Some stood in the street; others sat on the stone steps eating sandwiches.[32]

Soon the regular noontime crowd of Wall Street appeared alongside the students. Men in suits emerged from the New York Stock Exchange for their lunch break. Some listened to the speaker; some ignored him since protests were common on Wall Street. Sidewalk vendors did a brisk business from under their striped umbrellas.

Then the construction workers arrived: a wave of steelworkers, elevator mechanics, carpenters, and crane operators. They wore brown bib overalls and plaid shirts, yellow hard hats, and tool belts. Wire-snippers, pliers, and hammers clanked as the men surged forward. They emerged out of the narrow streets, flooded around the corners of Federal Hall, converged on the stone steps from all directions. At the police barricade on the west side of the building, they slowed to a halt, forming a milling pool of about two hundred men.

Two incongruously dressed men appeared among the workers. Both wore gray suits and gray hats; both wore matching patches on their lapels. They moved busily through the gathering throng, handing something out. In their wake, as if by magic, dozens of American flags appeared. The workers pushed forward against the police barricade. A line of a dozen officers in dark helmets separated them from the rally. The workers shook their flags. "U.S.A., all the way!" they shouted. "Love it or leave it!"[33]

The students were sprawled along the east side of the building's steps, which reached to the giant bronze statue of George Washington in the center. "Peace now!" they shouted back. "Motherfucking fascists!" One of them waved a Vietcong flag.[34]

A partner in a brokerage firm, watching with binoculars from the thirty-second floor of 63 Wall Street, saw the men in gray suits directing the crowd with hand signals. All of a sudden, the workers pushed forward and the police line dissolved. Construction workers swelled across the western part of the steps, reaching the Washington statue and pushing the students away from it. Workers swarmed up onto the statue and placed flags on it, then raced to the top of the steps and mounted their flags there. The men in gray suits shouted orders. The workers pushed the students back to the eastern margin of the steps, away from the statue. Said one witness, "it was just like John Wayne taking Iwo Jima."[35]

An unidentified man in a suit, neither worker nor student, climbed up onto the pedestal of Washington's statue. Standing between the president's huge bronze legs, he cursed out the construction workers and spit on the flag. The crowd roared in anger: "He spit on the flag! He spit on the flag!" A construction worker leaped up after him and punched him, sending the man flying into the crowd. A man in a bow tie cowered on the other side of the pedestal, clutching the statue's enormous thigh for support. Students started chanting, "Hell no, we won't go! Hell no, we won't go!" infuriating the workers.[36]

Then there was mayhem. Workers took off their yellow helmets and lashed out with them, beating indiscriminately at the protesters. Others smashed students with wire clippers and lead pipe, gashing foreheads. Office clerks and the backroom help from the financial district began to egg the workers on. And quite a few of the white-collar workers—nearly as many as the blue-collar ones—began to beat the students as well.[37]

Long-haired men were special targets. One was thrown to the ground and kicked by four pairs of steel-toed boots. Others were chased through the canyon-like streets of the financial district. A partner at Lehman Brothers tried to stop a worker from beating a youth and was himself pushed up against a telephone pole; a man who came to his aid, in turn, was bashed in the head with a pair of pliers. Stunned observers couldn't believe what they were seeing. The event seemed suspiciously choreographed. Police officers had been warned of a possible attack, but they seemed to melt away, leaving the protesters to the mercy of the beatings.[38]

Spectators dragged as many of the wounded as they could into nearby Trinity Church. Bloody noses and black eyes were common; more than seventy students were beaten so badly they had to be taken to the hospital. Then the mob turned north on Broadway, marching straight for City Hall.[39]

❦

President Nixon's chief domestic affairs adviser, John Erlichman, later said that he had always "assumed" that the hard hat demonstrations were "laid on" by the White House. By 1970, the Nixon White House already had an established track record of infiltrating civilian groups. Since the inauguration in 1969, the FBI and CIA had focused heavily on domestic intelligence and set up surveillance on activists. Agents had infiltrated Students for a Democratic Society, the largest student group, posing as members of the antiwar movement. Some even went further and became agents provocateurs, pushing the limits of protest to generate backlash.[40]

There was strong circumstantial evidence that the Hard Hat Riot was one of these instances. In early March 1970, two months before the incident, Nixon's vice president, Spiro Agnew, had written a memo suggesting that CIA operatives might organize counterprotests to the student demonstrations in various American cities. These protests, the memo stated, could feature construction workers. When confronted with the memo by a tiny muckraking magazine *Scanlan's Monthly*, the White House denied everything. It then spent the following six months putting the magazine out of business, investigating its IRS records and arranging for the Royal Canadian Mounted Police to shut down further printing.[41]

Most of the evidence emerged only much later. A Nixon aide admitted to pushing the Veterans of Foreign Wars to create "counter demonstrations," activities that may well have included the Hard Hat Riot. Nixon himself was caught on tape, plotting with his chief of staff, H. R. Haldeman, to use "thugs" to break up demonstrations. Their conversation described how they had previously used steelworkers—construction workers—to do the same thing.[42]

During the riot, there had been hints of backroom organization. The heavy pressure from the Building and Construction Trades Council suggested some vested interest. Later developments confirmed a deal between Peter Brennan, the powerful union boss, and President Nixon. The American flags, generously provided by the two men in gray hats and suits, gave a focal point to the protest: one that made the outrageous beatings more acceptable by clothing them as a defense of the flag. The middle-aged man who spat on the flag might well have been a secret agent: As he was neither student nor construction worker, his action was senseless unless he was trying to incite further anger and violence.

∽○∽

Bearing their American flags proudly before them, the rioters strode up lower Broadway. This half mile, where the avenue forms a deep and narrow gorge between the tall buildings, is known as the Canyon of Heroes. It is the city's traditional parade ground; the Apollo mission astronauts had marched there the summer before. In 1970, hundreds of construction workers and several thousand office workers made their own parade: American flags, brown overalls, yellow hard hats, white dress shirts, swinging ties. "U.S.A., all the way," the men chanted, and then began to sing. The words of "The Marines' Hymn" echoed from the tall buildings and resonated through the marching crowd. A half dozen mounted police on glossy horses trailed alongside. Office workers along the route threw open their windows and flung out handfuls of ticker tape—the traditional parade response—which twirled through the air.

From Broadway, the crowd marched under the budding trees in City Hall Park and brought their flags directly up to the stately structure of City Hall. High on the roof, just below the domed cupola, rose the city's official flagpole. The flag hung at half-staff, the mayor's tribute to the Kent State victims. The men surged around the building's pink granite base and up the front steps. They stopped in front of the central doors, while one man slipped inside and found his way to the roof. The people in the crowd craned their necks to watch, as the man appeared above and then untied the halyards and pulled the ropes. Foot by foot, the flag rose to its full height. Within minutes, one of the mayor's aides appeared on the roof and stalked over to the flagpole. He hauled the flag back to half-staff.[43]

From the steps and portico, the construction workers and clerks howled in anger. Some leaped onto parked cars and ran over the hoods; other men scrambled over the police barricades and stormed toward the building. They reached the tall doors and heaved themselves against the heavy wood, using their bodies as battering rams. It looked for a moment as though the men would splinter through and take over City Hall.

Frightened, the deputy mayor announced that the flag would be raised to its full height. The crowd quieted and watched as two plainclothes officers and the building custodian walked out onto the roof. The trio grasped the halyards and slowly raised the flag. As it ran up the pole, the crowd began to sing:

*Oh say can you see*
*By the dawn's early light*

Hands moved to hearts. Construction workers pulled their yellow helmets off.

*What so proudly we hailed*
*By the twilight's last gleaming*

A dozen police officers lined the stairs, their black helmets glinting in the sun. "Get your helmets off!" one of the workers shouted at them. The cops looked at one another. Grinning a little foolishly, about half of them pulled off their helmets and laid them over their hearts.

*And the rockets' red glare*
*The bombs bursting in air*
*Were proof through the night*
*That our flag was still there*

The flag on top of City Hall moved gently in the breeze. Just above the men's heads, the workers' flags fluttered in response. The reverence was palpable: a striking contrast to the violence of an hour before.

*Oh say does that star-spangled banner yet wave*
*O'er the land of the free*
*And the home of the brave?*[44]

∽∾

The Hard Hat Riot, also known as Bloody Friday, marked the beginning of the flag's intense repoliticization as a prowar symbol. Before that day, many construction workers and longshoremen had had a personal relationship with the flag, because of their military service. Now, the flag was something that belonged to the construction workers, *as workers*. Many of the men began to embrace the flag, especially as part of their workplace identity. Some decorated their hard hats with flag decals; others inscribed slogans like "For God and Country." This aggressive celebration of the flag was a form of class consciousness, a response to student protesters' perceived disrespect for the flag and working-class culture.[45]

The Hard Hat Riot was antiprotester, but after the event, it was not immediately clear that the construction workers had a political agenda beyond that. Did the workers support Nixon's war policy? There was no evidence to suggest that they did. Within days, however, a political program became apparent as the unions pushed their workers to more flag demonstrations. For more than a year, the Nixon administration had been advocating for what it called the Philadelphia Plan, which required specific quotas of minority workers on jobs involving the federal government. The overwhelmingly white unions, especially New York's Building and Construction Trades Council, opposed the plan fiercely. Immediately after the Hard Hat Riot, President Nixon met with union leaders in a secret session. Afterward, he quietly dropped his Philadelphia Plan, and Peter Brennan's union, representing 250,000 workers, brought the flag to the streets as a symbol of support for Richard Nixon.[46]

Ordinarily, a construction worker got half an hour for lunch, enough time to eat a sandwich, possibly drink a beer, and listen to Paul Harvey's *News and Comment* on the radio. If a man was late returning to work, justice was swift and severe. His pay was docked and his job was on the line: The foreman could easily send out to the union hall for another man to take his place. But for two weeks after Bloody Friday, the rules were different. Construction workers and longshoremen were paid for marching at lunchtime nearly every day, often for as long as two or three hours.[47]

These marches were spectacular affairs. Between two thousand and three thousand workers hit the street, generating enormous publicity and snarling traffic throughout Lower Manhattan. Construction workers marched from City Hall to Bowling Green, carrying foot-long American flags. Brooklyn longshoremen marched over the Brooklyn Bridge carrying flags to City Hall in a parade that featured pretty young women, a motorcycle escort, and a twelve-piece brass band. Workers even threatened the offices of the *Wall Street Journal* with violence, demanding that they fly their flag; despite objections from reporters and editors, management duly hung one out.[48]

The flag appeared in the Manhattan marches as a symbol of support for Nixon's prowar policies. "We Support Nixon and Agnew: God Bless the Establishment" proclaimed a large, printed sign. A young man who waved a peace sign to marchers was surrounded by men in business suits. "Go back to Germany and take your chances, you commie Jew!" one of the suits shouted at him. Another bystander, who formed a peace sign with his index and middle fingers, was attacked and punched out by marchers.[49]

Analogies to Nazi Germany were common among observers, especially those who opposed the war. "We won't be intimidated," said an antiwar speaker in the wake of the riots. "This is not the Weimar Republic." One woman, after seeing the workers punch a bystander, announced: "The new Nazis: They're here." Some of the construction workers made the same connection. "These are people I know well," said one worker. "They were nice, quiet guys until Friday. But I had to drag one fellow away from attacking several women. They became storm troopers."[50]

The culminating event two weeks later was a huge rally on Broadway in Lower Manhattan, encompassing all the members of the Building and Construction Trades Council. The May 20 rally was ostensibly an apolitical demonstration for "love of country and love and respect of our country's flag." The union told all the men in the building trades to drop their tools and go. As one union member experienced it:

> The word was passed around to all the men on the jobs the day before. It was *not* voluntary. You *had* to go. You understand these are all jobs where the union controls your employment absolutely. . . . We were told that if we got back to the job a half-hour after the parade ended, we'd be paid for a full day's work. Of course, the parade lasted until 3:30 and by the time the guys got back, the day was done. But everybody got paid.[51]

Nearly one hundred thousand people, many of them construction workers and longshoremen, most of them white, gathered on Broadway. Many carried flags; others wore red, yellow, and blue hard hats with flag decals. Signs bobbed across the crowd: "We Love Our Police, Flag and Country; We Hate Our Commie Mayor." A band played World War II fighting songs and "God Bless America"; then, as everyone stood and doffed their hard hats, it played "The Star-Spangled Banner." No patriotic detail was left out: music, the Pledge of Allegiance, the flag—it was all there.[52]

Peter Brennan, the handsome, ruddy head of the Building and Construction Trades Council, stood on the podium and addressed the crowd. "This symbol, this flag," his voice rang out, "is more than just a piece of cloth!" The crowd cheered and cheered. Throughout the noon hour and into the afternoon, ticker tape and computer punch cards were tossed out of the office buildings of lower Broadway in celebration. One man was hit on the head by a falling cardboard box of confetti and taken to the hospital.[53]

Amid this manufactured demonstration, it was hard to tell what the workers really felt. There was plenty of support for

Nixon, although it was the kind of support that came from having a common enemy. Given the alternatives—Nixon and the antiwar protesters—many construction workers chose Nixon. A union official summed up the feelings of his electrical workers: "Sure, a lot of workers feel Nixon should have gone to Congress before the Cambodia thing. But they go right back to supporting the President when they see what's happening on campus."[54]

Reporters who interviewed the workers after the events realized that they were in the presence of something they did not fully understand. Many of the workers felt a connection to the troops in Vietnam and had long personal histories with the flag, imbuing it with all the complex emotions of American pride and working-class grief. The journalists were struck by the particular reverence with which these men spoke of the flag. One worker said of the flag, "Outside of God, it's the most important thing I know." He elaborated, "I know a lot of good friends died under this. It stands for the greatest: America."[55]

One after another, the workers connected the flag with their military service, their dead buddies, their purple hearts, their sons in East Asia. One man, a veteran who had lost a son in Vietnam, spoke of an almost corporeal connection: "It's me. It's part of me." Seeing the flag violated was like seeing all that service, all that sacrifice, disrespected. And the anger that welled up in them was particularly intense because the flag burners were upper-middle-class young men and women who would never know what it was like to find themselves in a jungle being shot at by an unknown enemy.[56]

But there were also fault lines among the construction workers. One of the Twin Towers men, a construction worker in his twenties, had marched on Washington, protesting the U.S. move into Cambodia. "I don't think you honor America by beating someone over the head with a flag," he said. Another agreed. "I hate to even dignify these men by calling them construction workers. I'm a construction worker and proud of it. These guys are cowards who feel threatened, so they hit people. It makes them feel good and gets them time off of work."[57]

Black construction workers opposed the riots and the marches by a margin of fifteen to one. "These men are make-believe patriots and cowards," said one older carpenter, who wore both an American flag pin and a black nationalist button. "I fought in World War II also, but I don't go around beating up young kids and girls." A younger man, an electrician's apprentice at the World Trade Center, also kept his distance from the marchers. "None of the black workers want anything to do with them. How many blacks did you see in the march the other day? We counted five. And some of them weren't even Americans."[58]

The evening after the big rally, President Nixon phoned Brennan and spoke to him for over an hour. The next week, Brennan was invited to a reception at the White House. In front of other labor leaders, he stepped forward to present the president with two gifts. He handed Nixon a hard hat reading "Commander in Chief." Then he pinned an American flag pin on the president's lapel.[59]

Not surprisingly, the biggest winner from the Hard Hat Riot was Richard Nixon. Before the riots, he had been the president of a rapidly disintegrating country, having lost the confidence of most of his citizens. The national guard was shooting at students, and there were major protests against his policies nearly every day. As a result of the riots, Nixon found himself with unexpected sources of support. The press seized on the riots in New

York and similar riots in St. Louis, Missouri, and Tempe, Arizona, as a way to give popular face to the "silent majority" that Nixon claimed. By August, *Newsweek, Business Week, Time,* and a number of major newspapers had all published articles pitting blue-collar workers against student protesters.

Polls showed that 53 percent of the public disapproved of the hard hat violence, but they sympathized more strongly with the hard hats than they did with the students, by 40 percent to 24 percent. To most Americans, the flag was not just a symbol. Reflecting back, Nixon pinpointed the Wall Street events as a turning point in marshaling popular support. "I remember then that it seemed I was virtually alone," he said, "and then one day a very exciting thing happened: the hard hats marched in New York City."[60]

The Hard Hat marches epitomized a deepening split between the left and the right in American political culture, a split that centered around the flag. It was a split that would dominate American political culture for nearly the next four decades, as the right took hold of the flag and the left grew increasingly alienated from the symbol. When Peter Brennan pinned a gift of the flag on Nixon's lapel, the action proved deeply symbolic: The Hard Hat Riot gave the American flag to Nixon and the Republican Party, establishing its cultural politics through the end of the millennium.

Of all the presidents during this period, Ronald Reagan was the most gifted in his political use of the flag. In his 1980 and 1984 campaigns, he invoked the symbol frequently, though its political uses were often unspoken. With hundred-foot-long flags hanging behind them, the president and his wife Nancy appeared at rallies, waving smaller flags in hand. His television commercials, in particular, made heavy use of flag imagery, and publicity firms still view the "Morning in America" series—with its images of going to work, getting married, and Boy Scouts raising the flag—as one of the best advertising campaigns in history. It communicated, in visual shorthand, a rich and promising sense of a nation on the rise. There were a handful of negative ads, as well, ones that evoked the specter of Middle Eastern instability by showing a crowd of angry Iranians gathered around a flaming flag. These proved an effective foil to the optimistic patriotism that infused most of the campaign; together, both approaches pulled "Reagan Democrats" in large numbers from opponent Walter Mondale.[61]

One particular event during Reagan's presidency reestablished the political import of the flag, redrawing the lines that had been set during the Hard Hat demonstrations. On a sweltering day in late August 1984, a group of about a hundred protesters marched through the streets of Dallas. Most were members of the Revolutionary Communist Party, and they were on what they called the Republican War Chest Tour. They barged into department stores, kicking over trash cans and falling to the floor in a "die-in" protest against nuclear weapons. In a bank, they threw deposit slips in the air, overturned potted plants, and splattered red paint on the floor to symbolize blood.[62]

At one of the buildings, the demonstrators pulled an American flag off a flagpole. They carried it through the streets as they marched, chanting:

*America, the red, white and blue*
*We spit on you.*[63]

One of the protesters was a young man named Gregory Lee Johnson. When the group reached Dallas City Hall, someone handed him the flag. He poured kerosene on it and then set it ablaze.

Johnson was convicted under Texas law for vandalizing respected objects. He appealed the case all the way to the U.S. Supreme Court. The *Texas v. Johnson* decision, released in June 1989, reflected the division in American life over the flag: The justices split, five to four. The majority opinion held that flag burning was protected speech. "We do not consecrate the flag by punishing its desecration, for in doing so we dilute the freedom that this cherished emblem represents," wrote Justice Anthony Kennedy. "It is poignant but fundamental that the flag protects those who hold it in contempt."[64]

The dissent, written by Justice William Rehnquist, held that the flag was not simply an idea but rather a powerful collective symbol, viewed by millions of Americans with "an almost mystical reverence." It argued that burning the flag was not so much free speech as "the equivalent of an inarticulate grunt or roar that, it seems fair to say, is most likely to be indulged in not to express any particular idea, but to antagonize others."[65]

The *Texas v. Johnson* decision shocked many Americans. It also tapped into a political debate about patriotism that had sharpened with the 1988 campaign, when Republican George H. W. Bush hammered on Democrat Michael Dukakis's veto of an obscure bill that would have required all Massachusetts students to recite the Pledge of Allegiance every morning. "What is it about the American flag which upsets this man so much?" Bush had gibed. It was a revisiting of the Hard Hat dynamics.[66]

Television anchors and newspaper reporters covered the case prominently. Thousands of Americans wrote letters to their representatives in Washington, demanding action. Senator Strom Thurmond said the ruling had "opened an emotional hydrant across our country demanding immediate action to overturn it." Polls showed that 65 percent of the public disagreed with the ruling. One and a half million people signed petitions in favor of a constitutional amendment to overturn it. Opponents of the measure also jumped into action. Over five hundred law professors signed a public letter opposing a constitutional amendment. In September, Congress passed the Flag Protection Act, which made it a federal crime to desecrate the flag.[67]

When the law went into effect in late October 1989, opponents protested by setting fire to the flag in Seattle; New York; Berkeley, California; and Fort Collins, Colorado. It was the greatest profusion of flag burnings in American history. In Seattle, protesters set fire to one thousand small paper flags and a large cloth banner that had flown over a post office. In Fort Collins, on the campus of Colorado State University, a counter-protester blew out the flames of a burning flag and then grasped it in his hands, exclaiming, "My father fought in World War Two. I'm not going to let what he did go by the wayside." One of the protest organizers responded, "That's what your father fought for, the Constitution and freedom of the United States." The exchange encapsulated the emotions and arguments of the whole national debate.[68]

From 1989 to 2006, Congress debated the question of flag burning seven times, each time polarizing the American people with a largely theoretical discussion about what it meant to be a true patriot. On the one side stood those who considered flag burning a paradox. "Which is more important: the flag, or the free speech it symbolizes?" they asked. Nearly all were happy to sacrifice the symbol for the substance. On the other side were those who approached the flag not merely as a symbol, interchangeable with others, but also as an icon. Many veterans groups were in this number. For them, flag burning was an outrage, a desecration of an emblem as sacred as the cross. The flag had become a relatively static symbol of American conservativism, flown by certain groups and watched suspiciously by others. Its political meanings were more stable than at any other time in our history.

That is where things stood on September 10, 2001.

# ~8~

# FLAG OF REBIRTH

*Patriotism in the Twenty-First Century*

In the days after the fall of the Twin Towers in 2001, Americans hung out hundreds of thousands of flags. In New York, flags fluttered from baby carriages and taxi antennae; they decorated sidewalk memorials, propped on the ground next to candles and cards. A huge flag, five stories high, was hung from a building overlooking Ground Zero. Apartment dwellers suspended strings of red, white, and blue lights from their balconies. Flags sold for five times their usual value. Two weeks after the September 11 attacks, Asian manufacturers had sold out of American flags. Flag suppliers saw sales increase by 200 percent. Businesses offered an American flag contact lens. Flag pins sold for $4.95 in *TV Guide* and for $60,000 from Tiffany's. Over 80 percent of Americans polled said that they planned to fly the flag.[1]

Official flags flew at half-staff around the world, and citizens of other countries also hung out American flags, in a tacit declaration that the flag belonged to us all. An editorial in the French newspaper *Le Monde* declared: "*Nous sommes tous Américains.*" Italian and Swedish papers expressed similar sentiments. The moment was an unparalleled opportunity to claim common cause with others around the globe. In Greenwich Village, activist Todd Gitlin was moved to express that feeling through a symbol that had once seemed very alien. After years of disappointment during the Vietnam era, Gitlin had come to understand that hatred for his country could act "like a cleansing flame." Now, he and his wife hung an American flag from their balcony. "Our desire was visceral," he wrote, "to express solidarity with the dead, membership in a wounded nation, and affection for the community of rescue that affirmed life in the midst of death, springing up to dig through the nearby ashes and ruins."[2]

Within weeks, however, the post-9/11 flag of unity began to harden again into the flag of war. Aggressive foreign policy became the language of patriotism. There were constant comparisons to Pearl Harbor, with the implied need for military retaliation. Within a week, President George W. Bush had declared a national emergency, and the Senate had adopted a resolution authorizing the use of armed forces against those responsible for the attacks. Fifty thousand members of the National Guard and reserves were mobilized. Less than ten days after the fall of the Twin Towers, President Bush used the phrase "war on terror."

Almost immediately, the American flag was employed as the president and his staff appeared on television wearing flag pins and as CNN, Fox News, and MSNBC redesigned their logos to include the American flag. At the same time, the talk shows hosted administration officials who began to warn about biological and chemical weapons and who yoked patriotism to their political program. In response to *Real Time* host Bill Maher's comment that the hijackers were not cowards, White House spokesman Andrew Card announced that "Americans ... need to watch what they say, watch what they do ... this is not a time for remarks like this; there never is." In early October 2001, U.S. forces began bombing Afghanistan in Operation Infinite Justice, an attempt to locate and destroy Osama bin Laden. When CNN reported the civilian casualties there, the network got calls from corporations and the administration saying, "You're being un-American here." The CEO, Walter Isaacson, responded with a memo to staff to minimize such reports and balance them with reminders of the attacks.[3]

On *The Late Show with David Letterman*, CBS anchor Dan Rather announced, "George Bush is the president, he makes the decisions; and you know, as just one American, he wants me to line up. Just tell me where." Marching orders followed swiftly as administration officials began identifying suspects in Afghanistan and Iraq, and the flag's military connotations, which run below the surface in times of peace, stood once again revealed.[4]

Congress authorized the use of force again in October 2002. In the months before and after the United States invaded Iraq in March 2003, prowar rallies were held in Chicago, Richmond, and other cities. Flags were featured in abundance, as well as chants of "U.S.A." The largest demonstration, held in April in New York City, was startlingly reminiscent of the Hard Hat pro-Nixon rallies. Organized by the city's labor unions and attended by construction workers, pipefitters, and ironworkers, it was held at Ground Zero. Fifteen thousand workers, almost all of them men, crowded into the area. Seven-foot flags waved from poles in the air, their long, looping strands of red and white grazing the heads below. Many demonstrators wore hard hats, some of which were painted blue and covered in white stars. A large, handmade sign proclaimed: "We GAVE Peace a Chance. We Got

9/11! Support Our Troops!!" Smaller ones showed images of Saddam Hussein's statue tumbling to the ground. Mostly, there were flags: large, commercial flags; the standard five-by-three-foot household size; and smaller ones for hand waving. There were so many flags that you could reach out and touch one from almost anywhere you stood.[5]

Much larger marches protested the invasion. The demonstrations of February 15 were the largest in world history, with gatherings in over six hundred cities by more than six million participants. In Antarctica, several dozen research scientists in red parkas protested in an arc on the edge of the Ross Sea. In London, a million demonstrators marched under the clock tower of Big Ben with white and green signs reading, "Don't Attack Iraq" and "Not in My Name." In Rome, a crowd of three million—the largest antiwar rally in human history—wove its way past the Coliseum with a colorful assortment of flags: red for the Communists, green for the Green Party, and billowing rainbow banners reading *PACE*: Italian for "peace." In Tokyo, protesters carried purple balloons; in Buenos Aires, fifty thousand marched under umbrellas; in Jakarta, men in white suits released a dove.[6]

In the United States, people protested in at least 150 communities. Tens and even hundreds of thousands gathered in the larger cities: New York, Seattle, San Francisco, Los Angeles. Smaller communities held their own protests: Portland, Maine; Normal, Illinois; Bellingham, Washington. The crowds were large and colorful. In Northern cities, where the temperatures dropped far below the norms, protesters swathed themselves in parkas and scarves to keep out the cold. Mittened hands clutched steaming cups of coffee and cardboard placards. There were thousands of the rectangular signs distributed by the Stop the War Coalition:

"No Iraq War" emblazoned in red, white, and blue. Handmade messages read "Peace is patriotic."

But among the millions who gathered to protest the invasion, the American flag was conspicuously absent. At the larger U.S. demonstrations, only a handful could be seen: a quick glimpse of the Stars and Stripes amid the thousands of signs and banners. Those rare few who carried flags were taken aback by the suspicion with which they and their flags were greeted. As one woman wrote in a letter to the *New York Times*:

> I despair. At the war protest on Thursday in Times Square, I waved an American flag because I am a patriot.
>
> I revere the principles on which this country was founded. Our flag belongs to Americans of every stripe—even to its critics.
>
> I stood on Broadway with a flag and a sign that said, "I do not support this war."
>
> How sad that despite my wearing an antiwar sign, most people who passed by assumed that because I carried an American flag I support this war.
>
> This symbol of America has been co-opted by those who believe that dissent is un-American.[7]

Almost no one recognized the sailors' flag of participatory democracy; almost none claimed the flag of civil protest. In San Francisco, it was the dark and hooded figure of the Grim Reaper that carried the flag—gripped between his teeth.

∽∽∽

On February 28, 2003, journalist Bill Moyers appeared for his PBS television show *Now with Bill Moyers* wearing an uncharacteristic ornament: a flag pin on his brown crewneck sweater. "I wore my flag tonight," he began. "First time. Until now I haven't thought it necessary to display a little metallic icon of patriotism for everyone to see." Moyers said he had always thought it was enough to vote, pay taxes, speak out, and participate in the life of the democracy. "It no more occurred to me to flaunt the flag on my chest," he said, "than it did to pin my mother's picture on my lapel to prove her son's love. Mother knew where I stood; so does my country." Why the flag pin, then? he asked. "I put it on to take it back."[8]

The flag pin had reentered modern American politics as a cynical tribute to a Hollywood film. Nixon had worn a flag pin occasionally after the Hard Hats gave him one in 1970; for his reelection campaign two years later, his cabinet and staff all joined him. The idea came from the decorated lapel of the main character in *The Candidate*, a film that critiqued just such trappings by chronicling the main character's loss of integrity as he focuses on the image-making necessary to get elected. Nixon's chief of staff, H. R. Haldeman, was inspired not by this message, however, but by the perfect election ploy: ostensibly patriotic, the flag pin also possessed an unparalleled capacity to divide. At a cabinet meeting, Haldeman urged everyone to wear pins "to stick it to the liberals." Nixon agreed, even sending a memo to his staff in support of the idea. Republican congressional representatives followed. "American flag lapel pins," wrote conservative pundit Richard Brookhiser, "became a sort of GOP costume."[9]

Like the flag, pins carried multiple, and conservative, connotations: allegiance to country and support of U.S. foreign policy. But donning a pin was also somehow different, more possessive, than flying the flag. To wear a flag on one's suit jacket was to make a personal statement embedded in a political one. Wearing one was a branding: a claim that not only did you belong to the country, but the country also belonged to you. And it was a statement of identity, reminiscent of the nativists' secret passwords, which drew a magic line between self-described patriots and the outsiders who did not subscribe to their values. The flag pins were a signal to Nixon's "silent majority" that he was one of them, and they reelected him handily with one of the largest popular margins in presidential history.

In the wake of Watergate, however, flag pins lost their luster. When Haldeman testified before the Senate committee in the summer of 1973, perjuring himself, he wore his customary flag pin. When Nixon resigned from the Oval Office on August 9, his flag pin reflected the glare of television lights; it again flashed on his chest at the November press conference where he declared, "I am not a crook." When his successor, Gerald Ford, took the oath of office with the words "Our long national nightmare is over," Ford's navy suit had an undecorated lapel. There would have been no way to heal the country with the symbol that had become so divisive.[10]

Flag pins sprouted on political lapels again after the fall of the Twin Towers. The president and his cabinet wore them. White House Budget Director Mitchell Daniels owned a whole assortment of them and chose a different one each day. It seemed as though every politician wore them. These flags were meant to be an expression of patriotic unity, but as the administration began to talk about war, it was clear that the pins' apolitical connotations were matched by a deeply political agenda. Many television broadcasters began wearing flag pins on the air, and a debate broke out in the press corps. Some news directors encouraged the practice—the entire staff of Fox News appeared with pins—while others banned it. As 2001 gave way to 2002 and then 2003, it became clear that flag pins had become a symbol of war.[11]

So when Moyers told his television audience in early 2003 that "the flag's been hijacked and turned into a logo—the trademark of a monopoly on patriotism," his words rang true. Even as 180,000 American troops waited in the Gulf region, Moyers refused to relinquish the flag:

> The flag belongs to the country, not to the government. And it reminds me that it's not un-American to think that war—except in self-defense—is a failure of moral imagination, political nerve, and diplomacy. Come to think of it, standing up to your government can mean standing up for your country.[12]

Moyers's comments flew around the Internet, a tacit acknowledgement of the power of his words, but few Americans followed his example. Instead, the country's tradition of humanitarian patriotism all but disappeared between 2001 and the election of 2008, behind a nationalist agenda led by the Republican Party in power and assisted, initially enthusiastically, by congressional Democrats. The USA Patriot Act, passed in October 2001 in response to 9/11, radically expanded government powers and curtailed individual liberties: It authorized indefinite detention of noncitizens suspected of involvement in domestic terrorism, expanded law enforcement's ability to search private property without the owner's knowledge, and excused the FBI from obtaining court orders before investigating citizens for "intelligence purposes." The Bush administration also increased government

surveillance, putting in place both the National Security Administration electronic surveillance program, which established a
bank of phone records with the secret help of telecommunica-
tions companies, and the top-secret Total Information Awareness
program, which was intended to detect patterns of terrorist organization but which allowed the government to develop
dossiers on hundreds of millions of citizens.

Accompanying the destruction of civil liberties at home was a
growing contempt for the rule of law, witnessed most egregiously
abroad. At Abu Ghraib prison in Baghdad, detainees were tortured and humiliated; some died in custody. While the abuses
were committed by soldiers, the actions pointed to interrogation
methods sanctioned by higher-ups, including Attorney General
Alberto Gonzales. Called to task before the Senate Armed Services
Committee, even Secretary of Defense Donald Rumsfeld admitted that the abuses were "un-American" and "inconsistent with
the values of our nation." Prisoners held at Guantánamo Bay,
Cuba, were indefinitely detained and allegedly tortured, in violation of the Geneva Convention and American law.[13]

The nation that had stood for participatory democracy and
the rule of law now appeared as a symbol of mass wiretapping,
illegal detention, lack of habeas corpus, preventive war, rendi-
tion, and torture. Like the World Trade Center, the Constitution
stood in ruins.

∽∾∽

The 2008 election did not redefine American patriotism. The
two familiar patriotic traditions wound their way through it, and
familiar issues—the flag pin, the question of loyalty during time
of war—resurfaced. But it did change the politics of patriotism in

a way not witnessed in presidential campaigns of the past forty years. As the Republican candidate, John McCain was expected to make the case for patriotism, and he did, in the familiar terms of "putting the country first, before party or personal ambition, before anything."[14] But Democratic candidate Barack Obama also cast his vision in deliberately patriotic terms: a patriotism that acknowledged the nationalist claim while pushing to expand the definition of the American nation. "This is the America we love," he declared in his stump speech:

> We're one nation, all of us proud, all of us patriots.
>
> There are patriots who supported this war in Iraq and patriots who opposed it, patriots who believe in Democratic policies and those who believe in Republican policies.
>
> The men and women who serve in our battlefields, some may be Democrats, some may be Republicans, others independents, but they've fought together and they bled together and some died together under the same proud flag. They have not served a red America or a blue America; they've served the United States of America.[15]

His vision enabled an extraordinary reclaiming of humanitarian patriotism even before the election, as was witnessed by crowds of Democrats waving flags and chanting, "U.S.A., U.S.A." These were the Americans who had nodded at Moyers's words in 2003; now they themselves picked up the flag. It was not yet a full embrace—campaign workers reported thousands of flags discarded after Obama rallies—but it marked a real change.

Obama's victory, on the other hand, did remake American patriotism. For five years, patriotism had entailed supporting an administration committed to war and the rollback of civil liberties, but the Obama campaign was unambiguously critical of the war. One immediate consequence was that many activists who had played the role of outsiders for decades, always in protest, had to reorient their relationship to Washington. "For ... those of us who are on the left," asked professor Manning Marable, "how do we relate to the government?" It was a genuine question. Others on the left were surprised at the patriotism that welled up within them on November 4. As one voter noted, "I, for the first time, want to hang an American flag. Please don't say I'm being negative; I don't mean it that way. I mean I feel it. I feel that I want to hang a flag, that I'm a part of the United States and that we matter, all of us."[16]

On election night, Obama stood on the outdoor stage in Chicago's Grant Park in the lights and the breeze and declared it was the fundamental humanitarian ideals—"democracy, liberty, opportunity, and unyielding hope"—that formed "the true strength of our nation." The volunteers who had made his candidacy possible by organizing and registering and making phone calls had proved, he said, that "a government of the people, by the people and for the people has not perished from this Earth." But at the same time, Obama summoned "a new spirit of patriotism, of service and responsibility where each of us resolves to pitch in and work harder and look after not only ourselves, but each other." This call to nationalist patriotism was apparent, too, in the repeated references to "one people," "our union," and—most profoundly— his inclusive use of "we."[17]

In some ways, Obama's vision recalled Ronald Reagan's, not least because of its extraordinary optimism. His "Yes, we can" campaign mantra conveyed a sense of possibility curiously reminiscent of Reagan's "Morning in America" promise of new beginnings. Obama's nationalist emphasis on a single, united people echoed Reagan's. But while Reagan's "we" was overwhelmingly white and middle-class, Obama's "we" was profoundly diverse, encompassing all races, political parties, ages, orientations, and abilities. This reformulation of patriotism was compelling, in part, because as the first African American to be elected to the presidency, Obama was living testimony of the extension of rights to ever-larger circles of citizens. His election allowed non-white citizens of many communities, especially African American, to see themselves reflected in the polity, and it allowed all Americans committed to the extension of civil rights to take pride in the actions of their country.

Most clearly, Obama's vision called on the legacy of Abraham Lincoln. Like Lincoln, Obama sought to pull a deeply divided country together by invoking both patriotic traditions. And like Lincoln, he recognized that they are not necessarily opposed. Humanitarianism and nationalism do not stand on the ends of a spectrum, but on different axes entirely. When Lincoln invoked the ideals of liberty, he appealed to each citizen's sense of civic morality; when he called on the spirit of union, he appealed to the powerful sense of the group. His nationalism was not necessarily conservative; while it limited liberty in some ways—by, for example, suspending habeas corpus—it extended it in others, of which the Emancipation Proclamation was the most powerful example. Like Lincoln, his political hero, Obama framed his call for national unity as essential, not simply in and of itself, but rather to build a society around humanitarian values. "For that is the true genius of America," he said in his victory speech, "that America can change. Our union can be perfected. And what we have already achieved gives us hope for what we can and must achieve tomorrow."

∽◦∾

The defining image of the flag in our era is the one rising over the rubble of September 11, 2001. On that day, as the emergency vehicles raced through the city and the sirens rose and fell, three men working in the wreckage of Ground Zero found a flagpole in the concrete rubble. A local newspaper photographer caught the moment. The three men stand under the pole with a flag: one man pulling the halyards, one supporting the ropes, one squinting upward ready to lend a hand. Their black helmets and a reflective neon stripe mark them as firefighters; the white dust that covers their trousers and gilds their forearms gives testimony to their work that day. Around them lies a landscape of desolation: a gray background of concrete and steel and a mountain of beams piled in the rubble. The photograph centers on the American flag as it rises slowly from these ruins. The flag holds the memory of chaos: Its presence and the men who raise it are a silent tribute to what happened here. And it stands outside and above that memory. It is a timeless symbol, familiar and classic, a symbol of hope and promise against a background of despair.

In the famous Iwo Jima photo of the twentieth century, the pole also rose at an angle, the flag formed the same apex of a rough triangle, and the heroism of ordinary people was exalted: Americans as everyman, working together, raising a beacon of hope above a landscape of destruction. But the firefighters at the Twin Towers are not soldiers; they are civil servants, men whose business it is to save lives. They are not imposing order on a foreign land; they are clearing out a space for order in our own country. They are not planting a flag on new territory, claiming it for the United States; they are raising a flag as a memorial and a gesture of reclaiming. Whereas the Iwo Jima photograph conveys triumph, the photo of Ground Zero evokes a more complex set of emotions: grief, respect, determination, and hope. It is an image of a country united not in war but in rebuilding.

It is tempting to view our two historical patriotic traditions in moral terms and applaud our recent turn toward humanitarianism. Broadly speaking, humanitarian patriotism has been good for our democracy. By emphasizing key values—liberty, egalitarianism, respect for the individual—it established a long political tradition of dissent necessary for returning power to the people. It also inspired many of the moments in which our national circle has been expanded and our liberties granted to a wider group of people. This is the patriotism of the Revolutionary sailors, who saw themselves as practitioners of democracy and the rightful heirs to the civic promise of participation; it is the patriotism of the end of the Civil War, when the Union cause became synonymous with emancipation, and of the civil rights movement, when black Americans were finally able to exercise the voting rights that they had been denied so long. It is the patriotism invoked by Bill Moyers, whose flag drove a wedge between the country and the government, claiming the tradition of dissent amid the drumbeats of war.

Nationalist patriotism, in contrast, conflates a country's ideals and its politics, wrapping both in the flag and making it difficult to separate love of country from support for government policy. The loyalty and faith that nationalists prize facilitate unity but provide little room for the skepticism that the founding fathers valued so highly. At their worst, like the Hard Hats and the Klan in World War I, nationalist patriots exacerbate the worst excesses of democracy. Theirs is the impulse that Alexis de Tocqueville was thinking of when he warned in 1835 against "the tyranny of the majority" in American democracy. It is also the impulse that, despite Moyers's almost lone resistance, defined American patriotism between 2001 and 2008.

But an easy characterization of one form of American patriotism as constructive and another as destructive does not, in fact, hold. Nationalist patriotism also calls us to service, to sacrifice; it calls on our sense of belonging to a larger whole. This was the patriotism that inspired the firefighters and rescue crews of 9/11; it was the patriotism that caused Todd Gitlin to hang out the flag of solidarity. For its part, humanitarian patriotism can fail to honor the sacrifice of those who worked to procure the rights we now have. When humanitarians insist on the right to burn the flag, they risk dismissing the real emotions and real sacrifice that coalesce in that symbol. Left-leaning dissidents have learned, to their chagrin, that rejecting patriotism is deeply counterproductive. As Gitlin wrote, looking back on the 1960s: "Many Americans were willing to hear our case against the war, but not to forfeit love of their America." To fight patriotism is to run up against that insurmountable love, while to make the case against war—or for civil liberties or for the extension of rights to others—in terms of patriotism is to invoke the power of that love. Too much nationalism, and patriotism may well devolve into "my country right or wrong," but too much humanitarianism, and sense of community diffuses into the ether—a consequence that invariably ends in conflict.[18]

It is not just the two patriotic traditions that are morally ambiguous; patriotism as a whole is deeply flawed. It is inevitably exclusive. As flags unite, they necessarily divide, and to pledge allegiance to one group is to shut others out of the magic circle. No matter how many times we say "never again," human beings commit atrocities regularly in the name of love of country. And wherever humanitarian forms of patriotism do rise, they are vulnerable to takeover by illiberal nationalist forces. Our own post-9/11 period is a prime example.

Yet patriotism has a productive power that continues to surprise. The swift and overwhelming popularity of the firefighter photograph among Americans of many political beliefs reveals a resonance among Americans that is not always apparent. As often as patriotism has divided our nation, it nonetheless also serves as a shared language among people from very different cultures and political backgrounds, enabling a vast diversity of citizens to draw their personal values from a shared wellspring. There *are* American values, liberty and democracy among them, values that have been enshrined in our founding documents and at key points throughout our history. And even when those values manifest in very different ways, as they inevitably do, they serve as a moral compass. Patriotism provides an ongoing obligation to hold that moral compass; American patriotism, with its tradition of patriotic dissent committed to civil liberties, also provides the means and obligation to correct our path when we find ourselves off course. Because of our history of dissent tied to uncontested common values, we can stray from those values—as we have throughout American history—and still right ourselves in the end. Just as American society found its way back from the repression of World War I, so can we return from the policies of the Bush administration.

To say "I am a patriot" is an act of political engagement. In the United States, it is to acknowledge that we are part of a large and powerful nation—one among others—whose force can be directed for good or for ill. "The cause of America is in a great measure the cause of all mankind," Thomas Paine wrote in 1776. "We have it in our power to begin the world over again." To fly the flag is to stake an active claim to the promise of an American dream that draws its inspiration from the founders and is continuously renewed. It is to seize on the symbol that has always been claimed by ascending groups and to employ its power in service to our common values. A patriotism founded in democratic egalitarianism has the singular ability to cut across lines of geography, race, and class. This patriotism can, with encouragement, create a shared political culture of liberty and justice. In a world as diverse and multifaceted as ours—and as in need of renewal—it is, perhaps, the only thing that can.

# ACKNOWLEDGMENTS

This book grew out of my doctoral research on the patriotic groups of the late nineteenth century. As I answered the inevitable questions about my work at parties and family gatherings, it quickly became evident that not everyone shared my fascination with the Daughters of the American Revolution. I did, however, have many lively conversations about patriotism, its role in politics, and the American flag: conversations which were the genesis of this book. Everyone has their own flag stories and I thank those who have shared them with me over the past decade.

Numerous people went out of their way to help me with historical details. Lenny Rotman willingly shared his VVAW experiences with a curious stranger on the other end of the telephone; his work, both past and present, inspires me. Rusty Sachs has my eternal gratitude for many things; I thank him now for helping me do justice to the takeover of Lady Liberty with his vivid stories and sharpened pencil. Hunter Bear (John Salter) not only wrote the best account of the Jackson movement, he graciously responded to my inquiry about flag use during that time. Shawn O'Sullivan of the New York *Daily News* helped me track down the famous photograph of the Sheep's Meadow flag burning when all sources suggested it had been lost. Charlene Mires kindly responded to my inquiry about flags on the Pennsylvania State House. Rebecca Noel received a message in her inbox after three years of silence and shot back with an impressive catalog of information on Boston schools during the Revolutionary period; her acuity and generosity are unmatched.

I want to thank my colleagues at Harvard and at Vermont College/ Union Institute for their interest and support: Nathan Alexander, Elden Golden, Crystal Gray, Loree Miltich, John Stauffer, Brian Webb, and Diana Williams. David Hall has continued to offer wisdom and good counsel, far beyond the statute of limitations. Thanks to Tess Zimmerman, for ordering countless books and rolls of microfilm through interlibrary loan; to Stacey Knight, for her inspired and creative work as a research librarian; and to Matt Pappathan, for pulling up a chair and helping me find the sources I knew were out there.

Sarah Burnes believed in this project from the beginning and took me on in an impressive leap of faith; she has been a superb agent, bringing warmth and intelligence to every interaction. I first realized that Lara Heimert was an extraordinary editor when she confessed her fascination with elephant lynching stories; I re-realized it as she worked her magic on the manuscript, shearing off unnecessary paragraphs and transposing whole sections. It was a pleasure working with her. I am thankful to editorial assistant Brandon Proia for making it all possible, to Patty Boyd for careful copyediting and her patience with my dangling modifiers, and to production editor Michelle Welsh-Horst for her wonderful clarity and responsiveness.

Many friends tolerated my peculiar fascination with the flag. Rowan Jacobsen encouraged me through the whole process over dozens of cups of coffee—and occasionally something stronger—with his trademark wit and good humor. I am grateful to Laura DeBonis for the affectionate amusement with which she approached the project and the thoughtful encouragement with which she read it; to the warm and wonderful Gia Lee, for helping me think through key issues as she whizzed through L.A. traffic; to Katherine Mooney for the right words at the right time and thirty-five years of friendship; to Heidi Holland for the margaritas, high humor, and emotional clarity. Bronwyn Becker arrived on the scene in a heroic gallop: she was able to see the book hidden within the sheaf of draft pages and to help it emerge. My greatest debt is to Ann Armbrecht, who shared the crucible of writing and full-on motherhood: reading drafts after midnight, pushing me to find the time I needed, and inspiring me continually toward greater honesty and complexity. Her friendship has been a deep privilege, and her influence appears on every page.

Thanks also to the friends who didn't read the manuscript but who took my lively band of children so I could write: to Melissa Schaefer, who continues to be my personal hero, and Lila Bennett and Barbara Elliot, whose generosity and goodwill brighten my world nearly every day.

My family has been extraordinary, giving me the time and space to make this happen. My parents, Peter and Mary Teachout, spent countless summer weekends riding my children around the lawn on the tractor and countless winter ones strapping on skis and calling out "bend your knees!" while I tapped away furiously on the laptop. Thanks also to Chelsea and Sam, Dillon and Brian, Cabot and Meghan, for being the best aunts and uncles—and siblings—imaginable: my life is far richer for your presence. A special thank you goes to Zephyr, who helped me think about writing and gave that secret sustenance that only sisters can. My grandmother, Mollie Miles, was a constant source of inspiration, as well as providing a steady stream of patriotic treasures through the mail. My greatest gratitude goes to Mark, for his infinite patience and good humor and for holding it all together: his steadfast sense of what it means to live ethically continues to sustain me. And finally, all my love and thanks to Alyssa, Waylon, Jed, Celia, and Angus, for the infinite distractions and for reminding me why it all matters. May your generation guide this country a little closer toward its promise.

# NOTES

## INTRODUCTION

1. Rusty Sachs, interview with author, Norwich, Vermont, November 26, 2007; Lenny Rotman, telephone interview with author, October 28, 2008; Don Bristow-Carrico, "Seizing the Statue of Liberty 1971: Three Days with a Lady," *The Veteran* 29, no. 1 (spring/summer 1999), www.vvaw.org/veteran/article/?id=195.

2. Ibid.

3. Ibid.

4. Ibid.; Robert D. McFadden, "War Foes Seize Statue of Liberty," *New York Times*, December 27, 1971, 1.

5. Ibid.

6. Ibid.; Michael T. Kaufman, "15 Veterans Leave the Statue of Liberty, Claiming a Victory in Take-Over," *New York Times*, December 29, 1971, 32. See also Lawrence Van Gelder, "War Foes Reject U.S. Compromise to Reopen Statue of Liberty to the Public," *New York Times*, December 28, 1971, 1. The official National Park Service account appears in Barbara Blumberg, "The Statue of Liberty: Monument to an Expanding Set of Ideals," in *Celebrating the Immigrant: An Administrative History of the Statue of Liberty National Monument, 1952–1982*, Cultural Resource Management Study no. 10 (National Park Service, 1985), chapter 1, www.nps.gov/history/history/online_books/stli/adhi1.htm.

7. The literature on patriotism is vast, partly because it so often overlaps the literature on nationalism. In its simplest formulation, patriotism is love of country. Yet the term *country* may have a kaleidoscope of meanings (e.g., geographical territory; political territory; a shared history; a "people" defined by language, religion, ethnicity, or race; a set of articulated values), and *love* differs in its intensity, its exclusiveness, and its conditionality. We tend to think of patriotism as inherently conservative, dependent on a fundamental connection to

a nation's past, but national history is an infinitely variable terrain, and patriots have mapped different courses across the landscape of their history, from politically conservative to deeply radical. Moreover, Greek and Enlightenment thinkers addressing patriotism before the rise of modern nation-states emphasized devotion to a common good over national identification.

Nonetheless, patriotism can be viewed in terms of two basic categories. The first is a sentiment that privileges commitment to ideas and values, usually humanitarian, over commitment to nation; the second is a sentiment that seeks to promote one's nation politically, socially, or economically within the context of other nations. These categories have been described in various ways, most of them variations on a civic-versus-ethnic distinction. Maurizio Viroli's *For Love of Country* (New York: Oxford University Press, 1995), one of the most important recent works on patriotism, defined these two categories as, respectively, patriotism and nationalism. Others have viewed the sentiments as subcategories of nationalism, with the subcategories approximating the distinctions between liberal and illiberal nationalism and between voluntaristic (also called civic or civil) nationalism and ethnic nationalism. All of these sentiments pertain in American history also, but my work presents the two key categories as modes of patriotism because, like Viroli, I believe that both represent genuine emotions of love. Unlike Viroli, I believe that both deserve the positive connotations of the term *patriotism* (as opposed to the negative connotations of *nationalism*).

To distinguish between the two modes of patriotism as they appear in American history, I add the adjective *humanitarian* to the first because of the fundamental compassion of this kind of patriotism and because the "human" root of the word *humanitarian* underscores the centrality of the individual within this sentiment. I term the second category *nationalist patriotism* because nationalism has played an increasingly powerful role in the history of the United States, so much so that it has only recently become accepted to think of political dissidents as patriots. There remains no perfect word for this type of patriotism. Early iterations of this strain of American patriotism focused on ethnic groups, but *ethnic patriotism* is insufficient for describing the experience of culturally diverse Americans who nonetheless count loyalty to the state as the most fundamental patriotic virtue. In his seminal work *The Roots of Loyalty* (New York: Columbia University Press, 1946), Merle Curti used the term *organic*. While his attempt to encompass both the ethnic and the nationalist qualities was an important one, the term itself lacks explanatory power. Naturally, the classification system used here is only one of many that could be employed to explain the shifts in American patriotism over the past 250 years.

CHAPTER 1

1. On the Franklin-Folger map, see Joyce Chaplin, "Distance," in *The First Scientific American: Benjamin Franklin and the Pursuit of Genius* (New York: Basic Books, 1996), chapter 6.

2. William Rea Furlong and Byron McCandless, *So Proudly We Hail: The History of the United States Flag* (Washington, D.C.: Smithsonian Institution Press, 1981), chapter 1.

3. Jesse Lemisch, "Jack Tar in the Streets: Merchant Seamen in the Politics of Revolutionary America," *William and Mary Quarterly*, 3rd ser., 25 (July 1968): 371–407; Paul A. Gilje, *Liberty on the Waterfront: American Maritime Culture in the Age of Revolution* (Philadelphia: University of Pennsylvania Press, 2004), 101.

4. As a seventeenth-century minister remarked: "God sifted a whole nation that He might send Choice Grain over into this Wilderness" (William Stoughton, quoted in Merle Curti, *The Roots of American Loyalty* [New York: Columbia University Press, 1946], 5). As early as 1751, Benjamin Franklin, in *Observations Concerning the Increase of Mankind*, had pointed to the colonies' exceptional population growth as a source of pride. In the same vein, Thomas Jefferson sought natural history for evidence of the superior climate of the Americas.

5. John Adams, quoted in Marcus Rediker, *Between the Devil and the Deep Blue Sea: Merchant Seamen, Pirates, and the Anglo-American Maritime World* (New York: Cambridge University Press, 1987). See also Peter Linebaugh and Marcus Rediker, *The Many-Headed Hydra: Sailors, Slaves, Commoners, and the Hidden History of the Revolutionary Atlantic* (Boston: Beacon Press, 2000).

6. Jesse Lemisch, *Jack Tar Versus John Bull: The Role of New York's Seamen in Precipitating the Revolution* (New York: Garland, 1997).

7. Quoted in ibid., 36.

8. British newspapers condemned it, arguing that impressment was "inconsistent with Civil Liberty, and the natural Rights of Mankind" (ibid.).

9. Pauline Maier, "Poverty, Mobility, and the Problem of Class in Colonial Cities," review of Gary Nash, *The Urban Crucible: Social Change, Political Consciousness, and the Origins of the American Revolution* (Boston: Harvard University Press, 1979), in *Reviews in American History* 8, no. 4 (December 1980): 471; Gilje, *Liberty on the Waterfront*, 101. See also Linebaugh and Rediker, *The Many-Headed Hydra*, 168–169; and Lemisch, "Jack Tar in the Streets," 383–394.

10. Carl Bridenbaugh, *Cities in Revolt: Urban Life in America, 1743–1776* (London, New York: Oxford University Press, 1971), 234, 256; Marcus

Rediker, "A Motley Crew of Rebels," in *The Transforming Hand of Revolution: Reconsidering the American Revolution as a Social Movement*, ed. Ronald Hoffman and Peter J. Albert (Charlottesville: United States Capitol Historical Society by the University Press of Virginia, 1996), 190–191.

11. Dirk Hoerder, *Crowd Action in Revolutionary Massachusetts, 1765–1780* (New York: Academic Press, 1977), 89. A terrible trade deficit with Great Britain meant that it was nearly impossible to get currency in the colonies: Even people willing to pay their debts found themselves in danger of being hauled off to debtors' prison.

12. James Otis, quoted in Bernard Bailyn, *The Ordeal of Thomas Hutchinson* (Cambridge, Mass.: Belknap Press of Harvard University Press, 1974), 72; Jason Shaffer, *Performing Patriotism: National Identity in the Colonial and Revolutionary American Theater* (Philadelphia: University of Pennsylvania Press, 2007), 81, 86; Alfred Young, *The Shoemaker and the Tea Party: Memory and the American Revolution* (Boston: Beacon Press, 1999).

13. Russell Bourne, *Cradle of Violence: How Boston's Waterfront Mobs Ignited the American Revolution* (New York: Wiley, 2006), 102.

14. Peter Charles Hoffer, *Sensory Worlds in Early America* (Baltimore: Johns Hopkins University Press, 2003), 208; Hoerder, *Crowd Action in Revolutionary Massachusetts*, 97.

15. Quoted in John C. Miller, *Sam Adams: Pioneer in Propaganda* (Boston: Little, Brown, 1936), 61.

16. Bridenbaugh, *Cities in Revolt*, 307; Hoerder, *Crowd Action in Revolutionary Massachusetts*, 98; Furlong and McCandless, *So Proudly We Hail*, 78–79. The flag may also have been a liberty flag—a single color, with the word *liberty* written across it—or a pine tree flag (Boleslaw Mastai and Marie-Louise D'Otrange Mastai, *The Stars and the Stripes: The American Flag as Art and as History from the Birth of the Republic to the Present* [New York: Knopf, 1973], 16–20).

17. Hoerder, *Crowd Action in Revolutionary Massachusetts*, 99–100.

18. Ibid., 102; Andrew Oliver, quoted in Bourne, *Cradle of Violence*, 106.

19. For a fuller discussion of the two threads of patriotism, please see note 7 of the introduction. Humanitarian patriotism overlaps liberal, civic, or civil nationalism insofar as the category postulates a form of nationalism that is inclusive and seeks to extend the values of equality, individual rights, freedom, and tolerance to all those within a given nation's borders (and, frequently, to those beyond those borders). Humanitarian patriotism overlaps cosmopolitanism insofar as it insists that moral duties—and individual rights—apply to all people equally. As I use the categories, humanitarian pa-

triotism is distinct from, but can coexist with, the second major impulse: nationalist patriotism.

20. Quoted in Bourne, *Cradle of Violence*, 116.

21. Hoerder, *Crowd Action in Revolutionary Massachusetts*, 100; quoted in Howard Zinn, *A People's History of the United States* (New York: Harper Perennial, 1995), 66.

22. "War of plunder" quoted in Bourne, *Cradle of Violence*, 109; "that they lookt upon this" quoted in Hoerder, *Crowd Action in Revolutionary Massachusetts*, 113.

23. Ray Raphael, *A People's History of the American Revolution: How Common People Shaped the Fight for Independence* (New York: New Press, 2001), 13.

24. Ibid.; Pauline Maier, *From Resistance to Revolution: Colonial Radicals and the Development of American Opposition to Britain, 1765–1776* (New York: Vintage Books, 1972), 57; Lemisch, *Jack Tar Versus John Bull*, 90–92.

25. Furlong and McCandless, *So Proudly We Hail*, 61.

26. Ibid.

27. Ibid., 59.

28. Quoted in Maier, *From Resistance to Revolution*, 54.

29. Mastai and Mastai, *The Stars and the Stripes*, 62.

30. Observer and Jones both quoted in Furlong and McCandless, *So Proudly We Hail*, 90. This similarity caused a military debacle in January 1776, when General George Washington triumphantly raised the Continental Colors on a wintry hill in Boston. Washington meant the flag as a symbol of defiance, a statement of military independence. The British troops who peered at it through spyglasses, however, interpreted it as a parochial version of the Union Jack, raised in tribute to King George. "It was received in Boston as ... a signal of Submission," noted Washington several days later. "[B]y this time I presume they begin to think it strange that we have not made a formal Surrender" (Scot M. Guenter, *The American Flag, 1777–1924: Cultural Shifts from Creation to Codification* [Rutherford, N.J.: Fairleigh Dickinson University Press; London: Associated University Presses, 1990], 28).

31. Furlong and McCandless, *So Proudly We Hail*, 98; Mastai and Mastai, *The Stars and the Stripes*, 19–39.

32. Gilje, *Liberty on the Waterfront*, 106; John Shy, *A People Numerous and Armed: Reflections on the Military Struggle for American Independence* (New York: Oxford University Press, 1976), 248–249. Shy cites a population of 2.5 million at the outbreak of the Revolutionary War (*A People Numerous and Armed*, 122).

33. Gilje, *Liberty on the Waterfront*, 1–3, 112.

34. Ibid., 112.

35. Francis D. Cogliano, "We All Hoisted the American Flag: National Identity Among American Prisoners in Britain During the American Revolution," *Journal of American Studies* 32, no. 1 (April 1998): 20. Revolutionary sailor quotation from Charles Herbert, *A Relic of the Revolution* (Boston: published for the Proprietor, by Charles H. Pierce, 1847), 44. Jesse Lemisch, "Listening to the 'Inarticulate': William Widger's Dream and the Loyalties of American Revolutionary Seamen in British Prisons," *Journal of Social History* 3, no. 1 (1969): 7, 15.

36. Sheldon S. Cohen, *Yankee Prisoners in British Gaols: Prisoners of War at Forton and Mill, 1777–1783* (Newark: University of Delaware Press; London: Associated University Presses, 1995); Herbert, *A Relic of the Revolution*, 123, 183.

37. Herbert, *A Relic of the Revolution*, 111, 140–142, 161.

38. Lemisch, "William Widger's Dream," 14. Of the sailors, 92 percent stayed in prison; fewer than 8 percent defected. Of the defectors, many were foreign-born (Cohen, *Yankee Prisoners in British Gaols*, 104–105). "True sons of America" quoted in Herbert, *A Relic of the Revolution*, 177.

39. Herbert, *A Relic of the Revolution*, 142.

40. Ibid.

41. The men wore their flags in the cockades until the end of the day. In the nautical language of one seaman, "We kept our colors hoisted till sunset, and then took them down" (ibid.).

42. Ibid., 119.

43. Ibid., 79; Harvey J. Kaye, *Thomas Paine and the Promise of America* (New York: Hill and Wang, 2005), 43.

44. Quoted in Kaye, *Thomas Paine*, 48–50; Herbert, *A Relic of the Revolution*, 79.

45. Herbert, *A Relic of the Revolution*, 104.

46. Herbert himself used the term *gauntlet* (ibid., 32, 128, 163, 145–146).

47. Ibid., 202.

48. Quoted in Lemisch, *Jack Tar Versus John Bull*, 153.


CHAPTER 2

1. David Montgomery, "The Shuttle and the Cross: Weavers and Artisans in the Kensington Riots of 1844," *Journal of Social History* 5 (1972): 412.

2. Ibid., 414–415; Michael Feldberg, *The Philadelphia Riots of 1844: A Study of Ethnic Conflict* (Westport, Conn.: Greenwood Press, 1975), 100.

3. *Philadelphia Public Ledger,* May 4, 1844, quoted in Feldberg, *The Philadelphia Riots of 1844,* 102; John Hancock Lee, *The Origin and Progress of the American Party in Politics: Embracing a Complete History of the Philadelphia Riots in May and July 1844, with a full description of the Great American Procession of July Fourth, and a Refutation of the Arguments Founded on the Charges of Religious Proscription and Secret Combination* (Philadelphia: Elliott and Gihon, 1855), 45.

4. Boleslaw Mastai and Marie-Louise D'Otrange Mastai, *The Stars and the Stripes: The American Flag as Art and as History from the Birth of the Republic to the Present* (New York: Knopf, 1973), 61.

5. Ibid., 19.

6. *Philadelphia Public Ledger,* quoted in Feldberg, *The Philadelphia Riots of 1844,* 102.

7. On the Irish as nonwhite, see Noel Ignatiev, *How the Irish Became White* (New York: Routledge), 1995.

8. Quoted in Feldberg, *The Philadelphia Riots of 1844,* 102.

9. Quoted in ibid. See also Montgomery, "The Shuttle and the Cross," 431; and Lee, *Origin and Progress,* 45.

10. Quoted in Alfred Young, *The Shoemaker and the Tea Party: Memory and the American Revolution* (Boston: Beacon Press, 1999). See also Sean Wilentz, *Chants Democratic: New York City and the Rise of the American Working Class, 1788–1850* (New York: Oxford University Press, 1984).

11. Montgomery, "The Shuttle and the Cross," 419. See also Bruce Laurie, *The Working People of Philadelphia, 1800–1850* (Philadelphia: Temple University Press, 1980); and Feldberg, *The Philadelphia Riots of 1844,* 47.

12. Alexander McClure, quoted in Montgomery, "The Shuttle and the Cross," 422.

13. Ray Allen Billington, *The Protestant Crusade, 1800–1860: A Study of the Origins of American Nativism* (New York: Macmillan, 1938).

14. Lewis Levin, quoted in Lee, *Origin and Progress,* 107–108.

15. Ibid., 36; Montgomery, "The Shuttle and the Cross," 429. See especially Feldberg, "The Nativists," in *The Philadelphia Riots of 1844,* chapter 3.

16. Mastai and Mastai, *The Stars and Stripes,* 26–27; Jean Baker, *Ambivalent Americans: The Know-Nothing Party in Maryland* (Baltimore: Johns Hopkins University Press, 1977), 37.

17. Feldberg, *The Philadelphia Riots of 1844,* 87; Montgomery, "The Shuttle and the Cross," 426.

18. Feldberg, *The Philadelphia Riots of 1844*, 96; Lee, *Origin and Progress*, 39, 42.

19. Vincent P. Lannie and Bernard C. Diethorn, "For the Honor and Glory of God: The Philadelphia Bible Riots of 1840," *History of Education Quarterly* 8 (1968): 48, 61, 64.

20. Lee, *Origin and Progress*, 45–46.

21. Quoted in ibid., 40.

22. Ibid., 46.

23. "The Philadelphia Riots," *New Englander and Yale Review* 2 (1844): 475.

24. Feldberg, *The Philadelphia Riots of 1844*, 103; Lee, *Origin and Progress*, 52.

25. Feldberg, *The Philadelphia Riots of 1844*, 103; Lee, *Origin and Progress*, 49–50.

26. Feldberg, *The Philadelphia Riots of 1844*, 35; Montgomery, "The Shuttle and the Cross," 431.

27. Lee, *Origin and Progress*, 53; Feldberg, *The Philadelphia Riots of 1844*, 35, 37.

28. "The Philadelphia Riots," 476; Lee, *Origin and Progress*, 53.

29. Lee, *Origin and Progress*, 54; Montgomery, "The Shuttle and the Cross," 433; Robert Francis Hueston, *The Catholic Press and Nativism, 1840–1860* (New York: Arno Press, 1976), 85.

30. Lee, *Origin and Progress*, 56–57.

31. Ibid., 54–55; "On, On Americans" quoted in Billington, *The Protestant Crusade*, 224.

32. Feldberg, *The Philadelphia Riots of 1844*, 105–106; Lee, *Origin and Progress*, 63–65.

33. Lee, *Origin and Progress*, 69; Lannie and Diethorn, "Honor and Glory of God," 44; Feldberg, *The Philadelphia Riots of 1844*, 108.

34. Lee, *Origin and Progress*, 70; Feldberg, *The Philadelphia Riots of 1844*, 108.

35. Feldberg, *The Philadelphia Riots of 1844*, 108–109; Lee, *Origin and Progress*, 72; Montgomery, "Shuttle and the Cross," 432.

36. Lee, *Origin and Progress*, 79–80; Montgomery, "The Shuttle and the Cross," 433; Lannie and Diethorn, "For the Honor and Glory," 75; Feldberg, *The Philadelphia Riots of 1844*, 111.

37. Lee, *Origin and Progress*, 79; Feldberg, *The Philadelphia Riots of 1844*, 112.

38. Lee, *Origin and Progress*, 77–78.

39. Thomas P. Cope, *Philadelphia Merchant: The Diary of Thomas P. Cope, 1800–1851* (South Bend, Ind.: Gateway, 1978), 438; Feldberg, *The Philadelphia Riots of 1844*, 112–113; Lee, *Origin and Progress*, 81.

40. Lee, *Origin and Progress*, 79, 83.

41. "Crumbled ruins" through "houseless and homeless" from *Philadelphia Spirit of the Times*, quoted in Lee, *Origin and Progress*, 116; "Look at these things" from *Philadelphia Dollar Newspaper*, May 15, 1844, quoted in Lee, *Origin and Progress*, 83.

42. *Philadelphia Dollar Newspaper*, quoted in Lee, *Origin and Progress*, 83.

43. Cope, *Philadelphia Merchant*, 438; Sidney George Fisher, *A Philadelphia Perspective: The Diary of Sidney George Fisher Covering the Years 1834–1871* (Philadelphia: Historical Society of Pennsylvania, 1967), 169.

44. *Philadelphia Daily Sun*, May 11 and 13, 1844, quoted in Lee, *Origin and Progress*, 106–107.

45. Lee, *Origin and Progress*, 91, 132; Feldberg, *The Philadelphia Riots of 1844*, 135–136.

46. Lithograph reproduced in Mastai and Mastai, *The Stars and the Stripes*, 27. See also Feldberg, *The Philadelphia Riots of 1844*, 169; Scot M. Guenter, "The American Flag and the 1844 Kensington Riots," *Flag Bulletin* 139 (1991): 29; "George Shiffler," leaflet printed in Philadelphia by G. S. Harris, no date (but sometime after May 6, 1844), available at http://memory.loc.gov/cgi-bin/ampage?collId=amss&fileName=as1/as104410/amsspage.db&recNum=0&itemLink=S?ammem/amss:@field(TITLE+@od1(George+Shiffler++Printed+and+for+sale+at+G++S++Harris,+S+E++cor++of+4th+and+Vine+Sts+,+Phila+[n++d+])).

47. Lee, *Origin and Progress*, 137, 140, 142.

48. Ibid., 137–152; Lannie and Diethorn, "For the Honor and Glory of God," 83; Bruce Laurie, *The Working People of Philadelphia* (Philadelphia: Temple University Press, 1980), 131.

49. Feldberg, *The Philadelphia Riots of 1844*, 164–171.

50. Ibid., 180–181.

51. *New York Herald*, May 9, 1844, quoted in Terry Golway, *So Others Might Live: A History of New York's Bravest* (New York: Basic Books, 2003), 79.

52. The Know-Nothing nickname came from the American Party's heavy secrecy, as its elected candidates frequently claimed to know nothing about their organization's activities and positions.

53. Jean Baker, *Ambivalent Americans*, 37.

CHAPTER 3

1. George H. Preble, *History of the Flag of the United States of America*, 2d rev. ed. (Boston: A. Williams and Company, 1880), 421; Abner Doubleday, *Reminiscences of Forts Sumter and Moultrie in 1860–1* (Hartford, Conn.: American Publishing Company, 1882), 71.

2. Congressman Lawrence M. Keitt, quoted in James McPherson, *Battle Cry of Freedom: The Civil War Era* (New York: Ballantine Books, 1989), 229.

3. Doubleday, *Reminiscences*, 21.

4. Robert N. Rosen, *Confederate Charleston: An Illustrated History of the City and the People During the Civil War* (Columbia: University of South Carolina Press, 1994), 18; Maury Klein, *Days of Defiance: Fort Sumter and the Coming of the Civil War* (New York: Alfred Knopf, 1997).

5. Robert E. Bonner, *Colors and Blood: Flag Passions of the Confederate South* (Princeton, N.J.: Princeton University Press, 2002), 20–21; Rosen, *Confederate Charleston*, 39, 47; Doubleday, *Reminiscences*, 27.

6. Rosen, *Confederate Charleston*, 44–46; Klein, *Days of Defiance*, 145.

7. Doubleday, *Reminiscences*, 43–44.

8. W. A. Swanberg, *First Blood: The Story of Fort Sumter* (New York: Scribner, 1957), 37; Klein, *Days of Defiance*, 106.

9. Rembert Wallace Patrick, *Aristocrat in Uniform: General Duncan L. Clinch* (Gainesville: University of Florida Press, 1963), 54–66; Klein, *Days of Defiance*, 106. See also Eba Anderson, *Major Robert Anderson and Fort Sumter* (New York: Knickerbocker Press, 1911).

10. Doubleday, *Reminiscences*, 126; "Corrections in the First Edition," in *Battles and Leaders of the Civil War*, ed. Robert Underwood Johnson and Clarence Clough Buel (New York: Century Co., 1894), xii; Willie Lee Rose, *A Documentary History of Slavery in North America* (New York: Oxford University Press, 1976); Swanberg, *First Blood*, 366–367n.

11. James M. McPherson, *For Cause and Comrades: Why Men Fought in the Civil War* (New York: Oxford University Press, 1997).

12. Marc Leepson, *Flag: An American Biography* (New York: Thomas Dunne Books/St. Martin's Press, 2005), 86; Boleslaw Mastai and Marie-Louise D'Otrange Mastai, *The Stars and the Stripes: The American Flag as Art and as History from the Birth of the Republic to the Present* (New York: Knopf, 1973), 124.

13. James M. McCaffrey, *Army of Manifest Destiny: The American Soldier in the Mexican War, 1846–48* (New York: New York University Press, 1992),

181. See also Robert Anderson, *An Artillery Officer in the Mexican War, 1846-7* (New York, London: G. P. Putnam's Sons, 1911).

14. Quoted in Cecilia Elizabeth O'Leary, *To Die For: The Paradox of American Patriotism* (Princeton, N.J.: Princeton University Press, 1999), 22.

15. Doubleday, *Reminiscences*, 74; Anderson, *An Artillery Officer*, 71.

16. "The clouds are threatening" quoted in Klein, *Days of Defiance*, 108; "We appreciate your position" quoted in Doubleday, *Reminiscences*, 47–48.

17. The move also smacked strongly of betrayal. A party of secessionists had visited President Buchanan and reached an understanding with him that both the federal government and the South Carolinians would maintain a wary status quo. In their eyes, Anderson had violated that gentleman's agreement, moving into the very fort that Southern forces had hoped to possess.

18. Klein, *Days of Defiance*, 165.

19. Mastai and Mastai, *The Stars and the Stripes*, 79, 124.

20. Thomas Campbell, quoted in Robert Bonner, "Star-Spangled Sentiment," *Common-place, the Interactive Journal of Early American Life* 3, no. 2 (January 2003), available at www.historycooperative.org/journals/cp/vol-03/no-02/bonner/; abolitionist flag featured in Gilder Lehrman Institute of American History, "Freedom: A History of US," exhibit available at www.gilderlehrman.org/collection/freedom/freedom.html; Mastai and Mastai, *The Stars and the Stripes*, 148–149.

21. *Harper's Weekly*, quoted in Leepson, *Flag*, 101; McPherson, *Battle Cry*, 308.

22. Bonner, *Colors and Blood*, 11–12; Jefferson Davis, quoted in Leepson, *Flag*, 93. Other Confederates sought to downplay the importance of the Stars and Stripes. In the Confederate Congress, the chairman of the flag committee took the opposite tack, calling the American flag "a mere piece of striped bunting" (Leepson, *Flag*, 97).

23. Bonner, *Colors and Blood*, 28–29.

24. Doubleday, *Reminiscences*, 116.

25. Ibid., 110, 121–122.

26. Ibid., 100, 111.

27. Mary Boykin Miller Chestnut, *Mary Chestnut's Civil War*, ed. C. Vann Woodward (New Haven, Conn.: Yale University Press, 1981), 5.

28. Preble, *History of the Flag*, 409–411.

29. Quoted in ibid., 411.

30. Ibid.

31. Doris Kearns Goodwin, *Team of Rivals: The Political Genius of Abraham Lincoln* (New York: Simon and Schuster, 2005), 327–328. Abraham Lincoln inaugural speech quoted in Klein, *Days of Defiance*, 317–318.

32. Chestnut, *Mary Chestnut's Civil War*, 40.

33. Doubleday, *Reminiscences*, 159.

34. Ibid., 173.

35. Francis Pickens, quoted in Roy Meredith, *Storm over Sumter: The Opening Engagement of the Civil War* (New York: Simon and Schuster, 1957), 184.

36. Quoted in McPherson, *For Cause and Comrades*, 16.

37. "A thrilling and almost supernatural thing" quoted in Mark Neely, *The Union Image: Popular Prints of the Civil War* (Chapel Hill: University of North Carolina Press, 2000), 4; "It was impossible" quoted in Doubleday, *Reminiscences*, 175.

38. Alice Fahs, *The Imagined Civil War: Popular Literature of the North and South, 1861–1865* (Chapel Hill: University of North Carolina Press, 2003), 68; Neely, *The Union Image*, 4–5; "Broadway was almost hidden" quoted in Mark Summers, "'Freedom and Law Must Die Ere They Sever': The North and the Coming of the Civil War," in *Why the Civil War Came*, ed. Gabor S. Boritt (New York: Oxford University Press, 1996), 188–189; Harold Holzer, "New Glory for Old Glory: A Lincoln Era Tradition Reborn," in *White House Studies Compendium*, volume 2, ed. Robert Watson (New York: Nova Publishers, 2007), 316.

39. Scot M. Guenter, *The American Flag, 1777–1924: Cultural Shifts from Creation to Codification* (Rutherford, N.J.: Fairleigh Dickinson University Press; London: Associated University Presses, 1990), 70–71; Summers, "Freedom and Law," 188.

40. "Most immense" quoted in Neely, *The Union Image*, 4; "Rally to the star-spangled banner" quoted in Holzer, "New Glory for Old Glory," 316.

41. Mary A. Livermore, quoted in Guenter, *The American Flag*, 70–71.

42. Leepson, *Flag*, 108–109; song quoted in Guenter, *The American Flag*, 74–75.

43. Guenter, *The American Flag*, 73. Soldiers composed songs to the flag, borrowing existing melodies and adding their own words.

44. "I hope that from heaven" quoted in Guenter, *The American Flag*, 77.

45. Quoted in McPherson, *For Cause and Comrades*, 118, 122.

46. Both quotations from ibid., 121–123.

47. Ibid., 121; "I have always been opposed" quoted in ibid., 125; "if by so doing" quoted in McPherson, *Battle Cry*, 559.

48. Charles A. Dana, quoted in McPherson, *Battle Cry*, 634.

CHAPTER 4

1. Quoted in Donald L. Miller, *City of the Century: The Epic of Chicago and the Making of America* (New York: Simon and Schuster, 1996), 191.

2. Ibid., 186.

3. Richard Jensen, *The Winning of the Midwest: Social and Political Conflict, 1888–1896* (Chicago: University of Chicago Press, 1971), xv. There was a third Republican office in McKinley's hometown of Canton, Ohio, and the Democrats also had an auxiliary office in Washington, D.C. (Stanley L. Jones, *The Presidential Election of 1896* [Madison: University of Wisconsin Press, 1964], 277, 300).

4. Jensen, *The Winning of the Midwest*, 286; Marcus Alonzo Hanna, "William McKinley As I Knew Him," in Mark Hanna, *Mark Hanna: His Book* (Boston: Chapple Publishing, 1904), 71.

5. Paul W. Glad, *McKinley, Bryan and the People* (Philadelphia: Lippincott, 1964), 27–28.

6. Miller, *City of the Century*, 535.

7. Quotations from Glad, *McKinley, Bryan and the People*, 74. The most famous such army was headed by Jacob Coxey, who led a band of desperate veterans from his home in Ohio to the White House. There they found little help: At the Capitol, they were arrested for walking on the grass and carrying banners.

8. On the Pullman strike, see David Ray Papke, *The Pullman Case: The Clash of Labor and Capital in Industrial America* (Lawrence: University Press of Kansas, 1999).

9. William McKinley, quoted "They Came in Thousands," *New York Times*, September 6, 1896, 5.

10. William Jennings Bryan, quoted in Glad, *McKinley, Bryan and the People*, 139.

11. Ibid., 169.

12. John McElroy, quoted in David Blight, *Race and Reunion: The Civil War in American Memory* (Cambridge, Mass.: Belknap Press of Harvard University Press, 2003), 201.

13. John R. Paxton, quoted in Scot M. Guenter, *The American Flag, 1777–1924: Cultural Shifts from Creation to Codification* (Rutherford, N.J.: Fairleigh Dickinson University Press; London: Associated University Presses, 1990), 105.

14. "We give our Heads!" quoted in ibid., 117; Cecilia O'Leary, *To Die For: The Paradox of American Patriotism* (Princeton, N.J.: Princeton University Press, 2000), 151–153; "In and About the City: Patriotism in the Schools; Results of the Investigations of Col. George T. Balch," *New York Times*, June 29, 1889, 2.

15. O'Leary, *To Die For*, 157–158.

16. Ibid., 161.

17. Ibid., 129–130, 169.

18. Charles Kingsbury Miller, *Desecration of the American Flag and Prohibitive Legislation* (Chicago, 1898), 2–3, pamphlet available in Baldwin-McDowell Papers, New York Public Library.

19. "Hoped the American people" quoted in National Flag Committee of the Society of Colonial Wars in the State of Illinois, *Misuse of the National Flag of the United States of America (Chicago, 1895)*, 12–13. All other quotes from Marc Leepson, *Flag: An American Biography* (New York: Thomas Dunne Books/St. Martin's Press, 2005), 158.

20. William Allen White, *Masks in a Pageant* (Whitefish, Mont.: Kessenger Publishing, 2005), 215.

21. Herbert Croly, *Marcus Alonzo Hanna: His Life and Work* (New York: Macmillan, 1912), 41; Hanna, "William McKinley As I Knew Him," 21.

22. Croly, *Marcus Alonzo Hanna*, 116; "He believed in monopoly" from Frederic C. Howe, quoted in Matthew Josephson, *The Politicos* (New York: Harcourt Brace, 1938), 640. See also Josephson, *The Politicos*, 292. Hanna's political convictions symbolized the shift from the old Republican Party of abolitionism to the new one of business. His brother had fought in the Civil War on the side of the Union, and his family had all been staunch Republicans. His father-in-law, a Democrat, rebuffed his advances at first, telling him, "I like you very well, Mark, but you are a damned screecher for freedom" (Croly, *Marcus Alonzo Hanna*, 47).

23. H. Wayne Morgan, *William McKinley and His America*, rev. ed. (Kent, Ohio: Kent State University Press, 2003), 34; Jones, *Presidential Election*, 105; Glad, *McKinley, Bryan and the People*, 97; Thomas Beer, *Hanna* (New York: A. A. Knopf, 1929), 168.

24. Lawrence Goodwyn, *Democratic Promise: The Populist Moment in America* (New York: Oxford University Press, 1976), 527; "He has advertised McKinley" quoted in Morgan, *William McKinley and His America*, 173; Croly, *Marcus Alonzo Hanna*, 217; Jones, *Presidential Election*, 279–280; Morgan, *William McKinley and His America*, 173.

25. Charles G. Dawes, *A Journal of the McKinley Years*, ed. Bascom Timmons (Chicago: Lakeside Press, 1950), 97.

26. Hanna was worried about Bryan's speaking tours and urged McKinley to do something similar. But McKinley responded: "I might just as well put up a trapeze on my front lawn and compete with some professional athlete as go out speaking against Bryan. I have to *think* when I speak" (quoted in Morgan, *William McKinley and His America*, 176). See also Margaret Leech, *In the Days of McKinley* (New York: Harper, 1959), 89.

27. McKinley, quoted in Morgan, *William McKinley and His America*, 179; "The republican form of government" quoted in Jones, *Presidential Election*, 336; Roosevelt quoted in Henry Pringle, *Theodore Roosevelt: A Biography* (San Diego: Harcourt Trade, 2003), 107.

28. E. C. Wall, quoted in Jones, *Presidential Election*, 338. On Debs's articulation of patriotism, see especially Nick Salvatore, *Eugene V. Debs, Citizen and Socialist* (Urbana: University of Illinois Press, 1982).

29. *New York Journal*, September 26, 1896, quoted in Josephson, *The Politicos*, 697.

30. Jones, *Presidential Election*, 291.

31. Glad, *McKinley, Bryan and the People*, 17.

32. Admiral Richard Meade, quoted in Stuart McConnell, *Glorious Contentment: The Grand Army of the Republic, 1865–1900* (Chapel Hill: University of North Carolina Press, 1992), 228.

33. "Greatest train of its character" quoted in "Fire Guns for Tanner," *Chicago Tribune*, October 8, 1896; "1896 is as vitally important" quoted in Patrick J. Kelly, "The Election of 1896 and the Restructuring of Civil War Memory," *Civil War History* 49, no. 3 (September 2003): 16; Robert Justin Goldstein, *Saving Old Glory: The History of the American Flag Desecration Controversy* (Boulder, Colo.: Westview Press, 1995), 19; Jones, *Presidential Election*, 285; Goodwyn, *Democratic Promise*, 529.

34. McKinley, quoted in Jones, *Presidential Election*, 285.

35. McKinley, quoted in ibid., 292

36. Hanna, "William McKinley As I Knew Him," 53; Jones, *Presidential Election*, 291–292; "Tribute to the Flag," *Chicago Tribune*, November 1, 1896, 6.

37. *New York Tribune* quoted in Goldstein, *Saving Old Glory*, 20.

38. "Peck Wants to Share Flag Day," *Chicago Tribune*, October 21, 1896, 3; "Milwaukee in Gala Attire," *Chicago Tribune*, November 1, 1896, 6; Mr. Jones, quoted in "Bryan Welcomed at Battery D," *Chicago Tribune*, October 28, 1896, 2; "Big Parade in St. Louis," *Chicago Tribune*, November 1, 1896, 6.

39. Kingsbury Miller, *Desecration of the American Flag;* "Cut Down a Flag in Florida," *Chicago Tribune*, November 1, 1896, 8; "Popocrats Burn the American Flag," *Chicago Tribune*, October 25, 1896; "Big Parade in St. Louis," *Chicago Tribune*, November 1, 1896, 6; "Flags Trampled in the Dust," *Chicago Tribune*, November 1, 1896, 8; "Advocates Pulling Down Flags," *Chicago Tribune*, October 23, 1896, 2.

40. "Pops Burn Old Glory," *Chicago Tribune*, November 1, 1896, 8; "How They Hate the Flag! Unknown Popocratic Rascal Mutilates One in Brooklyn," *New York Press,* November 3, 1896.

41. *The Critic*, October 23, 1897, quoted in Goldstein, *Saving Old Glory,* 20.

CHAPTER 5

1. Nancy MacLean, *Behind the Mask of Chivalry: The Making of the Second Ku Klux Klan* (New York: Oxford University Press, 1995), 23; Wyn Craig Wade, *The Fiery Cross: The Ku Klux Klan in America* (New York: Simon and Schuster, 1987), 140.

2. Wade, *The Fiery Cross*, 140–141.

3. Ibid., 140–142.

4. William Joseph Simmons, quoted in David Mark Chalmers, *Hooded Americanism: The History of the Ku Klux Klan* (Durham, NC: Duke University Press), 1987, 28.

5. Wade, *The Fiery Cross*, 143.

6. The film would not arrive in Atlanta until December, but it was widely reported and celebrated in the print media beforehand. On *Birth of a Nation*, see Melvyn Stokes, *D.W. Griffith's* The Birth of a Nation: *A History of "The Most Controversial Motion Picture of All Time"* (New York: Oxford University Press, 2007).

7. James Michael Martinez, *Carpetbaggers, Cavalry, and the Ku Klux Klan* (Lanham, Md.: Rowan and Littlefield, 2007), 246–248; Wade, *The Fiery Cross*, 144.

8. Stokes, *D.W. Griffith's*, 233; Walter Clark, quoted in Wade, *The Fiery Cross*, 145.

9. Simmons, quoted in Wade, *The Fiery Cross*, 145.

10. Ibid.

11. Wade, *The Fiery Cross*, 146–7; Stokes, *D.W. Griffith's*, 233.

12. In 1912, with the addition of New Mexico and Arizona to the Union, President William Howard Taft had designated a single official design. Scot M. Guenter, *The American Flag, 1777–1924: Cultural Shifts from Creation*

*to Codification* (Rutherford, N.J.: Fairleigh Dickinson University Press; London: Associated University Presses, 1990), 165–166.

13. Nancy C. Unger, *Fighting Bob La Follette: The Righteous Reformer* (Chapel Hill: University of North Carolina Press, 2000), 248–249; Woodrow Wilson, quoted in Marc Leepson, *Flag: An American Biography* (New York: Thomas Dunne Books/St. Martin's Press, 2005), 90. See also David M. Kennedy, *Over Here: The First World War and American Society* (New York: Oxford University Press, 1980), 25, 79–80; and Cecilia Elizabeth O'Leary, *To Die For: The Paradox of American Patriotism* (Princeton, N.J.: Princeton University Press, 1999), 227.

14. O'Leary, *To Die For*, 229; George Creel, *How We Advertised America* (New York: Arno Press, 1972), 74, 122–129; David Holbrook Culbert, ed., *Film and Propaganda in America: A Documentary History* (New York: Greenwood Press, 1990), xxiii–xxvi.

15. Hiram Johnson, quoted in O'Leary, *To Die For*, 230, 240, 242. See also Mitchell Yokelson, "The War Department: Keeper of Our Nation's Enemy Aliens During World War I," paper presented at Society for Military History Annual Meeting, April 1998, available at http://net.lib.byu.edu/estu/wwi/comment/yockel.htm.

16. O'Leary, *To Die For*, 229; George Creel, *How We Advertised America* (New York and London: Harper and Brothers, 1920), 85–87.

17. Simmons, quoted in Wade, *Fiery Cross*, 150. See also Rice, *The Ku Klux Klan in American Politics* (Washington, D.C.: Public Affairs Press, 1962), 6; Chalmers, *Hooded Americanism*, 31; Wade, *The Fiery Cross*, 149; and *New York Times*, September 1, 1918.

18. Guenter, *The American Flag*, 163–170; Leepson, *Flag*, 180, 208–209.

19. Kansas Supreme Court ruling, quoted in Guenter, *The American Flag*, 168. See also Kennedy, *Over Here*, 80–83; and O'Leary, *To Die For*, 234.

20. Leepson, *Flag*, 191; Kennedy, *Over Here*, 68.

21. Quoted in O'Leary, *To Die For*, 236. See also Guenter, *The American Flag*, 169–170.

22. Kennedy, *Over Here*, 290.

23. Chalmers, *Hooded Americanism*, 32. "Better Babies" parades were initially part of a government campaign against infant mortality, one that emphasized sanitation, the elimination of germs, and scientific motherhood. However, the events very much resonated with the 1910s fascination with eugenics, and many fed into the Fitter Family Contests at agricultural fairs during this period.

24. Wade, *The Fiery Cross*, 157; Chalmers, *Hooded Americanism*, 33.

25. Wade, *The Fiery Cross*, 155.

26. Rice, *The Ku Klux Klan in American Politics*, 28–29; Chalmers, *Hooded Americanism*, 40–41; Wade, *The Fiery Cross*, 160.

27. Chalmers, *Hooded Americanism*, 33. From 1920 to 1921, the Klan gained 1.1 million new members (Rice, *The Ku Klux Klan in American Politics*, 8).

28. Chalmers, *Hooded Americanism*, 85–87; Wade, *The Fiery Cross*, 159.

29. *New York World* quoted in Wade, *The Fiery Cross*, 160.

30. Quoted in ibid., 251.

31. Mencken quoted in Chalmers, *Hooded Americanism*, 1.

32. Wade, *The Fiery Cross*, 159.

33. Ibid., 157–159, 239–245; J. Michael Martinez, William D. Richardson, and Ron McNinch-Su, eds., *Confederate Symbols in the Contemporary South* (Gainesville: University Press of Florida, 2000), 263.

34. Quoted in Wade, *The Fiery Cross*, 251.

35. Ibid., 246, 253–254.

## CHAPTER 6

1. Maryanne Vollers, *Ghosts of Mississippi: The Murder of Medgar Evers, the Trials of Byron de la Beckwith, and the Haunting of the New South* (Boston: Little, Brown, 1995), 15; Medgar Evers, *The Autobiography of Medgar Evers: A Hero's Life and Legacy Revealed Through His Writings, Letters and Speeches*, ed. Myrlie Evers-Williams and Manning Marable (New York: Basic Civitas Books, 2005), 5.

2. John Dittmer, *Local People: The Struggle for Civil Rights in Mississippi* (Urbana: University of Illinois Press, 1994), 13; Vollers, *Ghosts of Mississippi*, 14.

3. Adam Nossiter, *Of Long Memory: Mississippi and the Murder of Medgar Evers* (New York: Da Capo Press, 2002), 35.

4. Howard Zinn, *A People's History of the United States: 1492–Present* (New York: Harper Perennial, 1995), 398; Marc Leepson, *Flag: An American Biography* (New York: Thomas Dunne Books/St. Martin's Press, 2005), 209–215; Scot M. Guenter, *The American Flag, 1777–1924: Cultural Shifts from Creation to Codification* (Rutherford, N.J.: Fairleigh Dickinson University Press; London: Associated University Presses, 1990), 167.

5. Will Rogers, quoted in Wyn Craig Wade, *The Fiery Cross: The Ku Klux Klan in America* (New York: Simon and Schuster, 1987), 266. See also Leepson, *Flag*, 208–209.

6. Soldiers' reply quoted in Wade, *The Fiery Cross*, 333. Medgar Evers, "Our Need for Political Participation," address given October 25, 1959, at the Vesper Services of J. P. Campbell College, reprinted in Evers, *Autobiography*, 161.

7. Dittmer, *Local People*, 17; student quote from Zinn, *People's History*, 410.

8. Vollers, *Ghosts of Mississippi*, 31.

9. Dittmer, *Local People*, 3; Myrlie Evers-Williams, *For Us, the Living* (Garden City, N.Y.: Doubleday, 1967), 26.

10. There are multiple versions of the courthouse story, including Evers-Williams, *For Us, the Living*, 26–27; Evers, *Autobiography*, 7; and Vollers, *Ghosts of Mississippi*, 8–9. Theodore Bilbo, quoted in Evers-Williams, *For Us, the Living*, 26. "We split up" quotation from Evers-Williams, *For Us, the Living*, 27.

11. Dittmer, *Local People*, 29–31.

12. After the army, he had attended college on the GI Bill and then sold insurance to African Americans in one of the poorest parts of the state. His insurance-selling work had radicalized him. For a while, he dreamed of a freedom movement based on the independence movements in Africa.

13. Dittmer, *Local People*, 139; Nossiter, *Of Long Memory*, 44–47.

14. See the following in Evers, *Autobiography*: "Celebration of the Brown Decision's Fourth Anniversary" (May 18, 1958), 106; address to the Area Conference of the Florida State Conference of NAACP branches, Panama City, Florida, September 6, 1959, 159; and press release, August 30, 1960, 194.

15. See the following in Evers, *Autobiography*: "Introduction of Congressman Charles C. Diggs, Jr." (May 19, 1957), 72; "Celebration of the Brown Decision's Fourth Anniversary" (May 18, 1958), 102–106; "With Liberty and Justice for All," Mississippi NAACP branch newsletter, December 20, 1960, 202. See also Medgar Evers (as told to Francis H. Mitchell), "Why I Live in Mississippi," *Ebony*, November 1958, quoted in Evers, *Autobiography*, 119.

16. On membership figures, see Cynthia Griggs Fleming, *In the Shadow of Selma: The Continuing Struggle for Civil Rights in the Rural South* (Lanham, Md.: Rowman and Littlefield, 2004), 127; Vollers, *Ghosts of Mississippi*, 51.

17. James Eastland, quoted in Dittmer, *Local People*, 37. See also Neil R. McMillen, *The Citizens' Council: Organized Resistance to the Second Reconstruction, 1954–64* (Urbana: University of Illinois Press, 1971), 17; Evers-Williams, *For Us, the Living*, 175; and Rosalind Urbach Moss, "'Yes, There's

a Reason I Salute the Flag': Flag Use and the Civil Rights Movement," *Raven: A Journal of Vexillology* 5 (1998): 19.

18. Robert Patterson, quoted in Evers-Williams, *For Us, the Living*, 176. The Dixiecrats used the Confederate flag in the late 1940s, when they broke from the national Democratic Party in support of segregation, and so did the States Rights Party when it criticized the increasing concentration of federal power at the expense of the states (McMillen, *Citizens' Council*, 189; see also Moss, "'Yes, There's a Reason'").

19. Clayborne Carson, *In Struggle: SNCC and the Black Awakening of the 1960s* (Cambridge, Mass.: Harvard University Press, 1981), 10. On the Greensboro sit-ins, see also Miles Wolff, *Lunch at the Five and Ten, the Greensboro Sit-ins: A Contemporary History* (New York: Stein and Day, 1970); and William H. Chafe, *Civilities and Civil Rights: Greensboro, North Carolina, and the Black Struggle for Freedom* (New York: Oxford University Press, 1981).

20. Carson, *In Struggle*, 10, 14.

21. Ibid., 12; Moss, "'Yes, There's a Reason,'" 19; William H. Chafe, "The Sit-Ins Begin," in *Discovering North Carolina: A Tar Heel Reader*, ed. Jack Claiborne (Chapel Hill: University of North Carolina Press, 1993), 276.

22. Wolff, *Lunch*, 50; Chafe, *Civilities and Civil Rights*, 85.

23. Most accounts eliminate the word *are* in the quote, quoting the football players as responding, "We the Union Army." Chafe, *Civilities and Civil Rights*, 85; Chafe, "The Sit-Ins Begin," 277.

24. Carson, *In Struggle*, 11. See also Moss, "'Yes, There's a Reason.'"

25. Chafe, *Civilities and Civil Rights*, 118–199; Moss, "'Yes, There's a Reason,'" 21n.

26. John R. Salter, *Jackson, Mississippi: An American Chronicle of Struggle and Schism* (Hicksville, N.Y.: Exposition Press, 1979), 93.

27. Ibid., 65.

28. James Meredith had led a prior flag march in Jackson in 1961. Tim Spofford, *Lynch Street: The May 1970 Slayings at Jackson State College* (Kent, Ohio: Kent State University Press, 1988); Moss, "'Yes, There's a Reason,'" 28.

29. Salter, *Jackson, Mississippi*, 145.

30. Ibid., 131; Jack Langguth, "Jackson Police Jail 600 Negro Children," *New York Times*, June 1, 1963, 8.

31. Salter, *Jackson, Mississippi*, 149.

32. Ibid.

33. Ibid.; Evers-Williams, *For Us, the Living*, 259; Dittmer, *Local People*, 163.

34. Pete Seeger and Robert S. Reiser, *Everybody Says Freedom* (New York: Norton, 1989), 144.

35. Medgar Evers, quoted in Langguth, "Jackson Police," 1; Salter, *Jackson, Mississippi*, 150.

36. Langguth, "Jackson Police," 1; Jack Langguth, "Jackson Negroes Ease Picketing: Say Desegregation Drive Is Now in 'Second Phase'; Mayor Denies Concessions, N.A.A.C.P. Lawyers Gather," *New York Times*, June 4, 1963.

37. Salter, *Jackson, Mississippi*, 173, 177; Langguth, "Jackson Negroes Ease Picketing," 29; Moss, "'Yes, There's a Reason,'" 28; Ann Moody, *Coming of Age in Mississippi* (New York: Delta Trade Paperbacks, 2004).

38. Edwin King, quoted in Moss, "'Yes, There's a Reason,'" 28.

39. "Flag Day Affords Opportunity to Show Pride in National Heritage," *Jackson Clarion-Ledger*, June 13, 1963, 8-A, quoted in ibid., 29.

40. Salter, quoted in Moss, "Yes, There's a Reason," 28.

CHAPTER 7

1. Howard Zinn, *A People's History of the United States: 1492–Present* (New York: HarperCollins, 2003), 482–483.

2. Quoted in Tom Wells, *The War Within: America's Battle over Vietnam* (Berkeley: University of California Press, 1994), 133.

3. David T. Prosser, "Desecration of the American Flag," *Indiana Legal Forum* 3 (1969): 179; Wells, *The War Within*, 134.

4. Wells, *The War Within*, 134; photograph, Diana Davies Collection, Swarthmore College Peace Collection, reprinted in ibid., between 286 and 287.

5. A photo of the anti–Vietnam War demonstrators burning the American flag during a demonstration in Central Park, by Leonard Detrick, is available at http://www2.dailynewspix.com (search for "flag burning"). See also Robert Goldstein, *Saving Old Glory: The History of the American Flag Desecration Controversy* (Boulder, Colo.: Westview Press, 1995), 121.

6. Previous flag desecration bills had all been on the state level. Even the flag protection movement of the 1890s had been unable to pass a federal law, because the movement included commercial uses of the flag as "desecration." Quotes from Goldstein, *Saving Old Glory*, 119–131.

7. Prosser, "Desecration of the American Flag," 187, 190, 192.

8. Of the 20 percent who had enrolled in college, most attended two-year junior colleges rather than elite institutions (Christian Appy, *Working-Class War: American Combat Soldiers and Vietnam* [Chapel Hill: University of North Carolina Press, 1993], 26). Todd Dasher, quoted in ibid., 58.

9. Dan Shaw, quoted in ibid.

10. E. E. LeMasters, *Blue Collar Aristocrats: Life-Styles at a Working-Class Tavern* (Madison: University of Wisconsin Press, 1975), 173.

11. Zinn, *People's History*, 482; Philip Foner, *American Labor and the Indochina War: The Growth of Union Opposition* (New York: International Publishers, 1971), 81.

12. Quoted in LeMasters, *Blue Collar Aristocrats*, 173.

13. George Meany, quoted in Leonard S. Silk, "Is There a Lower-Middle-Class 'Problem'?" in *Blue-Collar Workers: A Symposium on Middle America*, ed. Sar A. Levitan (New York: McGraw-Hill, 1971), 9.

14. Quoted in Robert Coles, *The Middle Americans: Proud and Uncertain* (Boston: Little, Brown, 1971), 131–134.

15. Wells, *The War Within*, 24; Marilyn Milligan, quoted in ibid., 36.

16. Walter Cronkite, quoted in Bret Stephens, "American Honor," *Wall Street Journal*, January 22, 2008, 18.

17. Prosser, "Desecration of the American Flag," 179–180.

18. Ibid., 180–181.

19. Nancy Zaroulis and Gerald Sullivan, *Who Spoke Up? American Protest Against the War in Vietnam, 1963–75* (Garden City, N.Y.: Doubleday, 1984), 210; Prosser, "Desecration of the American Flag," 181–184.

20. Images of all three of these appear on the cover of Thomas Powers, *The War at Home: Vietnam and the American People, 1964–1968* (Boston: G. K. Hall, 1984). See also Prosser, "Desecration of the American Flag," 184.

21. Todd Gitlin, *The Intellectuals and the Flag* (New York: Columbia University Press, 2006), 133.

22. A similar dynamic occurred in the civil rights movement, as individual black activists began to rip flags off courthouses and refused to carry it at marches. Rosalind Urbach Moss, "'Yes, There's a Reason I Salute the Flag': Flag Use and the Civil Rights Movement," *Raven: A Journal of Vexillology* 5 (1998): 30–31.

23. Eric Darton, *Divided We Stand: A Biography of New York's World Trade Center* (New York: Basic Books, 1999), 106.

24. For percentages of various opinions, see Harris Poll, *New York Post*, May 28, 1970.

25. Kirkpatrick Sale, *SDS* (New York: Vintage Books, 1974), 636–637; Zaroulis and Sullivan, *Who Spoke Up?* 320.

26. Flags were hung on construction elevators ("Muscles and a Flag," *New York Post*, May 9, 1970, 2). Flags were also the centerpiece of the "topping out" ritual of steelworkers (Angus Kress Gillespie, *Twin Towers: The Life of*

*New York City's World Trade Center* [New Brunswick, N.J.: Rutgers University Press, 1999], 116; Mike Cherry, *On High Steel: The Education of an Ironworker* [New York: Quadrangle, 1974], 120).

27. Fred J. Cook, "Hard-Hats, the Rampaging Patriots," *Nation* 210 (June 15, 1970), reprinted in *Reporting Vietnam: American Journalism*, compiled by Milton J. Bates et al. (New York: Library of America, 1998), 100–101.

28. "After 'Bloody Friday,' New York Wonders If Wall Street Is Becoming a Battleground," *Wall Street Journal*, May 11, 1970.

29. *Wall Street Journal*, August 5, 1969, 1, quoted in Patricia Cayo Sexton and Brendan Sexton, *Blue Collars and Hard Hats: The Working Class and the Future of American Politics* (New York: Random House, 1971), 103. On dangers of construction work, see Cherry, *On High Steel*.

30. Homer Bigart, "War Foes Here Attacked by Construction Workers," *New York Times*, May 9, 1970. In the mid-1960s, when he testified before the city council in favor of the World Trade Center project, Brennan brought along several hundred of his union men. They stood outside in City Hall Park, waving flags and shouting their support of the project (Darton, *Divided We Stand*, 105).

31. Bigart, "War Foes."

32. Ibid.

33. Ibid.; Cook, "Hard-Hats," 102.

34. "The Hard Hats," *Newsweek*, May 25, 1970, 34.

35. "Those guys were directing the construction workers with hand motions," the man who was observing from the thirty-second floor told a reporter (*New York Times*, May 9, 1970; also quoted in Cook, "Hard-Hats," 104). "John Wayne" comment quoted in *Wall Street Journal*, May 11, 1970. One construction worker, an observer rather than a participant, told a reporter that these men "were shouting orders to the workers" (Bigart, "War Foes," 10).

36. The man who supposedly spat on the flag was in his forties and was wearing a coat and tie. Reports vary on what he did: spitting on the flag, blowing his nose, tearing it with his teeth, eating it. In any event, it was intended to be—and perceived as—an act of desecration ("Joe Kelly Has Reached His Boiling Point," *New York Times Magazine*, June 28, 1970).

37. "There [were] as many of these antiwar demonstrators whacked by Wall Street and Broadway office workers as there were by construction workers. The feeling seemed to be that the white-collar-and-tie-man, he was actually getting in there and taking as much play on this thing as the construction worker was" (ibid.).

38. Bigart, "War Foes," 10.

39. Ibid.

40. Wells, *The War Within*, 310–312, 426; Zaroulis and Sullivan, *Who Spoke Up?* 220–221. See also Laura K. Donohue, *The Cost of Counterterrorism: Power, Politics, and Liberty* (Cambridge and New York: Cambridge University Press, 2008), 223; James Kirkpatrick Davis, *Assault on the Left: The FBI and the Sixties Anti-War Movement* (Westport, Conn.: Greenwood Publishing Group, 1997), 108.

41. Philip Foner, "Bloody Friday: May 8, 1970," *Left Review* 4, no. 2 (spring 1980): 20; Stephen Ambrose, *Nixon*, vol. 2, *Triumph of a Politician* (New York: Simon and Schuster, 1988–1991), 374; William Gillis, "How to Infuriate a Bank, an Airline, Unions, Printing Companies, Immigration Authorities, Canadian Police, Vice President Agnew, and President Nixon in Ten Months: The Scanlan's Monthly Story," paper presented at the Association for Education in Journalism and Mass Communication, Toronto, Canada, 2004. Nixon was personally involved: In July, he sent a confidential memo asking staffer John Dean to investigate the company (John Dean, *Blind Ambition: The White House Years*, quoted in Jonathan S. Lynton and Terri Mick Lyndall, *Legal Ethics and Professional Responsibility* [Rochester: Lawyers Cooperative; Albany: Delmar Publishers, 1994], 4–5). That fall, after being rejected by a number of American printing firms, the magazine finally found a willing publisher in Canada. Montreal police seized eighty thousand copies from the publisher, ostensibly for lacking the proper printing registration; on the same day, customs agents in California seized copies that were being sent to the United States. The Montreal chief of police was reported as saying he did it because "the United States Government asked us to stop it" (Gillis, "How to Infuriate").

42. Seymour Hersh, "1971 Tape Links Nixon to Plan to Use 'Thugs,'" *New York Times*, September 24, 1981, 1.

43. Cook, "Hard-Hats."

44. Ibid.

45. "Marchers Go Uptown," *New York Post*, May 13, 1970. See also Fred Cook, "Hard-Hats," 111.

46. The assistant secretary of labor in the Nixon administration, Arthur Fletcher, suspected this immediately upon hearing of the demonstrations. He detected what he called an "ulterior motive." "I believe they feel that if they can support the President on this one issue, they can get inside the White House and be a formidable opponent of the Philadelphia Plan" (quoted in Joshua B. Freeman, "Hardhats: Construction Workers, Manliness, and the

1970 Pro-War Demonstrations," *Journal of Social History* 26, no. 4 [summer 1993]).

47. "Workers . . . have freely admitted taking time from their jobs to join demonstrations or battle with students, and they say they have not lost pay" (*New York Post*, quoted in Cook, "Hard-Hats," 114).

48. Homer Bigart, "Thousands Assail Lindsay in 2nd Protest by Workers," *New York Times*, May 12, 1970, 1; Sandor Polster, "U.S. Probing Violence Here," *New York Post*, May 15, 1970, 5; "Flag-Raising Brings Dispute Downtown," *New York Times*, May 19, 1970, 33.

49. Polster, "U.S. Probing," 5; Bigart, "Thousands Assail"; "Pro-War Rally Draws Huge Crowd," *New York Post*, May 20, 1970.

50. "These are people I know well" quoted in "After 'Bloody Friday'"; "The new Nazis" quoted in Bigart, "Thousands Assail"; "We won't be intimidated" quoted in Homer Bigart, "2 Protest Groups Meet on Wall Street," *New York Times*, May 13, 1970, 13.

51. Quoted in Cook, "Hard-Hats," 114.

52. "Pro-War Rally."

53. Ibid.

54. Agis Salpukas, "Unionists Say War Protestors Prompt a Backlash," *New York Times*, May 17, 1970.

55. Francis X. Clines, "For the Flag and for Country, They March," *New York Times*, May 21, 1970, 22.

56. Ibid.

57. Francis X. Clines, "Workers Find Protest a 2-Way Street," *New York Times*, May 13, 1970, 18; "The Blacks in the Hardhats," *New York Post*, May 14, 1970.

58. "Blacks in the Hardhats."

59. "Construction Men Give Head Man a Hard Hat," *New York Post*, May 26, 1970. Three years later, Nixon returned the favor, naming Brennan to his cabinet as secretary of labor (Foner, "Bloody Friday," 19).

60. Nixon quoted in Foner, "Bloody Friday," 20.

61. Marc Leepson, *Flag: An American Biography* (New York: Thomas Dunne Books/St. Martin's Press, 2005), 248. As Reagan's campaign aide Richard Darman described it, the goal was to create a mood "where a vote against Reagan is, in some subliminal sense, a vote against a mythic 'America'" (David Greenberg, "Waving the Flag," part 2, "How the 'Patriotism' Debate Might Actually Help Obama," *Slate*, July 3, 2008, available at www.slate.com/id/2194695/).

62. Robert Justin Goldstein, *Burning the Flag: The Great 1989–1990 American Flag Desecration Controversy* (Kent, Ohio: Kent State University Press, 1996), 33; "99 Arrested in Dallas Protest," *New York Times*, August 23, 1984, A26.

63. Goldstein, *Saving Old Glory*, 197; Goldstein, *Burning the Flag*, 33.

64. Quoted in Goldstein, *Burning the Flag*, 109–110. Flag desecration legislation had originated in the 1890s with the Flag Protection Movement. Many states passed laws banning defacement and contempt, laws that originated as a symptom of disgust at the way that the American flag had become commercialized, but quickly became used against immigrants with radical politics. Defacements and prosecutions spiked during World War I, with the repeal of civil liberties, but largely disappeared from the 1920s onward. It was only with the Vietnam era that the flag had again become a target for desecration. After the flag burning in Sheep's Meadow, Congress and state legislators passed anti-desecration laws: By 1984, fully forty-eight states had anti-desecration laws on the books. See especially Goldstein, *Saving Old Glory*. On the history of flag desecration, see also Prosser, "Desecration of the American Flag."

65. Quoted in ibid., 110–111.

66. Goldstein, *Burning the Flag*, 74.

67. Goldstein, *Saving Old Glory*, 205, 213.

68. Goldstein, *Burning the Flag*, 231–232.

## CHAPTER 8

1. Lynette Holloway, "Seeing the Green Amid the Red, White and Blue; Wholesalers, in Rush to Market, Got Sept. 11 Souvenirs on Street," *New York Times*, December 8, 2001, 1; John Simons, "Living in America," *Fortune*, January 7, 2002, 92–94; Tom Shales, "Stars and Stripes Turn into Dollars and Cents," *Electronic Media* 20, no. 41 (October 8, 2001): 6; Marc Leepson, *Flag: An American Biography* (New York: Thomas Dunne Books/St. Martin's Press, 2005), 256.

2. Todd Gitlin, "Liberal Activists Finding Themselves Caught Between a Flag and a Hard Place," *San Jose Mercury News*, October 28, 2001.

3. Andrew Card, quoted in Jim Rutenberg and Bill Carter, "Draping Newscasts with the Flag," *New York Times*, September 20, 2001, C8; Richard Reeves, "Patriotism Calls Out the Censor," *New York Times*, October 1, 2001, A23. Walter Isaacson, chairman and CEO of CNN, and Eric Sorensen, president of MSNBC, were later independently quoted as describing a "patriotism police" (Isaacson, interview by Bill Moyers, "Buying the War," *Bill*

*Moyers Journal*, PBS, April 25, 2007, available at www.pbs.org/moyers/journal/ btw/transcript1.html).

4. Rutenberg and Carter, "Draping Newscasts." It is no accident that the American flag first appeared in the context of the Revolutionary War or that the occasion that gave rise to our national anthem was the War of 1812. In all armed conflicts, from the Mexican-American war onward, the flag had always appeared first and foremost as an official symbol of American military forces.

5. Douglas Jehl, "Across Country, Thousands Gather to Back U.S. Troops and Policy," *New York Times*, March 24, 2003, B15; Greg Retsinas, "A Rally at Ground Zero for the Troops," *New York Times*, April 11, 2003, B12.

6. The BBC estimated between six and ten million worldwide ("Millions Join Global Anti-war Protests," BBC News Online, February 17, 2003, available at http://news.bbc.co.uk/2/hi/europe/2765215.stm). Lizette Alvarez, "Festive Gatherings, Somber Messages, from London to Berlin," February 16, 2003, *New York Times*, N20.

7. Rochelle Braunstein, "Here on the Home Front: Flags and Protests," *New York Times*, March 23, 2003, E12.

8. Bill Moyers, "On Patriotism and the Flag," February 28, 2003, available at www.pbs.org/now/commentary/moyers19.html.

9. Flag pins had originated in the 1896 election and had been a key hawkish symbol during the buildup to World War I. Some were campaign-style buttons with flag images printed on them; some were rhinestone-studded metal pins in the outline of the flag. Appearing most prolifically at moments when two patriotic visions clashed, flag pins had become widely popular during the conflicted spring of 1970. People who opposed the antiwar movement— even some officials, like the officers in the New York City Police Department— wore them. Nixon was wearing an American flag pin by October 1970. Robert M. Smith, "Nixon Will Offer 'Major' Proposal on War Tonight," *New York Times*, October 7, 1970, 1; Theodore White, *The Making of the President, 1972* (New York: Bantam Books, 1973); Elizabeth Drew, *Richard M. Nixon* (New York: Times Books, 2007), 33; "stick it to the liberals" quoted in Walter Isaacson, *Kissinger: A Biography* (New York: Simon and Schuster, 1992), 393; Stephen Ambrose, *Nixon, vol. 3, Ruin and Recovery 1973–1990* (New York: Simon and Schuster, 1988–1991); "American flag lapel pins" quoted in Richard Brookhiser, "Son of the Emerging Republican Majority," *National Review*, December 31, 1980, 1590.

10. David Greenberg, *Nixon's Shadow: The History of an Image* (New York: W. W. Norton, 2004), 207.

11. "Washington Whispers," *U.S. News and World Report*, October 7, 2002, 8.

12. Moyers, "On Patriotism."

13. Donald Rumsfeld, quoted in "'My Deepest Apology' from Rumsfeld; 'Nothing Less Than Tragic' Says Top General," *New York Times*, May 8, 2004, A8.

14. John McCain, "Putting the Country First," *Parade* Magazine, July 6, 2008.

15. Barack Obama, speech at Canton Memorial Civic Center, Canton, Ohio, October 27, 2008, transcript available at http://blogs.suntimes.com/sweet/2008/10/obama_closing_argument_speech_1.html.

16. Manning Marable, interview by Amy Goodman, *Democracy Now!* November 5, 2008, available at www.democracynow.org/2008/11/5/manning_marable_on_the_significance_of; Lynne Davis, quoted on *Democracy Now!* November 5, 2008, available at www.democracynow.org/2008/11/5/headlines.

17. Barack Obama, speech at Grant Park, Chicago, November 4, 2008, transcript available at www.barackobama.com/2008/11/04/remarks_of_president elect_bara.php.

18. "Many Americans were willing" quoted in Gitlin, "Liberal Activists."

# INDEX

# Index

Haldeman, H. R., 192, 212, 213
Hanna, Mark, 118–120, 122–127,
    129–130
Hard Hat Riots (New York City, N.Y.)
    alleged government involvement in,
        191–193, 200–201
    construction workers in opposition to,
        199–200
    construction workers paid to protest,
        187–191, 196–199
    flag as prowar symbol, 195–199
    march up Canyon of Heroes to City
        Hall, 193–195
    Nixon as big winner, 199, 200–201
Harding, Warren, 147
*Harper's Weekly,* 87, 103
Hearst newspapers, 119
Henry, Patrick, 35
Herbert, Charles, 35–36
Hierarchy in colonial America, 22–24
Hoffman, Abbie, 184
Hogan, William, 55
Humanitarian patriotism
    of antiwar activists, 174, 180–181
    Christian socialism, 114–115, 118
    colonial tradition of, 21–24
    emancipation of slaves, 100–103
    misuse by Republican Party, 129–130
    Obama's vision of, 216–219
    overview, 5–6, 7, 220, 221
    post-9/11 flag of unity, 207–208
    World War II as promise of, 154–155

Illinois, 141. *See also* Chicago, Illinois
Immigrants and immigration
    connotations of the flag, 45, 67–68
    ethnic basis for social class, 48–50
    flag as a tool for integrating, 113–114,
        115
    and flag protectionists, 129
    Germans during World War I, 139,
        141
    *See also* Irish in Philadelphia
Impressment of sailors, 15, 43
Industrial armies of mid-1890s, 108–109
Industrialization
    development of market economy, 50

as financial basis for the North, 74
of flag making, 81
spiritual salvation versus, 68–69
transition to, 43–44
Working Men's movement, 50–52, 69
International Workers of the World
    (Wobblies), 140, 142
Internment camps, 139
Intimidation and murders by KKK,
    144–145
Iraq invasion, 209
Irish in Philadelphia
    and ARP speech in their neighborhood,
        46–47, 48–50, 55–58
    ARP's three-day riot in Kensington,
        62–66, 70
    meaning of patriotism, 51–52
    and Nanny Goat Market, 58–59
    nativists compared to, 69
    riots against ARP in their
        neighborhood, 58–60
    strike supported by union, 51
Isaacson, Walter, 209
Iwo Jima flag-raising photograph,
    152–153, 219–220

Jackson, Mississippi, 164–170
*Jackson Clarion-Ledger,* 169–170
Japanese Americans, 154
Jefferson, Thomas, 5–6
Jews and anti-Semitism, 135, 143–144,
    146–147, 153–154, 197
Johnson, Gregory Lee, 203
Johnson, Hiram, 138–139
Johnson, Lyndon, 174, 181–182
Jones, John Paul, 29
*Journal of Commerce,* 96
July 4, 1778, in British prison, 28–29,
    33–36
July 4, 1844, in Philadelphia, 67–68
Justice Department, 139

Kansas penalty for flag desecration, 141
Kennedy, Anthony, 203
Kennedy, John F., 7, 164
Kent State massacre, 186–187, 188–189,
    193–194

# Index